HOWARD ST

THE ENGLISH WORLD CHESS CHAMPION

by

R.D.Keene and R.N.Coles

Howard Staunton
The English World Chess Champion

by

Raymond Keene and R. N. Coles

First published in 1975 by
British Chess Magazine

Current Edition Published in December, 2009
Ishi Press in New York and Tokyo

Copyright © 1975 by Raymond Keene and R. N. Coles

All rights reserved according to International Law. No part of this book may be reproduced by for public or private use without the written permission of the publisher.

ISBN 4-87187-860-0
978-4-87187-860-9

Ishi Press International
1664 Davidson Avenue, Suite 1B
Bronx NY 10453-7877
USA

1-917-507-7226

Printed in the United States of America

CONTENTS

Foreword	v
List of annotated games	vi
Other Staunton games quoted in the text	vii
Biography	1
Play at odds	26
Match and Tournament record	29
The 1843 World Championship match	30
Selected games	33
The Staunton System in defence	107
Index of openings	161
General Index	163
Illustrations	167
List of illustrations	181

FOREWORD

The English are much too diffident about Staunton. They have not made enough of him. The Russians have the great Tchigorin, who has been elevated by their writers into the exalted position of spiritual founder of the Soviet school of chess. The Germans have Tarrasch, Tchigorin's doctrinal rival, and they have not been slow to stress his status as a chess teacher of world prestige. The French have Philidor. The Austrian Steinitz is regarded as the 'founder of modern chess' and the Americans have heroes a-plenty, some of whom have been magnified into legendary figures. Denmark has given some recognition to Nimzowitsch who took refuge in Scandinavia in the 1920s. The Dutch have Euwe and they know it. But what have we done for Staunton?

A Staunton Memorial tournament was held in 1951 and occasional articles have appeared in praise of him, but that is all. Even Bobby Fischer's generous recognition of him in *Chess World* in 1964 went relatively unnoticed. Staunton was a major writer on the game, a profound thinker and the strongest player of his time, a master both of theory and practice. He was the inventor of many modern systems, especially those involving fianchettoes, and the precursor of numerous positional ideas only generally accepted when promulgated by the recognised 'great teachers' of later years. A striking example of his modernity can be seen in Game 23 in the present volume, where a modern World Championship game follows remarkably closely upon a game from his own World Championship match.

The English have adopted a strangely reserved attitude towards a man who should actually be regarded as the founder of our national school. Criticism of him has gone unanswered, and there has been all too ready an acceptance of the view that he held no more than a stop-gap position between the brilliant epochs first of Labourdonnais and McDonnell and then of Anderssen and Morphy. It is our hope that this volume will go some way towards redressing the balance.

R.D.K. R.N.C. 1974

LIST OF ANNOTATED GAMES

	Page
1. Staunton - Amateur, Casual game, London, c.1839	33
2. Staunton - Harrison, Casual game, London, c. Oct.1840 (ending)	35
3. Staunton - Popert, Match game, London, c. Nov.1840	36
4. Staunton - Popert, Match game, London, c. Nov 1840	38
5. Zytogorski - Staunton, Match game, London, c. Apr.1841	40
6. Stanley - Staunton, Match game, London, Dec.1841 (ending)	41
7. Staunton - Cochrane, Casual game, London, 1842	42
8. Staunton - Cochrane, Casual game, London, 1842 (ending)	43
9. Cochrane - Staunton, Casual game, London, 1842	44
10. Cochrane - Staunton, Casual game, London, 1842	46
11. Staunton - Amateur, Casual game, London, c. Dec.1842 (ending)	47
12. Cochrane - Staunton, Match game, London, Feb.1843	47
13. Cochrane - Staunton, Casual game, London, Mar.1843	50
14. Staunton - Saint-Amant, 4th Match game, London, May 1843	51
15. Saint-Amant - Staunton, 1st Match game, Paris, Nov.1843	53
16. Staunton - Saint-Amant, 4th Match game, Paris, Nov.1843	55
17. Saint-Amant - Staunton, 5th Match game, Paris, Nov.1843	58
18. Saint-Amant - Staunton, 7th Match game, Paris, Nov.1843	62
19. Staunton - Saint-Amant, 8th Match game, Paris, Nov.1843	64
20. Saint-Amant - Staunton, 9th Match game, Paris, Nov.1843	65
21. Saint-Amant - Staunton, 13th Match game, Paris, Dec.1843	67
22. Saint-Amant - Staunton, 15th Match game, Paris, Dec.1843	69
23. Saint-Amant - Staunton, 21st Match game, Paris, Dec.1843	72
24. Staunton - Amateur, Casual game, London, 1844	75
25. Staunton - Bristol Chess Club, Correspondence, 1844-5	78
26. Mongredien - Staunton, Match game, Liverpool, May 1845 (ending)	80
27. Williams - Staunton, Match game, Bristol, June 1845	81
28. Staunton - Amateur, Casual game, London, June 1845	83
29. Kennedy - Staunton, Match game, London, July 1845	84
30. Evans - Staunton, Casual game, London, Aug.1845 (ending)	85
31. Staunton - Amateur, Casual game, London, c. 1845	87
32. Horwitz - Staunton, 2nd Match game, London, Feb.1846	90
33. Horwitz - Staunton, 20th Match game, London, Apr.1846	93
34. Horwitz - Staunton, 24th Match game, London, Apr.1846 (ending)	95
35. Harrwitz - Staunton, 16th Match game, London, Sept.1846	97
36. Harrwitz - Staunton, 19th Match game, London, Sept.1846	99
37. Staunton - Harrwitz, 21st Match game, London, Oct.1846	101
38. Staunton - Amateur, Casual game, London, 1847	103
39. Lowe - Staunton, Match game, London, Dec.1847	104
40. Staunton - Amateur, Casual game, London, Dec.1850	105
41. Horwitz - Staunton, Casual game, London, May 1851 (ending)	106
42. Horwitz - Staunton, 2nd Match game, London Tournament, May 1851	109
43. Staunton - Horwitz, 7th Match game, London Tournament, June 1851	113
44. Anderssen - Staunton, 3rd Match game, London Tournament, June 1851	117
45. Staunton - Anderssen, 4th Match game, London Tournament, June 1851	119

LIST OF ANNOTATED GAMES

Page

46. Williams - Staunton, 1st Match game, London Tour. play-off, July 1851   120
47. Williams - Staunton, 5th Match game, London Tour. play-off, July 1851   122
48. Staunton - Williams, 8th Match game, London, July 1851   124
49. Williams - Staunton, 9th Match game, London, Aug.1851   129
50. Jaenisch - Staunton, 8th Match game, London, Aug.1851   133
51. Staunton - Jaenisch, 9th Match game, London, Aug.1851   137
52. Allies - Staunton, Exhibition game, Edinburgh, July 1852   138
53. Staunton - Amateur, Casual game, Scotland, Aug.1852   140
54. Staunton - Lowenthal, Casual game, London, Jan.1853   142
55. Staunton - von der Lasa, 5th Match game, Brussels, Aug.1853   143
56. von der Lasa - Staunton, 12th Match game, Brussels, Aug.1853   147
57. Staunton & Owen - Lowenthal & Barnes, London, Feb.1856   151
58. Lowenthal & Falkbeer - Staunton & Ranken, London, Aug.1856 (ending)   153
59. Anderssen & Allies - Staunton & Allies, Manchester, Aug.1857   154
60. Staunton - Worrall, Match game, London, 1859   158

OTHER STAUNTON GAMES QUOTED IN TEXT
(Games marked ✶ are quoted in full)

✶ Staunton - Popert, Match game, 1840	39
✶ Staunton - Popert, Match game, 1840	39
✶ Zytogorski - Staunton, Match game, 1841	27
Brown - Staunton, Match game, 1841	97
✶ Cochrane - Staunton, Casual game, 1842	46
✶ Cochrane - Staunton, Casual game, 1842	117
Cochrane - Staunton, Casual game, 1842	44
✶ Cochrane - Staunton, Casual game, 1843	7
✶ Cochrane - Staunton, Match game, 1843	48
Cochrane - Staunton, Match game, 1843	48
Staunton - Saint-Amant, 6th Match game, Paris, 1843	62
Staunton - Saint-Amant, 12th Match game, Paris, 1843	126
Staunton - Saint-Amant, 16th Match game, Paris, 1843	92
Saint-Amant - Staunton, 19th Match game, Paris, 1843	72
Allies - Staunton & Kennedy, Telegraph game, 1845	12
Staunton - Horwitz, 1st Match game, 1846	147
Horwitz - Staunton, 4th Match game, 1846	92,107
Staunton - Horwitz, 11th Match game, 1846	3
Horwitz - Staunton, 14th Match game, 1846	38
Horwitz - Staunton, 24th Match game, 1846	30,107
✶ Staunton - Kenny, Match game, 1847	14

* Staunton - Amateur, Casual game, c. 1850	8?
Brodie - Staunton, 2nd Match game, London Tournament, 1851	8?
* Horwitz - Staunton, 4th Match game, London Tournament, 1851	10?
Staunton - Horwitz, 5th Match game, London Tournament, 1851	?
Anderssen - Staunton, 1st Match game, London Tournament, 1851	14?
Anderssen - Staunton, 5th Match game, London Tournament, 1851	15?
* Williams - Staunton, 1st Match game, 1851	10?
* Staunton - Williams, 6th Match game, 1851	5,10?
Staunton - Jaenisch, 1st Match game, 1851	13?
Jaenisch - Staunton, 2nd Match game, 1851	13?
Staunton - Jaenisch, 5th Match game, 1851	13?
* Staunton - de Rives, Casual game, Brussels, 1853	3?
* Staunton - Rockferry Chess Club, 1853	2?
* Staunton - von der Lasa, 9th Match game, 1853	14?
* Staunton - Skipworth, Exhibition game, 1854	2?
* Staunton & Owen - Morphy & Barnes, 1858	2?
* Lowenthal - Staunton, Birmingham Tournament, 1858	2?

BIOGRAPHY

Howard Staunton is the only British chessplayer to have become the World Champion, yet he has been curiously neglected except by those who find more to condemn than to praise. There was in his day, it is true, no World Chess Championship as such, and it was left to Steinitz, prior to his 1886 match with Zukertort, to declare that the match would be for 'The Chess Championship of the World'. Before that date matches and tournaments alike were considered to indicate who held the palm at any given moment. Thus, some little while after his victory in the first 1851 London tournament, Anderssen was adjudged to have succeeded to Staunton's throne. Staunton's contemporaries had no doubts, after his defeat of Saint-Amant in 1843, that an Englishman was for the first time the World Chess Champion. Elijah Williams (1804-1854), President of the Bristol Chess Club, hailed Staunton as 'The Champion of Chess' at a dinner given especially in Staunton's honour early in 1844, and a speaker proposing Staunton's health at the 1845 dinner of the Yorkshire Chess Association said: 'The game (in earlier days) was practised in England, but the sceptre has always been wielded by a foreigner; now, however, we have the satisfaction of knowing that the Chess Champion is an Englishman.'

Staunton's unusual abilities were so little comprehended by his own age and his limitations so clearly seen that his genius by its very nature tended to obscure itself. In the 1840s the open game was predominant and had indeed been given new impetus by the publication in 1837 of the famous German *Handbuch*, which offered the first systematic analysis of the openings, based upon the researches of Bilguer, Bledow, von der Lasa, Horwitz and their associates into the prevalent open games. Though Staunton inevitably played a great deal of his chess with these openings, his development of the close game was an entirely new feature in chess history. It was his misfortune that he was to be followed by Morphy, who brought the open game to its highest pitch of perfection, thereby placing the emphasis firmly back on all those aspects in which Staunton was neither so especially interested nor so completely skilled. What Staunton had had to offer the chess world was forgotten, and when Steinitz revived the close game thirty years later, it was he and not Staunton who received all the credit for it.

In the *Dictionary of National Biography* the article on Staunton was written by Sir Sidney Lee (1859-1926), for many years an editor and for some time sole editor of the Dictionary. He was, like Staunton, a Shakespearean scholar of note and therefore, one might think, well fitted to write an obituary. He quotes his chess sources, none of which supplied him with the information he gives that Howard Staunton was the illegitimate son of Frederick Howard, 5th Earl of Carlisle, from whom, he adds, Staunton received a 'few thousands' when he came of age, money which he quickly squandered. Staunton left many detractors behind him when he died, and perhaps Sir Sidney listened too closely to some ill-disposed tongue.

The 5th Earl of Carlisle (1748-1825) had been a gay spark and a famous dandy in his youth, but he married, became a sober politician and was Lord Privy Seal by 1783. In 1793 he was made a Knight of the Garter. He wrote a tract on the state of the contemporary theatre early in the 19th century, as well as two five-act verse tragedies. Howard Staunton was similarly given to elegance in dress and interest in the theatre, so that it was easy for the name Howard to suggest a connection. Sixty year old Knights of the Garter are as capable as anyone else of fathering illegitimate children, though Staunton, completing the church register at the time of his marriage, described his father as 'William Staunton, gentleman'. Of course father William may have been a figment of Staunton's imagination, conveniently created to conceal the truth from his bride. But then there is the story of the money he came into at the age of twenty-one. 'A few thousands' was a very large sum at the time when money had at least ten times its present value and would have taken quite a bit of squandering. Perhaps the fact that Staunton died a poor man suggested this part of the story. Since the Earl predeceased Staunton's coming-of-age by six years, the money could only have been received if there had been a written instruction in the will or if a special trust had been created. So far the archives at Castle Howard have yielded no such corroborative evidence.

Whatever is the truth about his birth, Staunton's early life remains obscure. He was born in 1810 but neither the exact date nor the place are known. His education was neglected, and though he spent some years at Oxford it was not as a member of the University. Whether his father had died or abandoned his mother, the fact is that she was apparently left alone to bring him up and was unable to provide him with normal schooling. It was a beginning from which only strong character and great efforts could raise him. He had the character and he made the effort. In his later years he proved himself a man of no mean education and the grounding must have been laid fairly early in life, so he was presumably able to take some steps to educate himself. As a young man he drifted into the acting profession even, according to his own statement, playing Lorenzo to Edmund Kean's Shylock, and it was from this period of his life that his wide knowledge of, and interest in, Shakespearean and Elizabethan drama undoubtedly derives.

In 1836, however, Staunton became interested in chess and from that time his life took a new direction. A small thing which has done much to obscure the greatness of his qualities as a chessplayer is the much-quoted criticism of Morphy when a child that Staunton was the author, not only of the *Handbook*, but also of 'some devilish bad games'. Certainly he did not possess the consistent accuracy of Morphy. At times, particularly in his later years when he was in ill health, his power of concentration broke down. It is, however, recognised that those who possess the finest combinative skill are those who learn and play the game at an early age. Staunton did not begin to play chess until he was 26, at which age he admits that Saint-Amant could have given him a rook. To reach the top after so late a start is indeed proof of very exceptional chess powers.

It was to be said of his Shakespearean studies later that they 'combined commonsense and exhaustive research'. It was certainly those same two qualities which he brought to the chessboard. He did not seek the flashier variations beloved of the German school of the time, though he accepted them if he felt they were sound; he preferred to find the solid, commonsense move which he felt the situation demanded. Though by no means incapable of calculating the most intricate combinative variations, it was probably easier for one who had come to chess so late in life to avoid the more open games and to adopt a closer and more positional style. Philidor had been the master of pawn structures and pawn play, but Philidor had been dead some forty years when Staunton took up chess, and no one in the interval had taken up where Philidor left off. But now came Staunton, who developed within Philidor's ideas on pawn structures the optimum operation of the pieces. No one understood better than Staunton the power of the fianchettoed bishop, his first introduction of which into the Queen's Gambit Declined enabled him to make Saint-Amant look second-rate. His use of it as Black in the Sicilian Defence anticipated the play of a school later even than that of Steinitz. In the English Opening, so called from his adoption of it, his double fianchetto brought him to the fringes of the Reti System. Nimzowitsch's idea of outposts on open files, supported by the pawn structure, came quite naturally to him, as can be seen in the 15th and 21st games of the Saint-Amant match, and his use of prophylaxis might almost suggest that Nimzowitsch preceded him in time instead of being born 76 years later. It was Staunton, too, a strong supporter of the Sicilian Defence as a means of preventing White from forming a powerful centre, who first recognised that the ideal way of meeting the defence as White was with 2 N-KB3 and 3 P-Q4, although the line had occasionally been played before his time. Applying his treatment of the Sicilian Defence to the other wing, he evolved the Staunton Gambit as a means of playing against the Dutch Defence, a line he first tried in the 11th game of his 1846 match with Horwitz: 1 P-Q4, P-KB4; 2 P-K4, PxP; 3 N-QB3, N-KB3; 4 B-KN5, P-B3; 5 BxN, KPxB; 6 NxP, P-Q4; 7 N-N3, B-Q3; 8 B-Q3, O-O; 9 KN-K2, P-KB4; 10 P-KB4.

His modernity was never better realised and expressed than in *Chess World* in 1964 by Bobby Fischer: 'Staunton was the most profound opening analyst of all time. He was more theorist than player but none the less he was the strongest player of his day. Playing over his games I discover that they are completely modern. Where Morphy and Steinitz rejected the fianchetto, Staunton embraced it. In addition he understood all of the positional concepts which modern players hold so dear, and thus with Steinitz must be considered the first modern player.'

Certain players at widely separated stages of the development of chess have displayed a most remarkable affinity in their approach to the game, which goes much deeper than a similarity of style. One feels that Staunton, Nimzowitsch and Petrosian are such astrally related spirits. From an early age, thanks to his trainer Ebralidze, Petrosian was a devotee of the teachings of Nimzowitsch, but it is doubtful if either of those two 20th century grandmasters was in any degree aware of Staunton's exploits, which often anticipated later conceptions by something like a century.

Though he developed the play of the close game, Staunton was never a dull player and always preferred an opening which would lead to interesting situations. He condemned the Ruy Lopez as leading to tedious games, so that although he recognised it as White's strongest opening, there are but five examples of it in his recorded games, other than in consultation games — the 1st game of his 1846 match with Horwitz and four games of the 1853 match with von der Lasa. Bird in his *Modern Chess* relates that 'at a little chess

18_49_. Marriage solemnized at _St Nicholas Church_ in the _Parish_						
No.	When Married.	Name and Surname.	Age.	Condition.	Rank or
204	Feby 23	Howard Staunton	full age	Bachelor	Gent
		Frances Carpenter Nethersole	full age	Widow	

Married in the _Parish Church_ according to the Rites and Ceremonies of the

This Marriage was solemnized between us, { _Howard Staunton_ _Frances Carpenter Nethersole_ } in the Presence of us,

Copy of the actual marriage register signed by Staunton and his wife.

reunion between Staunton, Kolisch and Bird, three weeks before the death of the former, the Ruy Lopez was voted chessically a bore, and the unanimous opinion was that a player wishing to have a highly enjoyable game should scarcely ever open with a Ruy Lopez.' But Staunton recognised the force of the opening. In 1920 Breyer declared that after 1 P-K4 White's game was in the last stages of disintegration, a curious echo of the statement in Staunton's *Chess Player's Companion* that after 1 P-K4, P-K4 Black's game was embarrassed from the outset. But only Breyer was dubbed 'hypermodern'.

One of Staunton's most remarkable contributions to opening play, however, escaped the notice of his contemporaries as well as of later generations. It was a time when opening play was only beginning to be classified and to receive an approved nomenclature; many openings and defences which have since become standard were then grouped under the term 'irregular'. Eighty years were to elapse before chessplayers first conceived of a 'system', a group of moves which could remain valid against a variety of counter-moves, such as the Reti System, which could be employed whether Black's most forward early pawn move was P-Q4, P-QB4 or P-K4. The Staunton System escaped identification, for if books on openings noted the moves at all, they were dispersed under a number of different headings. The Staunton System began as a means of playing the Sicilian Defence as Black. He was working towards the idea in the 2nd and 4th games of his 1846 match with Horwitz, where the KB was developed by B-K2-B3. By the 24th game of the match he saw that the KB should be developed in fianchetto, and so the essential moves of the System, which were P-QB4, P-K3 and P-KN3, were established. (The relevant moves will be found quoted in the note on 'The Staunton System in Defence'). By 1851 Staunton was using this formation against various White methods of treating the Sicilian and he used it equally as a defence against Bird's Opening (refer again to 'The Staunton System' for the opening of the 1st game of his match with Williams). But the striking feature of the Staunton System was that he used it also as

White in his version of the English Opening. In the 1851 London Tournament the 5th game of his quarter-final match with Horwitz began: 1 P-QB4, P-KB4; 2 N-QB3, P-K3; 3 P-K3, N-KB3; 4 P-KN3, (See Diagram 1), while in the 6th game of his match with Williams the opening moves were 1 P-QB4, P-K4; 2 P-K3, N-KB3; 3 P-KN3, P-Q4.

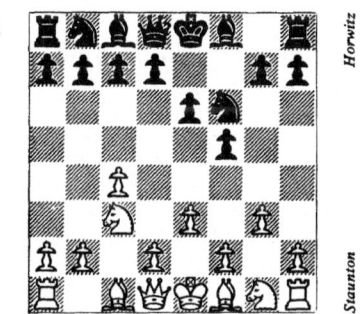

The subsequent Steinitzian theory of weak squares could not countenance such a formation because of the hole on KB3, so what had arrived unheralded died in infancy and was soon interred and forgotten. It is only in recent years that the formation has once more been frequently adopted by master players both as White and Black, and not infrequently by both sides simultaneously. If the Staunton System was stillborn some 120 years ago, it is showing distinct signs of life today, and the ghost of the old master must be having a quiet chuckle!

This was the player who at the age of 26 began as a mere novice to haunt the chess resorts of London — the Divan, Gliddon's, 'The Shades', Huttman's,

Goode's and others. He subscribed in 1836 to Greenwood Walker's *Games by the late Alexander McDonnell*, but he himself never met McDonnell, nor even his great antagonist Labourdonnais who survived until 1840. One of the problems facing the chess historian of this period is not only that many scores have not survived but that most of those which have, apart from games played in the more important matches, bear no indication of date. Normally one can safely assume that publication followed closely upon the actual playing of the game and in the case of Staunton's match with Buckle this presumption stands up even in the face of some contrary evidence.

It is not until 1840 that Staunton's career becomes at all well documented. We learn from a comment in *Bell's Life* in 1841 that he was the secretary of the Westminster Chess Club at the start of the '40s. At this time the strongest player in London was considered to be H.W.Popert, formerly of Hamburg, but temporarily resident in London as a merchant. In 1840 a match between Staunton and Popert took place at the old London Chess Club, and Staunton is said to have won by the odd game, although Bachmann quotes the result as 10-5 to Staunton with 6 drawn. The surviving scores are 8-3 in his favour with 2 draws. Not long after the match Popert resumed his residence in Germany.

But it was not primarily as a player that Staunton made his first impact upon the chess scene. The inclination he always had to earn a living with his pen was called in to capitalise his chess prowess. He founded the (*Chess Player's Chronicle* and edited it from 1840 until the beginning of 1854. This, the first regular chess magazine in the English language, if an abortive effort of George Walker's be excepted, was a considerable contribution to the cause of chess in England, and since it provided him with a regular income, enabled him to achieve the solidity and respectability which a man of those days had to attain if he was to be anybody at all.

His change of circumstances manifested itself in a certain sartorial ostentation. The Rev. G.A.MacDonnell describes him later in *Chess Life-Pictures* as 'wearing a lavender zephyr outside his frock coat. His apparel was slightly gaudy, his vest being an embroidered satin, and his scarf gold-sprigged, with a double pin thrust in it, the heads of which were connected by a glittering chain ... He was tall, erect and broad-shouldered, military in his air, and graceful in every movement'. In fact, as the Rev. J.Donaldson put it in the *B.C.M.* of October 1891, he was 'a fine princely-looking man, walking like a king amongst his fellows'. His leonine head alone, to which all his portraits testify, would have singled him out in a crowd.

In April 1841 Staunton played a match with Zytogorski, a Pole three years his senior who had fled to England after the 1830 Polish revolution. Staunton gave him the odds of Pawn and Two Moves, evidence of his increasing strength. In the *Chess Player's Chronicle* of 1854, when R.B.Brien had taken over the editorship, the match is erroneously ascribed to 1843 and was said to have been won by the Pole 6-0, which is manifestly untrue as the surviving scores are 2-1 in favour of Staunton. Brien was notoriously unreliable and, further, his dislike of Staunton often led him to pervert the truth, as P.W.Sergeant pointed out in his *Century of British Chess*.

Two other matches at the same odds were played in 1841, the first against J.Brown, Q.C., whom Staunton had first met on level terms at 'The Shades', in which the surviving scores are 5-3 to Staunton with 2 draws; and the second against the 22-year old C.H.Stanley, which Stanley is said to have won, the surviving scores showing him with an advantage of 3-2 and 1 draw. This latter was a far from discreditable result for Staunton since Stanley, who was soon to be appointed to a post with the British Consulate in New York, came to be regarded as the strongest player in America from 1846 until Morphy's appearance and his own first round defeat in the 1857 New York tournament.

As fortune would have it, just as Staunton was finding himself short of strong opposition, there returned to England on leave from India the brilliant John Cochrane, a barrister of the Middle Temple, who 20 years earlier had gone to Paris with Lewis to play Deschapelles and Labourdonnais. He was still no more than 43 years of age. Always dangerous, if at times unsound, Cochrane was possessed of a highly imaginative genius. From late 1841 until his return to India early in 1843 Cochrane met Staunton in endless casual games, and out of some 600 said to have been played between them nearly 130 have survived, some clearly no more than 'skittles' but many among the finest specimens of chess skill. This was just what Staunton needed to deepen and sharpen his play, which shows a marked improvement in this period. But any over-confidence was severely punished as in the following delightful miniature from early 1843.

      White: **Cochrane**   Black: **Staunton**   Q.P. Counter-Gambit
1 P-K4, P-K4; 2 N-KB3, P-Q4; 3 NxP, Q-K2; 4 P-Q4, P-KB3; 5 N-QB3, PxN; 6 NxP, Q-B2; 7 B-QB4, B-K3; 8 O-O, P-B3; 9 P-B4

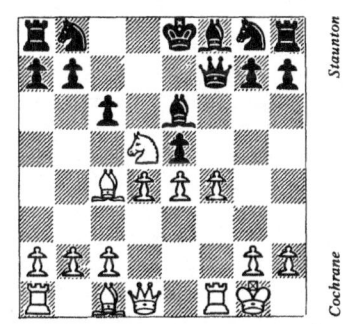

9 ..., PxN; 10 BPxP, Q-Q2; 11 PxP, BxP; 12 P-K6!, Q-B3; 13 Q-R5+, P-N3; 14 QxB, N-K2; 15 Q-K5, QxB; 16 QxR, N-B4; 17 B-R6, Q-N5; 18 QxB+, QxQ; 19 BxQ, KxB; 20 P-KN4, **Resigns**.

Soon after this little game the two men sat down to a set match of 18 games which Staunton won 14-4, and thereafter we find him giving even Cochrane the odds of Pawn and Move, on which terms each player won 3 and one was drawn. Also early in 1843 Staunton played a match against Taverner, an old opponent of McDonnell's, in which he gave Pawn and Move and won easily, the surviving scores being 5-1 in his favour.

In the spring of 1843 the French Champion, P.C.F. de Saint-Amant, in his capacity as a wine merchant, paid one of his frequent visits to London. On a visit in 1836 he had beaten George Walker 5-3 with one draw and Fraser 1-0 with 2 draws. In 1842 he had played Cochrane and lost 4-6 with one draw, so the opportunity was now taken of matching him with Staunton for a nominal stake of a guinea. P.W.Sergeant has suggested that these small matches were little more than 'skittles', but in the days before tournament play almost every casual game had an importance far greater than the casual games of today. And these were not casual games in the true sense, for a stake and indeed reputations were involved. Saint-Amant was regarded as the heir of Labourdonnais and he was surrounded by that special aura which attached itself to the leading representative of the greatest chessplaying nation of the world. Staunton may have tried, when he lost these little matches, to play them down as of small account, but Saint-Amant after this match and von der Lasa after the match of 1853 regarded them as serious contests. Saint-Amant, who was ten years Staunton's senior, won the present match 3-2 with one draw, a result sufficiently encouraging both to Staunton and to the general body of English chessplayers for a challenge to a further and longer serious match to be issued. The challenge was accepted.

During the summer of 1843 Staunton undertook a match against Brooke Greville, the first portion for the first five won games at Pawn and Move, and the second for the first five games at Pawn and Two Moves. According to *La Regence* he resigned the first part of the match when 0-3 down, and though no record of the second part exists, it seems likely that Staunton won, since there are six surviving games at the greater odds of which Staunton won five. One of the most striking features of Staunton's play was his remarkable ability to give the odds of Pawn and Two Moves more successfully than those of Pawn and Move.

One other match of interest occurred in London in 1843, in which Staunton gave Pawn and Move to Buckle, who was soon to be ranked as second only to Staunton himself in British chess. Henry Thomas Buckle (1821-1862) was a most remarkable character; in spite of missing almost all his normal schooling through ill health, he so mastered these early disadvantages that by the age of thirty he spoke seven and read twelve languages. The first part of his great *History of Civilisation*, so highly praised by Bernard Shaw, appeared in 1857 and it was said of him that after Macaulay he possessed the most tenacious memory and amply-stored mind of any man. Chess he feared because of its fascination and the exhaustion it induced, yet he frequently missed appointments by becoming engrossed in a game. He won the first of all tournaments, a domestic affair at the Divan in 1849. He contested friendly matches with Kieseritsky in Paris in 1848 and with Lowenthal in London in 1851, winning the first 3-2 with 3 draws and the second 4-3 with one draw. Buckle claimed to have won the 1843 match with Staunton by 6-1, and the surviving scores are 2-1 in his favour. According to MacDonnell in *Chess Life-Pictures*, Buckle claimed to have won the match in 1838, but three games appeared in the *Chess Player's Chronicle* in 1843, and in support of the assumption that publication normally followed closely after the play there is on this occasion conclusive corroborative evidence in *Bell's Life* of 1st October 1843. Buckle complained that only two games were ever published, presumably basing this statement on the two which appeared in the *Chess Player's Companion* and overlooking the *Chronicle*'s three.

Howard Staunton

By November Staunton, with Capt. Wilson and Mr. Worrel as his seconds, was in Paris for the match with Saint-Amant, and on the 14th the contest began with the Frenchman a strong favourite. The stakes were £100 a side and four games were to be played each week, the winner of the first eleven to be the victor. There was no provision for adjournments, each game being played right through without a break, and the spectators were allowed to crowd the players as closely as in any cafe chess. The progress of the match revealed both the strength and weakness of Staunton as a chessplayer. He staggered the chess world by conceding only one draw in the first eight games, and the excitement back in England can only be compared to the excitement which prevailed during the 1972 Fischer - Spassky match. 'In the chess clubs of the country,' wrote Tomlinson, 'the greatest excitement prevailed, and the games, as and when received, played over and over.' All over the country there were converts to the game of chess, demanding particulars of the games of the 'Grand Match'. Even the Press suddenly found that chess was news. In the 9th game Staunton blundered in a won position, and of the next three he won two and only lost the other by going wrong again after recovering to a won position from an inferior opening. But for his two errors he might after twelve games have scored 11-0 with one draw, but as it was he stood at 9-2 with the one game drawn. It was this intermittent lack of accuracy that was beyond the comprehension of so phenomenally accurate a player as Morphy. At this point in the match Saint-Amant staged a remarkable recovery and at the start of the 19th game, when the score stood at 10-4, and 4 draws, in favour of Staunton, 'such was the anxiety of the public to witness the skill of Mr. Staunton and the heroic resistance of Saint-Amant, that both parties suffered terribly from the heat, and gendarmes had to be posted at the club doors to refuse further admittance.' Staunton had been further upset that Capt. Wilson had not been able to stay with him during the last few games, but after losing the 20th game, 'the worst-played partie of the match', he pulled himself together for a final effort in the 21st. Only 29 moves were completed in the first eight hours and for the first time the no-adjournment rule was waived and the players allowed an hour's rest. They resumed and reached the 54th move some time after midnight, so once more it was decided that an adjournment, this time till the following morning, should be allowed. Finally, on 20th December, after fourteen hours play the game and the match went to England by 11-6 with 4 draws. British chess stood at its highest level.

More than that, Staunton's victory made London instead of Paris the Mecca of international chess masters. Horwitz took up permanent residence in England in 1845. Harrwitz, after a visit in 1846, lived in England from 1849 to 1856. And later still came Lowenthal, Steinitz and others. Even home players were attracted to London. Elijah Williams left Bristol and moved to the capital to the great benefit of his play. The debt owed to Staunton by English chess was incalculable.

As has so often happened since when the chess title has changed hands, an acrimonious correspondence developed between the principals, Saint-Amant claiming that contests between them stood at one each and Staunton dismissing the earlier match as of no consequence at all. The argument persisted through the early part of 1844, but finally an arrangement was made with the French for a return — or deciding — match. But first, in September, as mentioned in *Bell's Life* of 20th October, Staunton won a match at the odds of Pawn and Two against Tuckett, the surviving games being 7-1 in his favour with one draw. In October Staunton travelled once more to Paris. Unhappily he developed pneumonia and was desperately ill for some time, 'a terrible malady', he described it afterwards, 'which brought me to death's door.' After recovery he was left with a permanently weak heart. The projected match was necessarily abandoned.

That his heart now considerably affected him was shown by his speech at the Yorkshire Chess Association's 1845 annual dinner. 'Prior to my late indisposition,' he said, 'an after dinner speech was an affair of little moment, and disconcerted me no more than would the giving a castle to some sixth or seventh rate chessplayer. Now I experience no difficulty in expressing my thoughts while seated, but somehow, when I rise, I find my tongue has lost its freedom, and my ideas lack something of their clearness.'

This illness undoubtedly had some effect upon his character. He had always been a man of determined opinions with a somewhat pontifical way of expressing them. Now the violence of his feelings became accentuated and he never hesitated to condemn in outspoken language anything of which he disapproved either through the *Chess Player's Chronicle* or through the weekly column in the *Illustrated London News* which he had just taken over. He showed an increasing lack of tact as the years went by, so that what began as outspoken comment was, because of the resentment it caused, allowed to develop into personal animosity and bitter feuds were born. H.J.R. Murray, in the *B.C.M.* of 1908, remarked: 'I regret to find the beginnings of those petty personalities, likes and dislikes, that were to accompany Staunton throughout his whole chess career. He hit out at his enemies, real or supposed, under the cover of answers to correspondents. There were people who refused to credit the existence of these correspondents ... He misused his editorial position again and again, and in this way gave his enemies openings of which they were not slow to avail themselves.' Horwitz, a most generous opponent, declared: 'I never liked Staunton's principles, but he was always a man.' The more generous of his enemies in fact always admired him even when they disliked him; his many friends loved him while admitting that he had his faults. MacDonnell again in his *Chess Life-Pictures*: 'His heart was naturally as tender as his intellect was vigorous ... He had neither the obtrusive bounce nor the cock-o'-the-walk strut which distinguish some chess magnates ... He never tramped about the room, nor unduly raised his voice ... never flaunted his superior knowledge before the public ... As a raconteur he was a king, and even aimed at being an autocrat ... He cared for no man's anecdote but his own; and listened with impatience, if not contempt, to the song or joke by any other member of the company to the general amusement. But though socially a tyrant, yet he was withal a very pleasant one ... Frequently he enacted a drama, in which he introduced half-a-dozen comic characters, portraying each of them in turn in the most lifelike and laughter-provoking manner ... His imitations of the great actors and humourists whom he had known — Edmund Kean, Maginn, Thackeray, Douglas Jerrold, etc., were simply perfect ... Had fortune not been, as I fancy, somewhat unkind to him, he might have been a very fine specimen of humanity.' Bird also noted his 'Munchausen anecdotes' as well as his 'elevated eyebrows and rolling forehead', not to mention his Havana cigars. W.N.Potter, in his obituary notice in the *City of London Chess Magazine*, was influenced no doubt by the excesses of Staunton's closing years by which alone he knew him, to say: 'The deceased often acted, not only with signal lack of generosity, but also with gross unfairness towards those whom he disliked, or from whom he suffered defeat, or whom he imagined likely to stand between him and the sun ... Nevertheless,' Potter adds, 'there was nothing weak about him and he had a backbone that was never curved with fear of anyone.' Ranken summed him up well in his article *Chess Reminiscences in the Victorian Era* in the 1897 *B.C.M.*: 'With great defects he had great virtues; there was nothing mean, cringing or small in his nature, and taking all in all, England never had a more worthy chess representative than Howard Staunton.'

He was alert to the changes going on in the world around him, and more than once showed a remarkable prescience and progressiveness of outlook. For example, the first electric telegraph was tried in 1838, and in 1846 the Electric Telegraph Company was formed to exploit it commercially. Yet as early as April 1845, almost as soon as he recovered from his illness, Staunton was proposing playing chess by telegraph — 'Messrs. Cooke and Wheatstone's marvellous messenger,' as it was described — and two games on successive days, between Staunton and Kennedy in Gosport and a team in London comprising Evans, Perigal, Tuckett and Walker, with Buckle occasionally making valuable suggestions, were played. The second game on 10th April, in which Staunton and his partner were Black, came quickly to a neatly drawn ending so that the Gosport players could catch the last (five o'clock) train back to London.

3 Staunton & Kennedy

Allies

The ending was **39 R-B3, R-N6; 40 R(2)-KB2, R-K7; 41 RxP, RxP; 42 RxR(K2), RxR; 43 R-Q2, R-K4. Drawn.**

The development of the railway system was rapidly linking hitherto distant localities. There were less than 500 miles of line when Staunton first took up chess, yet by 1849 the system was about as complete as it was to remain for the next hundred years. Staunton travelled by rail extensively and indefatigably, and it was not rail travel as we know it today. Rolling stock was still primitive and made rail travel quite an exhausting business. When Staunton went to Hull in 1847 for the annual chess festival there, he described himself as still 'suffering from the excitement of twelve hours rapid whirling through the air'. Yet he went not merely to Gosport in 1845, but to Liverpool and Bristol for matches, and attended various functions in other parts of the country as the guest of honour and as a crusader for the game. At Liverpool he played matches at Pawn and Two against Mongredien and Spreckley, who were respectively

President and secretary of the Liverpool club. Mongredien had only just come back from Germany where he had beaten Hanstein 3-1 with 2 draws, lost to Bledow 4-7 with one draw, and drawn with Mayet 3-3 and one draw, so he was no mean performer. A few years later Spreckley's commercial interests took him off to China, but Augustus Mongredien remained one of the country's most energetic and enthusiastic supporters of the game. Besides being President at Liverpool, he was also President of the London Chess Club from 1839 to 1870, and George Walker, at a London Chess Club dinner in 1848 when Mongredien was in the chair, said: 'I cannot be in two places at once like the President, who so ably keeps the cause alive both in Liverpool and London. If I were told that at this moment Mr. Mongredien is taking the chair at a dinner of the Liverpool club also, I should believe it.' Mongredien (1807-1888) played matches with Morphy in 1859 and Harrwitz in 1860, losing both 0-7 and one draw; he competed in the 1862 London tournament and lost a match with Steinitz in 1863 by 0-7. During his visit to Bristol Staunton played a match against Williams, again at odds of Pawn and Two. All this was apart from his London activities, which included a match at the St. George's Chess Club against Kennedy at the same odds again. Hugh Alexander Kennedy (1809-1878) was another of the enthusiastic chess organisers of the day. He founded the Brighton club in 1840, was later President of the club at Bath and a vice-president of the British Chess Association from 1862 to 1866. He was a frequent contributor to *Punch*. In 1858 he met Morphy over the board in casual games, but his only competitive chess was the London tournament of 1851 in which he came sixth.

The first serious challenge to Staunton's supremacy came in the spring of 1846 from the German master, Bernard Horwitz, one of the famous seven 'Pleiades' of the Berlin school, newly arrived in England. Staunton's play since his illness lacked some of the accuracy and decision of the Saint-Amant match; he was, as H.J.R. Murray observed, 'really unfitted for all serious match play from that time forward. Matches he certainly did play and win in the next few years but more and more he complained of 'my old enemy, palpitation' and excused himself at times from playing because 'the excitement could be too much for me'. 'Staunton was as aware as the Russians are today that good health was essential to success at chess. He quoted Marshal Saxe as saying that the attributes required in a commander-in-chief were genius, courage and health. 'The first of these qualities is unquestionably called for in the highest order of chess skill; and if by courage is implied, not so much mere physical bravery as entire self-possession, promptitude of decision and undaunted perseverance, and by health is meant the preservation of a sound mind, to which a sound body is so important an adjunct, then indeed both courage and health will be found to exercise a powerful influence upon the success of the chessplayer.' Yet he could never admit that his own ill health impaired his performance. Horwitz himself was always extremely nervous under match conditions and seldom did himself justice. In the end Staunton won their match comfortably by 14-7 with 3 draws. Horwitz (1807-1885) settled in England and married a Miss Priscilla Deykes. He practised as a painter of miniatures, but never forsook chess and gave England the inestimable gift of his *Chess Studies*, prepared in collaboration with Kling, the first of all the great books on the endgame. In June Staunton won a match at the odds of a knight against Hannah of Brighton by 5-2 with one draw. In the autumn the young German master, Daniel Harrwitz (1823-1884), who had lived most of his life in Paris and was regarded as a member of the French school, arrived in England. His fine reputation as a player was really still in the future and may be said to have begun when he drew a match with Anderssen in 1848, though he was to beat Horwitz by the odd game at the very end of 1846 and again by the same narrow margin in a further match in 1849. But when immediately after his arrival he beat Williams 3-0 and 2 draws with some very brilliant play, it was felt that he was a not altogether unworthy opponent for the World Champion, and Staunton offered odds in a curious match of 21 games, excluding draws, in which the odds of Pawn and Move, no odds, and Pawn and Two Moves were to be played in rotation. Staunton won the level series 7-0, lost at Pawn and Move 1-6 and one draw, but revealed his virtuosity at the odds of Pawn and Two by winning 4-3, thus winning the whole match, in which he first took the lead only in the 16th game, by 12½-9½.

Later, when Harrwitz took up residence in England, he often met Staunton in the club or at the Divan. The Englishman was tall by the standards of his age, while Harrwitz was small and in comparison seemed, as Bird put it, 'sinking to the ground, but the story that he once disappeared overawed by Staunton's style and manner of moving and was after a search found under the table, is a mere canard of Staunton's ... Staunton pretended sometimes not to see Harrwitz, and would look round the room and even under the chairs for him when he was sitting at his elbow, which greatly annoyed Harrwitz who, however, sometimes got a turn and was not slow to retaliate. In a game one day, Staunton materially damaged his own prospects by playing very tamely and feebly, and testily complained 'I have lost a move'. Harrwitz told the waiter to stop his work and search the room until he had found Staunton's lost move, and ... caused a degree of merriment by no means pleasing to the English Champion.'

After 1846 Staunton played less, partly because of deteriorating health and partly because he was immersed in the preparation of his first chess book, but even so there were matches in 1847 against Kenny, to whom he gave the huge odds of a rook and lost, and against the 53-year old Czech player, E. Lowe, long settled in London, to whom he gave Pawn and Two and lost 1-4 with 2 draws. The following is a neat little win from the former match:

White: (without QR) **Staunton**   Black: **Kenny**
1 P-K4, P-K4; 2 B-B4, B-B4; 3 N-KB3, P-Q3; 4 P-Q4, PxP; 5 NxP, BxN; 6 QxB, N-KB3; 7 B-N5, B-K3; 8 B-Q3, N-B3; 9 Q-B3, P-KR3; 10 B-KB4, Q-K2; 11 O-O, P-KN4; 12 B-N3, P-R3; 13 P-B4, O-O-O;

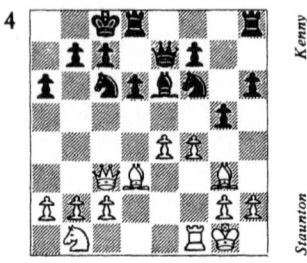

14 BxP, NxP; 15 QxN, N-B4; 16 BxP+, NxB; 17 R-K1, Q-Q2; 18 Q-R6, P-QB4; 19 N-B3, Q-B2; 20 P-B5, B-Q2; 21 N-Q5, Q-R4; 22 N-K7+, Resigns.

The latter of the two matches is the only minor match of Staunton's noticed by Murray in his 1908 *B.C.M.* article or by P.W.Sergeant in his *Century of British Chess*, perhaps because a certain Thomas Beeby issued an irate pamphlet about it, accusing Staunton of bad sportsmanship. Lowe had no hand in this attack, for the genial old Czech was much loved for his eccentricities and his character. He sat with a cigar permanently in his mouth, which he constantly tried to relight, but as he usually held the flame an inch from the weed, he only expended prodigious quantities of matches. He carried a box in every pocket, each one lasting him about an hour, while one cigar was said to have lasted him a week. Though he had been in England since 1838, he never mastered the language, and even just before his death in 1880 at the age of 86 he said that after all he had only been here forty years and would soon learn.

Staunton's *Chess Player's Handbook* appeared in 1847. In his article *Writers who have changed chess history* Harry Golombek ranks this work as number two in a series of five throughout the ages, which began with Philidor's *Analyse des Echecs* and continued with Lasker's *Commonsense in Chess*, Reti's *New Ideas in Chess* and Nimzowitsch's *My System*. It immediately became the standard textbook of English chessplayers and remained so for over half a century, being republished twenty-one times between 1847 and 1935. Staunton in his preface acknowledges his debt to the German *Handbuch* but adds that he had subjected every variation to the test of repeated investigation. As Golombek points out, it was not just what he added that counted, it was the cunning way in which he arranged his material, all subsequent manuals having, with only small differences, followed his model. Murray ranks him higher as an analyst than as a player. The power of analysis is equally, according to Murray, a special gift and this Staunton possessed in a very high degree. 'He made many important contributions to our knowledge of the openings and he was the pioneer in the scientific arrangement of that knowledge.' Morphy too made a similar assessment: 'His knowledge of the theory of the game was ... complete; his powers as an analyst were of the very highest order; his *coup d'oeil* and judgment of position and his general experience of the chess board great; but all these qualities, which are essential to make a great chessplayer, do not make him a player of genius. These must be supplemented by imagination and by a certain inventive or creative power, which conceives positions and brings them about; of this faculty I see no evidence in the published games. In a given position, where there is something to be done, no matter how difficult or recondite the idea, Mr. Staunton will detect it and carry out the combination in as finished a style as any great player that ever lived, but he will have no agency in bringing about the position. Therefore, in his best day, Mr. Staunton (in my opinion) could not have made a successful fight against a man who had the same qualities as himself and who, besides, was possessed of the creative power above-mentioned. Such were Anderssen, McDonnell and Labourdonnais.' Morphy may see no evidence of this 'creative faculty', but perhaps that was because in Morphy's open game such a faculty was inevitably fully exposed to view, whereas in Staunton's close style the creative faculty is concealed and slow to make itself felt. Morphy had the grace to admit that he was only giving 'his opinion', and we are convinced that the readers of this book will, as they close it after their study of the games quoted, be left with a very contrary point of view.

After some years of intensive chess play, followed by his *Handbook*, Staunton eased off in 1848, merely playing a small match against G.W.Medley at Pawn and Two, which he won 6-1 with 3 draws. The truth was that bouts of ill health and his weak heart made him conscious that he needed a helpmate and he had made the acquaintance in Brighton of a widow to whose hand he aspired. Mrs. Frances Carpenter Nethersole, then living at 1, Norfolk Square, Brighton, was the widow of William Dickerson Nethersole, a London solicitor from Essex Street, Strand, who had died in 1842. Born in 1805, she was five years older than Staunton. Financially he had little enough to offer her, for though he made a living out of his *Chess Player's Chronicle*, the fortune he might have made from his *Handbook* went to Bohn, his publisher, who had acquired the copyright outright for a lump sum. Nevertheless the lady smiled upon him and they were married on 23rd February 1849 at St. Nicolas's Church, Brighton. (The *D.N.B.* wrongly gives the date as 'about 1854'). She was ultimately to survive him by nearly nine years, dying on 7th May 1883. There is little doubt that he felt that with marriage he was putting his chessplaying days largely behind him, so later that year he published another book, the *Chess Player's Companion,* which in a later age might have been called *My Chess Career*.

About this time the firm of Jaques, workers in ivory and fine woods, had received from Nathaniel Cook, a friend of Staunton's, the design for a new set of chessmen which combined elegance, solidity and clarity to a degree hitherto unknown. Appreciating the sales value of Staunton's name, they requested permission to name the design after him and to use his autograph on the box, permission which Staunton, liking the design and in consideration of his friendship with the designer, readily gave. It says much for his good taste that the pattern persists today, not only in England but throughout the world, as the best available. His small *Chess Player's Textbook* was produced to be given free to every purchaser of the Staunton pattern chessmen. The firm still produces its fine quality sets with the boxes all bearing a replica of Staunton's signature, but ironically they are now hard to come by in England since almost the entire production goes for export.

When the Prince Consort a year later presided over the planning of the Great Exhibition to be held in Hyde Park in 1851, Staunton was stirred from his retirement because he conceived the idea of a parallel chess project which was ultimately to put chessplayers all over the world in his debt. Lands were everywhere being spanned by railways and iron vessels were crossing the seas. The time to New York had been cut from a month to twelve and a half days. The hitherto impossible idea of collecting under one roof all the world's most famous players seemed now to be practicable for the first time. In spite of indifferent health he went to work, having as his pattern the purely domestic tournament held in January 1849 at Ries's (later Simpson's) Divan, which had been won by Buckle. The initial stages of his project were marred by an unseemly squabble of rival chess factions, and the London Chess Club dissociated itself from the venture and held its own tournament for foreign masters only a little later in the year. But the difficulties were overcome and it is to Staunton that the chess world in the first place owes the international tournaments which are now one of the chief features of chess activity. Staunton had hoped at the same time to have an opportunity of standardising the laws in all countries, but this part of the project did not materialise.

The tournament was to begin in May 1851, the month in which the Exhibition was officially opened. The choice of time was a happy one. Never before had London been so thronged with visitors from the provinces and abroad. Not all the players who it was hoped would attend were able to be present. Petroff and Schumoff were absent, though the latter was expected, and von Jaenisch arrived late. von der Lasa and Hanstein could not come, but the Berlin school was represented by Horwitz and Mayet, while Anderssen represented the newer German school. Lowenthal and Szen came from the Austro-Hungarian Empire and there was the Czech, 'old' Lowe of London. Of the French school Saint-Amant was on consular duty in California and Harrwitz absented himself because of his association with the London club, but Kieseritsky arrived. The British representation was weakened by the absence of Buckle who arrived too late, but besides Staunton there were H.E.Bird, E.Williams, M.Wyvill, Capt. H.A.Kennedy, Newham, Mucklow, Brodie and E.S.Kennedy, the last three coming in as reserves for Buckle, von Jaenisch and Schumoff. One of the most striking things is the high age of the chief contestants compared with modern times. Bird 21, Anderssen 33 and Wyvill 36 were the three youngest. Staunton, Lowenthal and Mayet were 41, Kennedy was 42, Horwitz 44, Kieseritsky 45, Szen 46 and Williams 47, while Lowe was 57. The knock-out system was employed and the draw, in days before the invention of 'seeding', had the disadvantage that most of the strongest players were in one half of the draw. Matches were for the best of three games but after the first round, to reduce the element of chance, this was altered to the best of seven.

It seems almost strange now that Anderssen hardly came into the reckoning of a possible winner. Staunton's chief rival was thought to be Szen, with Lowenthal and Kieseritsky as the next most likely winners. Anderssen was unknown except for having drawn a match with Harrwitz in 1848 and as a problemist. Anderssen himself hardly expected to win, and it must be presumed that before this tournament he had not discovered his own strength; for even with Lowenthal and Kieseritsky knocked out in the first round, he still felt so uncertain about the outcome that he made a compact with Szen that should either of them win, the other was to receive a third of the prize money. Tournament ethics have developed since those days!

The tournament was opened on May 26th and play began on the following day. Capt. H.A.Kennedy described the scene in the rooms of the St. George's Chess Club: 'It is a sultry morning as we enter the ground floor of No.5 Cavendish Square — the arena of the chess tournament. Passing through a large outer apartment, appropriated to the provincial matches' (the Provincial Tournament actually began one week later) 'we find ourselves standing in a smaller room, which is devoted to the general contests. The fray has already commenced and some half-dozen tables are occupied by combatants ... In the composed and somewhat ascetic countenance of Herr Anderssen you may read a steady reliance on his own strength and resources that augurs well for his success; whilst the uneasy trepidation manifest in the manner of M. Kieseritsky seems almost to foretell defeat. In truth, Kieseritsky's miserable want of nerve rendered him wholly unfit for important match-play. This fatal defect in his chess organization overshadowed him like an incubus, paralysing his fine genius. The slight figure, dark lineaments, and keen intellectual expression of the far-famed Hungarian Herr Lowenthal, contrast strongly with the burly form, light hair and eyes, and florid complexion of Mr. Williams ... Szen was the most jovial of chessplayers. There was an air of insouciance about him; a rollicking good humour perpetually dancing in his large round eyes that contrasted strikingly with the care-worn looks of some of the other combatants. With an irresistible pawn he thrusts his opponent to death in the most affectionate manner possible; and when he himself is moribund, to look at his cheerful countenance, you would think that to be checkmated was the pleasantest thing in the world.'

Of the actual arrangements Anderssen at least was somewhat critical: 'The provision for our comfort was not remarkable; tables and chairs small and low; the large boards projected over the edges of the tables on both sides. In short, there was no room to support your weary head on your hands during the hard struggle. It must be confessed an English player stands in no need of more comfortable surroundings. He sits on his chair straight as a poker, sticks his thumbs in the pockets of his waistcoat and stares at the board for half an hour motionless before moving.'

Nevertheless the German master won, and won convincingly, having had the hardest draw of any competitor — Kieseritsky, Szen and Staunton in the first three rounds. The tournament table is sufficient comment on the surprises which occurred.

```
Kieseritsky  ⎫  Anderssen  ⎫
Anderssen    ⎭  2-0 =1     ⎪
                           ⎪  Anderssen
Szen         ⎫  Szen       ⎪  4-2       ⎫
Newham       ⎭  2-0        ⎭            ⎪
                                        ⎪  Anderssen
Horwitz      ⎫  Horwitz    ⎫            ⎪  4-1       ⎫
Bird         ⎭  2-1 =1     ⎪            ⎪            ⎪
                           ⎪  Staunton  ⎪            ⎪
Brodie       ⎫  Staunton   ⎪  4-2 =1    ⎭            ⎪
Staunton     ⎭  2-0        ⎭                         ⎪  Anderssen
                                                     ⎪  4-2 =1
Lowenthal    ⎫  Williams   ⎫                         ⎪
Williams     ⎭  2-1        ⎪                         ⎪
                           ⎪  Williams               ⎪
E.Kennedy    ⎫  Mucklow    ⎪  4-0       ⎫            ⎪
Mucklow      ⎭  2-0        ⎭            ⎪            ⎪
                                        ⎪  Wyvill    ⎭
Mayet        ⎫  Kennedy    ⎫            ⎪  4-3
H.A.Kennedy  ⎭  2-0        ⎪            ⎪
                           ⎪  Wyvill    ⎪
Lowe         ⎫  Wyvill     ⎪  4-3 =1    ⎭
Wyvill       ⎭  2-0        ⎭
```

Play-off matches:-

    3rd and 4th prizes — Williams beat Staunton 4-3 =1
    5th and 6th prizes — Szen beat Kennedy 4-0 =1
    7th and 8th prizes — Horwitz beat Mucklow w.o.

Wyvill, the member of Parliament for Richmond, Yorks, made on this occasion his solitary and glorious incursion into competitive chess. But almost equally striking was Williams's defeat of Lowenthal and then of Staunton in the play-off. Since his move from Bristol to London he had attained master status, as his play reveals. Both Wyvill and Williams, and to some extent Buckle also, had so far absorbed Staunton's principles as to be quite at home in the close style of play, a concept almost entirely unknown to the foreign masters. Examine, for example, the opening moves of an Anderssen - Wyvill game in the final: 1 P-K4, P-QB4; 2 B-B4, P-K3; 3 N-QB3, P-QR3; 4 P-QR4, N-QB3; 5 P-Q3, P-KN3; 6 KN-K2, B-N2; 7 O-O, KN-K2; 8 P-B4, O-O; 9 B-Q2, P-Q4; 10 B-N3, N-Q5. Horwitz alone among foreign masters, due to his years of residence in England, had to some extent begun to master the style by the time of his second match with Harrwitz in 1849, a game from which, with Horwitz White, had begun: 1 P-QB4, P-K4; 2 N-QB3, P-KB4; 3 P-K3, P-B4; 4 P-Q3, N-KB3; 5 P-KN3, N-B3; 6 B-N2, P-Q3; 7 N-R3, B-K2; 8 P-B4, O-O; 9 O-O, P-KR3; 10 P-N3, B-Q2; 11 B-N2, N-KN5; 12 Q-Q2, B-B3; 13 N-Q5, and White stands better. But the style had only brushed off on Horwitz superficially, for he failed badly with it whenever he met Staunton.

There were obvious reasons for Staunton's failure. Besides the ill health which told against him in a strenuous or prolonged contest, he was burdened with the organisation and administration not only of this tournament but also of the Provincial tournament of ten players which was conducted at the same time, in which the first and second prizes fell to S.Boden and C.E.Ranken. Everyone was prepared to admit these handicaps to Staunton's play, and no immediate suggestion was made that the tournament in any way provided a final and conclusive test of the relative strengths of Staunton and Anderssen. But Staunton, always somewhat testy in temper and jealous of his reputation, was nettled by his failure against Williams in the play-off and in a subsequent match, and his violent efforts to excuse himself merely succeeded in creating an uncomfortable atmosphere and in leaving behind a somewhat unpleasant flavour. With Williams indeed, who seven years earlier had been delighted to hail him as 'The Champion of Chess', there was a complete breach, to which it must be admitted Williams's inordinate slowness of play was a contributory factor. Unhappily, before there could be any reconciliation, Williams fell a victim to the London cholera epidemic of 1854.

After the start of the tournament Buckle and von Jaenisch arrived, so the meeting was concluded with a number of set matches. Many casual games between the masters were also played, among them the 'Immortal' game won by Anderssen from Kieseritsky. In the matches Buckle beat Lowenthal and Lowenthal beat Williams, Horwitz beat Bird and Deacon beat Lowe. Staunton played two matches. In the first he conceded three games start to Williams in a match for the first seven wins, and though he scored 6-4 with one draw, the handicap was just too heavy. In the second he played von Jaenisch (1813-1872), the Finnish player who had been closely associated in Warsaw with Petroff, when together they analysed the Petroff Defence. Staunton won the match decisively by 7-2 with one draw. This meeting of the two men must have occasioned considerable pleasure to each, for both were much concerned with the need for an internationally agreed code of rules.

After the London meeting Staunton had virtually been promised a match with Anderssen at a later date, so in 1852 he put out a general challenge but nothing came of it, though it looked for a time as if Harrwitz might take it up. His book of the *Chess Tournament*, containing all the games in both the tournaments and in the various matches, appeared during that year.

Clubs which looked to him for encouragement seldom did so in vain. In May 1853, for example, he visited the Rockferry Chess Club, Birkenhead, and met their leading players in consultation. The game, at the striking odds for such an event of QN, was won by a pretty, if not quite sound, combination.

White: (without QN) **Staunton** Black: **Rockferry Chess Club** Evans Gambit
1 P-K4, P-K4; 2 N-KB3, N-QB3; 3 B-B4, B-B4; 4 P-QN4, BxP; 5 P-B3, B-R4; 6 O-O, N-B3; 7 N-N5, O-O; 8 P-B4, B-N3+; 9 K-R1, P-Q4; 10 PxQP, NxP; 11 B-R3, NxKBP; 12 N-K4, R-K1; 13 P-N3, B-KB4; 14 Q-B3, BxN; 15 QxB, N-K3; 16 RxP! (the best chance), K-R1!; 17 QR-KB1, N-N4; 18 B-B8!, NxR? (RxB!); 19 BxP+, KxB; 20 RxN+, **Resigns.**

In August, as his health was still poor, he took a holiday in Brussels, where he met the local champion de Rives in some friendly games, first level and then at the odds of Pawn and Two. The chief event of his visit, however, was a series of games against von der Lasa, who was there in a diplomatic post. Staunton, as in the case of the first match against Saint-Amant, described the games as casual in the extreme; his opponent once again took the opposite view. Certainly it was not a match in the sense that any stake or title was involved. Staunton describes the 10th game as 'dashed off in a canter', but in other games as much as an hour was spent over some of the moves. The series was left unfinished in the middle of the 13th game as Staunton had to return to London. In the twelve games finished von der Lasa led by 5-4 with 3 draws.

Staunton now determined to give up chess and devote himself to the work which really absorbed his interest and to which he had long felt himself called. He was widely read in the drama of the time of Elizabeth I and James I, and Shakespeare was his especial forte, due no doubt in part to his earlier acquaintance as an actor with the works of the Bard. He had no doubts that there was something of value he could leave to the world in this field and he believed that it was by this rather than by chess that he would stake his claim to fame. He gave up the editorship of the *Chess Player's Chronicle* to R.B.Brien, with whom he then played a match at Pawn and Two, though there is no record of the result. Any chess he played henceforth would be purely recreational and in the event it consisted primarily of occasional consultation games. He kept an interest in the game chiefly by retaining his weekly column in the *Illustrated London News*.

His first production in the new field was a complete edition of Shakespeare for Messrs. Routledge with 824 illustrations by Sir John Gilbert. This handsome work appeared in serial form from 1857 to 1860, and then was collected in a three volume version. An unillustrated edition in four volumes appeared in 1864. It was now that he was said to have 'combined commonsense with exhaustive research' and to possess 'a thorough mastery of the literature of the period'. Golombek does him less than justice in suggesting that he is now quite discredited as a Shakespearean scholar. The Variorum edition still carries many Staunton references, and they are not all by any means prefaced by 'Staunton wrongly surmises', even though he is probably no more than a minor figure in Shakespearean criticism. The commonsense with which he is credited sometimes seems excessive: in Act II, Scene 1, of *Julius Caesar,* when Brutus says, 'Kneel not, gentle Portia,' and she replies, 'I should not need, if you were gentle Brutus,' Staunton's insertion of a comma between 'gentle' and 'Brutus' rather detracts from the effect of her riposte. But the exhaustive research and knowledge was certainly there, for not many commentators would have been able to quote as an analogy to a Shakespearean passage a piece from *Riche his Farewell to Militarie Profession* of 1581.

He still made a point of attending the more important chess gatherings, and in 1857 was in Manchester for the Northern and Midland Counties Chess Association meeting, though he did not play in the tournament, which was won by Lowenthal ahead of Anderssen, Harrwitz and Horwitz. Anderssen seemed to regard the tournament as subsidiary to the long consultation game he played against Staunton.

The extent to which Staunton had for so long towered over the chess scene was highlighted by the fact that when Morphy came to Europe in 1858, his one overriding wish was to meet him over the board. A match between the two men was never really on from the start. Staunton, apart from his occasional consultation games, had completely retired from chess, a fact of which Morphy was apparently quite unaware. The original challenge from Morphy to the best players in Europe had suggested that they should meet him in New York but, as Staunton rightly pointed out in his column, if it was indeed true that a chess genius had arisen in the New World, it was up to him to come to Europe, the centre of chess life, to play. Nothing in Staunton's comment suggested that he was one of the European masters who would meet Morphy, although Morphy seemed to take it so. When Morphy arrived in England and asked for a match, Staunton reasonably enough pleaded that he was both out of practice and committed to bringing out his illustrated edition of Shakespeare in monthly instalments, which had started appearing from the previous November. He did not say he would not eventually play and the evidence is that he hoped to get once more into fighting trim and play a match. Morphy's ardent but polemical supporter, F.M.Edge, a reporter for the American *Herald,* published his version of the letters between the two men in a form most damaging to Staunton and one which is by no means devoid of bias. The great majority of American chess writers since then, with the notable exception of Bobby Fischer, have suffered from what may be termed the Morphy - Edge syndrome. Staunton was an experienced campaigner but was still not immune to that 'chess fever' which Morphy said he felt so strongly before an important contest, and he so far succumbed to it that, unwisely as it turned out, he allowed himself to be lured out of his retirement to take part in the Birmingham tournament of August 1858, in which Morphy was also entered. But Morphy, as the world was soon to realise, was himself an incipient psychopath and so, undoubtedly influenced by Edge, he put the worst possible construction on the replies he had received from Staunton and withdrew from the tournament. After the Birmingham meeting Morphy went off to France intending, so it was said, to return in time to meet Staunton in November, which had provisionally been suggested as a possible date. But Staunton's disastrous performance in the second round at Birmingham showed him the red light.

White: **Lowenthal**   Black: **Staunton**   Centre Counter
1 P-K4, P-Q4; 2 PxP, N-KB3; 3 B-B4, NxP; 4 P-Q4, P-K3; 5 N-KB3, B-Q3; 6 O-O, O-O; 7 B-Q3, B-B5?; 8 QN-Q2, N-QB3; 9 P-QR3, N-B3; 10 N-K4, BxB; 11 RxB, Q-K2; 12 R-K1, P-QN3; 13 NxN+, PxN?; 14 P-Q5, N-K4; 15 NxN, PxN

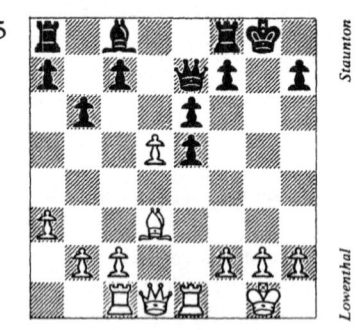

16 BxP+, KxB; 17 Q-R5+, K-N2; 18 R-K3, R-KN1; 19 R-N3+, K-B1; 20 Q-R6+, K-K1; 21 RxR+, K-Q2; 22 PxP+, QxP; 23 R-Q1+, K-B3; 24 QxQ+, PxQ; 25 R(1)-Q8, **Resigns**.

Staunton had to recognise that he was no longer the master he had been, so when Morphy wrote once more he declined a set contest altogether. It was not the most gallant of gestures, but it was certainly sensible. Had the two men met in a match in 1858 there is no doubt whatever that Morphy would have won, though he would have had a hard task against the Staunton of fifteen years earlier. As it was, a couple of consultation games, played in the month after his arrival in England, are all that came of the American's journey to meet the man who had been his great hero. Both were won by Morphy and his partner, and the following one is the more attractive of the two.

White: **Staunton & Owen**   Black: **Morphy & Barnes**   Philidor Defence
1 P-K4, P-K4; 2 N-KB3, P-Q3; 3 P-Q4, P-KB4; 4 QPxP, BPxP; 5 N-N5, P-Q4; 6 P-K6, N-KR3; 7 N-QB3, P-B3; 8 N(5)xKP, PxN; 9 Q-R5+, P-N3; 10 Q-K5, R-N1; 11 BxN, BxB; 12 R-Q1, Q-N4; 13 Q-B7, BxP; 14 QxNP, P-K6; 15 P-B3, Q-K2; 16 QxR

See Diagram 6 opposite

16 ..., K-B2; 17 N-K4, B-KB5; 18 B-K2, K-N2; 19 O-O, Q-QB2; 20 N-B5, BxP+; 21 K-R1, B-B1; 22 R-Q4, B-N6; 23 R-K4, K-R1; 24 R-Q1, Q-KN2; 25 R-KR4, BxR; 26 QxN, B-R3; 27 Q-R2, BxB; 28 R-Q7, Q-R3; 29 N-K4, B-B5; 30 N-B6, P-K7; 31 R-K7, Q-B8+; 32 Q-N1, QxQ+; 33 KxQ, P-K8/Q+; 34 RxQ, BxR; 35 **Resigns**.

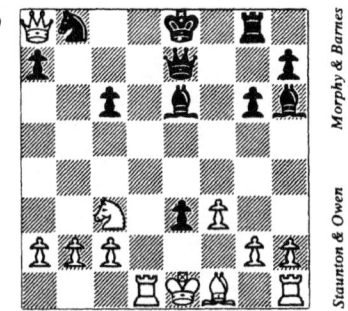

6 Morphy & Barnes / Staunton & Owen

That Staunton might have done better to refrain from being provoked into entering at Birmingham is clearly shown by the tournament table, though it was once more the eventual winner who put him out.

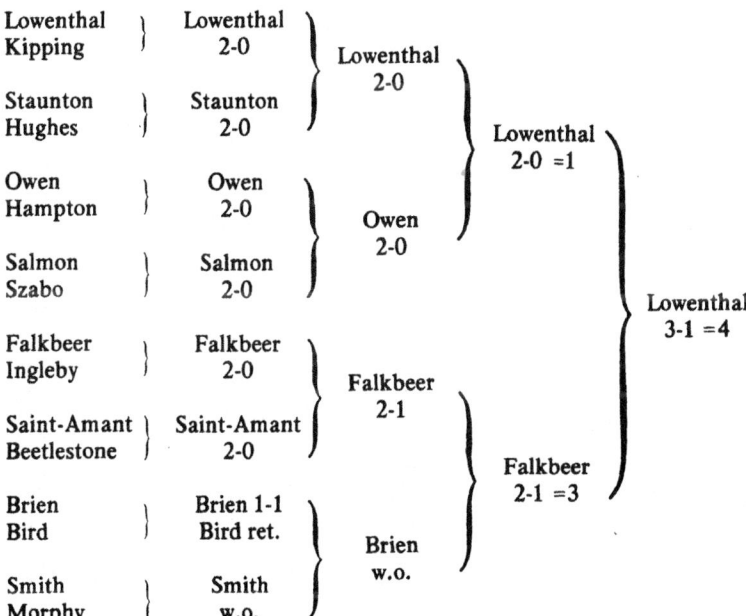

A tournament book was intended by Staunton but never appeared so that most of the scores are lost, the only source being the few in his *Chess Praxis*. Boden explained in his column in the *Field* that his periodical would refrain from publishing any games as Staunton would later produce them in book form, and the same no doubt applied to others. Neither the *Chess Player's Chronicle* nor *La Regence* was being published in 1858.

The only remaining record of chess activity by Staunton, apart from a few consultation games, was a so-called match early in 1859 in which he gave the odds of a knight to T.H.Worrall. The *Chess Monthly* mentions a match, but not the *Illustrated London News*, though the latter gives a game. Worrall was British Commissioner for the adjustment of Mexican claims, and was regarded as the champion of that country. He died in New York in September 1878 at the age of 71.

In 1860 Staunton's *Chess Praxis* appeared, which brought his *Handbook* up to date for, as he pointed out, 'certain systems of attack which were thought to be irresistible a few years ago, are now regarded as defective, and some lines of defence which the best authorities then deemed impregnable, are found to have their vulnerable points. Even in those openings of which the general principles are perhaps immutable, modifications have been suggested that materially affect their operation.' The book also included a very large collection of Morphy's games, including two apocryphal ones against Deacon, and also a selection from the Birmingham tournament.

He then reverted to his Shakespearean studies and in 1864 brought out a photolithographic reproduction of the Quarto edition of *Much Ado about Nothing*. In 1865 his versatile genius produced *The Great Schools of England*. He selected for this work ten of the leading endowed schools — Eton, Winchester, St. Paul's, Merchant Taylor's, Charterhouse, Harrow, Rugby, Shrewsbury and Christ's Hospital — but found he had to add five more in brief in an appendix — Cheltenham, Marlborough, Rossall, Wellington and Dulwich. The book contained descriptions of their foundation, endowments, organisation, curriculum and discipline. When a further edition came out in 1869, he included, in addition to his original fifteen, an appendix summarising some 800 other endowed establishments. For his time he had advanced views on education for, though he considered the great schools to be less intellectual than social agencies, he condemned fagging on the ground that, if power corrupted grown men, a mere adolescent could scarcely be preserved. If classics had to be taught — and in his day it was almost all that was taught apart from religion — he demanded that boys should be led to appreciate the heart, soul and whole organic existence of the ancients rather than just their grammar and vocabulary, but above all schools should come round to teaching the outlines of science, which was almost completely excluded. In fact, he declared that education in the natural sciences had not progressed in three centuries.

Meanwhile in 1866 he had produced a photolithographic facsimile of Shakespeare's *First Folio*, and from 1865 to 1869 had been editing *Chess World*, in which his irritable pomposity was given full rein.

Then in 1872 he began a series of papers in the *Athenaeum* on *Unsuspected Corruptions of Shakespeare's Text* which attracted attention even on the Continent and in America. These papers were intended to be merely preliminary to a new edition of Shakespeare, and in order to finance this project Staunton issued a prospectus which met with much verbal approval but insufficient help. He was, in fact, in low financial straits at this time and even asked the Government if his name might be put on the list of literary pensioners. Presumably his wife still had some small private means from her first marriage, for their house at 117, Lansdowne Road, Notting Hill, was in her name. Even so, they had to move to other accommodation nearby and it was soon after their arrival at 29, Elgin Road (now 27, Elgin Crescent) that a heart attack took him on 22nd June 1874 as he sat in his library chair working on the manuscript of a further chess book, which proved sufficiently advanced with the help of editing by R.B.Wormald, to appear in 1876 as *Chess: Theory and Practice*. Mrs. Staunton was left quite unprovided for, but the Government, in view of her late husband's recent request, made a donation of £200 from the Royal Bounty Funds.

So, at the age of 64, there passed from the scene a man who did some transitory damage but so much permanent good.

THE LATE MR. HOWARD STAUNTON.

PLAY AT ODDS

The practice of playing games at odds has so largely disappeared from the current chess scene that it seems desirable, when presenting a selection of Staunton's games, many of the best of which were not on level terms, to remind readers of the details of odds play.

For the purpose of calculating odds, players were divided into classes according to strength, and for all practical purposes five classes were recognised. Players in the same class met on level terms, the odds being increased as the difference in class increased.

Where the difference between the players was as much as four or three classes, the stronger player took White but started without his QR for a four-class difference, or his QN for a three-class difference. The absence of the QN is to some extent compensated by the speed with which White can achieve Q-side castling or otherwise get his QR into play. Where the QR is given, there has been a divergence of opinion as to whether Q-side castling is possible; the idea was generally rejected in England, but abroad the move K(K1)-QB1 was often permitted. White's problem at both these odds is to avoid excessive exchanges, every one of which tends to emphasise the weaker player's advantage. A remarkable example of this occurred when Staunton attended a chess meeting at Caistor on 25th October 1854. He took on, at the heavy odds of QN, one of the best provincial amateurs in the Rev. A.B.Skipworth (who later took part in the great 1883 London tournament, though he then had to retire half way through on account of ill health). In the following game Staunton departs from his normal treatment of the opening, presumably to avoid the exchanges which Skipworth may well have said he could pursue to victory.

White: (without QN) **Staunton**   Black: **Skipworth**   Sicilian Defence
1 P-K4, P-QB4; 2 P-KB4, N-QB3; 3 N-B3, P-Q3; 4 B-B4, P-K3; 5 O-O, B-K2; 6 B-N3, P-KR3; 7 P-B3, N-B3; 8 P-K5, PxP; 9 PxP, N-R2; 10 P-Q4, PxP; 11 PxP, N-N4; 12 B-K3, NxN+; 13 RxN, B-N4; 14 B-KB2, O-O; 15 B-B2, P-B4; 16 PxP e.p., BxP; 17 Q-Q3, R-B2; 18 Q-R7+, K-B1; 19 P-Q5, N-Q5; 20 PxP, BxP;

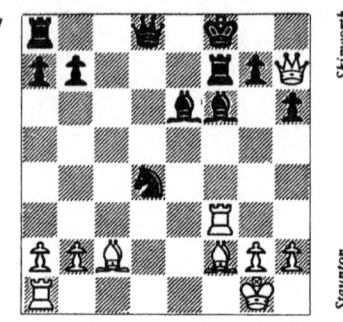

21 R-Q1, NxR+; 22 PxN, R-Q2; 23 RxR, BxR; 24 B-B5+, B-K2; 25 B-Q4, B-B3; 26 B-B5+, Drawn.

For a difference of two classes the odds were 'Pawn and Two Moves', where the stronger player took Black and started without his KBP. White then made two moves before Black made his first move, but was not allowed to invade his opponent's half of the board with his second move. It was not so much the material given up — a mere pawn — that constituted these odds as the fact that Black was forced into anti-positional moves from which it would take him all his skill to recover. As Staunton put it: 'These are very instructive odds; the attack they afford is sufficiently powerful to stimulate the inferior player to the utmost; and, on the other hand, to call into action all the skill and patient self-possession of his opponent, who for a long time, if the most is made of the opening, has quietly to submit to a galling fire from the enemy's forces, which he must be content to bear until the gradual development of his own pieces enabled him to change his defensive tactics and become the aggressor. There are no odds, however, so deceptive. An amateur, promoted from the ranks of Rook or Knight players, is so surprised at the apparent facility with which he can prosecute an assault, that he is very apt to overshoot his mark, and in the endeavour to crush his opponent in the outset permits the attack to be wrested from him before the game is half developed. The immense superiority in position which these odds afford, leads him also commonly into the error of believing that he must soon surmount them; that it is impossible for any player to continue giving him advantages of attack so striking for any length of time; experience, however, shows the contrary.' All the same, even so skilful a player at these odds as Staunton sometimes failed to survive the opening, as in the following game from his 1841 match with Zytogorski.

White: **Zytogorski**   Black: (without KBP) **Staunton**

1 P-K4, ——; 2 P-Q4, P-K3; 3 B-Q3, P-B4; 4 P-K5, P-KN3; 5 P-KR4, PxP; 6 P-KB4, Q-R4+; 7 B-Q2, Q-N3; 8 P-R5, QxP; 9 PxP, P-KR3; 10 P-N7, BxP; 11 Q-R5+, K-B1; 12 N-K2, QxR; 13 O-O, N-K2; 14 B-N4, N-B3; 15 BxN+, NxB; 16 N-Q2, QxP; 17 P-B5, NxP; 18 B-B4, QxP

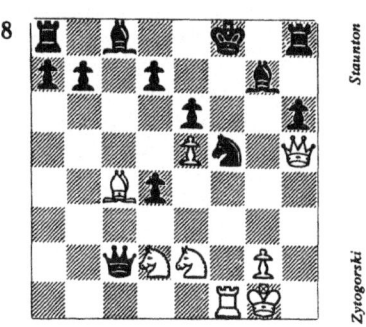

19 NxP, QxN; 20 NxN, BxP; 21 N-K3+, K-K2; 22 QxB, R-KN1; 23 N-Q5+, K-Q1; 24 Q-B7+, K-K1; 25 N-B6+, K-K2; 26 NxR+, **Resigns**.

For a difference of one class, the odds were 'Pawn and Move', with the same provisions except that White only makes one move before Black replies, and is therefore not restricted to his own side of the board for his second move. Staunton again: 'The difference between the odds of Pawn and Move and Pawn and Two Moves, though hardly appreciable by inferior players, is well known by proficients to be very great.' Yet, oddly enough, Staunton himself was much more successful when giving the heavier odds.

In the unlikely event of a difference of more than four classes, odds of QR plus QN, or of a Q, or of a 'capped' pawn (one predesignated to administer mate), are available. Other miscellaneous odds have been tried, such as giving the KN, or the QR in exchange for the QN, or even giving Pawn and Three Moves, or Two Moves without the Pawn, but all these can be disregarded.

There has been such a levelling up in master strength today that there is no longer even the difference of Pawn and Move between the strongest players, odds which were so often seen between some of the very best players 130 years ago. It may, however, be queried whether chess clubs in general should so completely have jettisoned odds play and the handicap tournament. Where there is a difference of, say, two classes in strength, it can do no good to either player to meet on level terms; the stronger puts no real effort into the game and the weaker starts with the conviction that he is beaten. It is rightly said to be the very best practice for young players to meet stronger opponents, but this assumes that their opponents will be forced to show their strength, so that the young player will learn by example. If the stronger were giving odds the example would be there. All that the young player would not then get would be practice in modern opening theory and, since that is so constantly volatile, excessive emphasis is all too easily placed on that.

The young player's weaknesses and the benefits he may derive from odds play were summarised by Staunton in his *Chess Player's Companion:* 'It is a great fault with many young players that they never know when they have sufficient force to win, and in their anxiety to save some Pawn or Piece which they might well spare, they afford an adversary time either to escape from an attack or to mature one, and finally lose the game. As far as our experience goes, and it extends over many years, we have always found that the amateur who most readily surmounted the large odds was not the one who tenaciously stuck to every Pawn as if its loss involved the game, but he who endeavoured to wrest the attack from his opponent and was always on the look-out to sacrifice his extra Piece for some decisive advantage in position.'

Thus it is with the best interests of young beginners at heart that the authors would like to see some revival of handicap play. One can be as fired with genuine ambition in trying to move from Class V to Class IV as one might be in competing for the Club Championship.

MATCH AND TOURNAMENT RECORD

* Scores marked by an asterisk are not final results, which are not known, but are totals of surviving games.

Place and Date	Opponent	Odds given by Staunton	Staunton's score + = −			Result
Oct-Nov. 1840, London	Popert	——	8	2	3 *	Won
Apr. 1841, London	Zytogorski	Pawn & Two	2	0	1 *	Won
Nov. 1841, London	Brown	Pawn & Two	5	2	3 *	Won
Dec. 1841, London	Stanley	Pawn & Two	2	1	3 *	Lost
Feb. 1843, London	Cochrane	——	14	0	4	Won
Mar. 1843, London	Taverner	Pawn & Two	5	0	1 *	Won
Mar-Apr. 1843, London	Saint-Amant	——	2	1	3	Lost
July, 1843, London	Brooke Greville	Pawn & Move	0	0	3	Lost
		Pawn & Two	5	0	1 *	Won
Sept. 1843, London	Buckle	Pawn & Move	1	0	2 *	Lost
Nov-Dec. 1843, Paris	Saint-Amant	——	11	4	6	Won
Sept. 1844, London	Tuckett	Pawn & Two	7	1	1 *	Won
May, 1845, Liverpool	Mongredien	Pawn & Two	2	3	0 *	Won
May, 1845, Liverpool	Spreckley	Pawn & Two	3	1	1 *	Won
June, 1845, Bristol	Williams	Pawn & Two	3	1	0 *	Won
Jun-July,1845, London	Kennedy	Pawn & Two	7	2	2 *	Won
Feb-Apr.1846, London	Horwitz	——	14	3	7	Won
June, 1846, Brighton	Hannah	Queen's N	5	1	2	Won
Sept-Oct.1846, London	Harrwitz	——	7	0	0	
		Pawn & Move	1	1	6	Won
		Pawn & Two	4	0	3	
July, 1847, London	Kenny	Queen's R	2	0	2 *	Lost
Dec. 1847, London	Lowe	Pawn & Two	1	2	4	Lost
1848, London	Medley	Pawn & Two	6	3	1	Won

1851 London International Tournament:

May.	Round 1	Brodie	——	2	0	0	
May-June	Round 2	Horwitz	——	4	1	2	4th prize
June.	Semifinal.	Anderssen	——	1	0	4	
July.	Play-off.	Williams	——	3	1	4	

July, 1851, London	Williams	3 games start	6	1	4	Lost on handicap
Aug. 1851, London	Jaenisch	——	7	1	2	Won
Aug. 1853, Brussels	von der Lasa	——	4	3	5	Lost (not finished)
Jan. 1854, London	Brien	Pawn & Two	?			?

1858 Birmingham International Tournament:

| Aug. | Round 1. | Hughes | —— | 2 | 0 | 0 | |
| Aug. | Round 2. | Lowenthal | —— | 0 | 0 | 2 | Unplaced |

1859, London	Worrall	Queen's N	?			?

| | | Total: | 146 | 35 | 82 | |
| | | Total on Level Terms: | 85 | 17 | 46 | |

THE 1843 WORLD CHAMPIONSHIP MATCH
described as 'The Grand Match between England and France'.

Staunton had Black in the odd-numbered games.

Game	Staunton's score	Moves	Opening	Duration (in hours)
1	1 - 0	33	Sicilian Defence (transposing to French Defence)	6
2	1 - 0	32	Benoni Defence	7
3	½ - ½	58	Sicilian Defence (transposing to French Defence)	7
4	1 - 0	28	Benoni Defence	4½
5	1 - 0	39	Sicilian Defence (transposing to French Defence)	9½
6	1 - 0	47	English Opening	4½
7	1 - 0	33	Queen's Gambit Declined	6
8	1 - 0	36	Sicilian Defence	7
9	0 - 1	35	Queen's Gambit Declined	8
10	1 - 0	61	Sicilian Defence	7½
11	0 - 1	50	Queen's Gambit Declined	8
12	1 - 0	89	English Opening	9
13	0 - 1	33	Queen's Gambit Declined	(No record)
14	½ - ½	62	English Opening	8¾
15	1 - 0	56	Queen's Gambit Declined	7
16	0 - 1	58	English Opening	(No record)
17	½ - ½	54	Queen's Gambit Declined	(No record)
18	½ - ½	57	English Opening (transposing to Q.G.D.)	(No record)
19	0 - 1	79	Queen's Gambit	(No record)
20	0 - 1	30	English Opening (transposing to French Defence)	(No record)
21	1 - 0	66	Queen's Gambit Declined	14

13 - 8   (Staunton: 11, Saint-Amant: 6, Drawn: 4).

Staunton was accompanied to Paris by two seconds, Capt. Wilson and Mr. J.Worrel. He partly attributed his poor showing in the last portion of the match to their absence from Paris in that period. Capt. Wilson with his chronometer kept a note of the duration of the games, except the 13th, until he left Paris. He also recorded the times taken by the contestants over individual moves in some of the games and, of those in our selection which were noted, the following details were recorded, showing Staunton as by far the quicker player:-

	Staunton	Saint-Amant
Game 4.	- - - - Under 5 minutes a move throughout.	18 minutes over move 9 20 - - - 15
Game 5.	- - - - 10 minutes over move 10	10 minutes over move 12 11 - - - 13 11 - - - 20 12 - - - 24 25 - - - 26 12 - - - 27 35 - - - 31 20 - - - 33 10 - - - 36 10 - - - 37
Game 7.	- - - - 16 minutes over move 21	10 minutes over move 11 15 - - - 14 15 - - - 20 14 - - - 22 12 - - - 23
Game 8.	- - - - 9 minutes over move 14 (all other moves less than 5)	12 minutes over move 11 45 - - - 14 14 - - - 16 10 - - - 17
Game 9.	- - - - 9 minutes over move 21	10 minutes over move 12 11 - - - 16 11 - - - 21 25 - - - 22 26 - - - 23 15 - - - 25 11 - - - 28 20 - - - 30 30 - - - 31 22 - - - 32
Game 13.	- - - - 10 minutes over move 24 25 - - - 25	10 minutes over move 24
Game 15.	- - - - 15 minutes over move 8 10 - - - 12 15 - - - 14 16 - - - 20 20 - - - 21	10 minutes over move 8 25 - - - 12 10 - - - 20 15 - - - 21 10 - - - 32 10 - - - 33 20 - - - 34 10 - - - 38 10 - - - 40 10 - - - 54

SELECTED GAMES

1
STAUNTON - AMATEUR
Casual game, London, c. 1839
Two Knights Defence

Morphy's description of Staunton as the author of some 'devilish bad games' may be forgiven as the exuberant utterance of childish immaturity, for when he came to manhood he admitted that there was no master whom he would sooner meet over the board. Fischer has ranked Staunton in his personal 'top ten'. But many mature men, and chessmasters at that, who should know better, have echoed Morphy's boyhood criticism. Horowitz, for example, inspired either by prejudice or sheer ignorance, wrote in his *History of the World Chess Championship:* 'About Staunton as a player it is perhaps impossible to be strictly objective; it is just too incredible that anyone seemingly so weak as he could have achieved such success and exerted such influence for so long.' Then, after quoting young Morphy, he adds: 'Devilish bad they are, and share with their author's prose style a turgidity that is truly exasperating.'

Seemingly weak to Horowitz he may have been perhaps, but he did achieve success and he did exert influence, and anyone who makes a proper study of his games will soon assess Horowitz's shallow criticism at its true value. The following devilish good game from his very early days displays not only a quality of high imagination but also a depth in analysis which is an impressive example of Staunton's powers in this respect.

1 P-K4	P-K4
2 N-KB3	N-QB3
3 P-Q4	PxP
4 B-QB4	N-B3

B-B4 would be the normal reply in the Scotch Gambit. Black's move turns the game into a Two Knights Defence, very little analysed at the time. The normal White continuations now are O-O or P-K5, more rarely N-N5. Staunton makes an unusual move, which may well be a valid idea to control his Q5 at the cost of a pawn.

5 B-KN5	P-KR3
6 BxN	

Or 6 B-R4?, P-KN4; 7 B-KN3, P-Q3; 8 O-O, B-N5!; 9 P-B3, PxP; 10 NxBP, B-N2; and Black stands better (Marshall - Smirka, 1925).

6 ...	QxB
7 O-O	B-B4
8 P-K5	Q-N3
9 P-B3	PxP
10 NxP	O-O
11 N-Q5	B-N3
12 P-QN4	K-R1

Against the threat of P-N5 and N-K7+.

13 P-N5	N-R4
14 B-Q3	Q-K3
15 B-B2	P-QB3

A natural enough reaction against White's grip on the centre, but he is never able after this to develop his Q-side, so P-Q3 was better.

16 N-B4, Q-B5; 17 P-N3, QxNP;

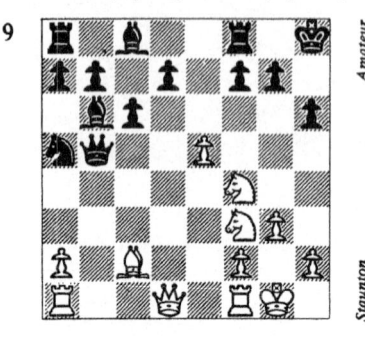

9

18 N-N6+

A highly imaginative sacrifice, indicating a young player of exceptional promise. Staunton's sacrifices in his maturer years could usually be found to secure a positional advantage or a calculable material one. The present offer is more speculative, and of absorbing interest and complexity. Staunton's own analysis reveals the profundity of thought which went into the move. He gives five main variations.

I — 18 ..., PxN; 19 N-R4, Q-B4; 20 Q-Q3, P-Q4; 21 NxP+, K-N1; 22 NxR, QxN; 23 Q-R7+, K-B2; 24 Q-N6+, with a draw.

II — 18 ..., PxN; 19 N-R4, K-N1; 20 Q-Q6, N-B5; 21 QxNP, NxP; 22 Q-R7+, K-B2; 23 N-B5

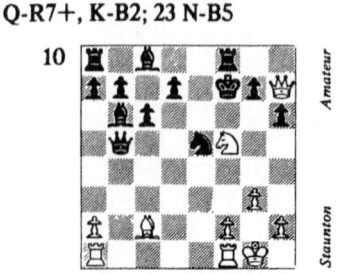

10

23 ..., N-B6+; 24 K-N2, Q-K4; 25 KR-K1, NxR+; 26 RxN, QxR; 27 QxP+, K-K3; 28 Q-K7+, K-Q4; 29 B-N3 mate.

III — 18 ..., PxN; 19 N-R4, R-K1; 20 Q-Q6, R-K3; 21 NxP+, K-R2;

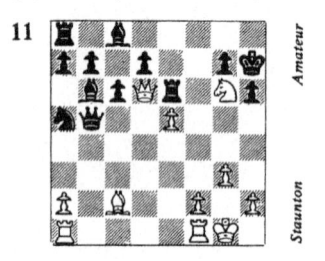

11

22 Q-B8, RxN; 23 Q-B7, Q-Q4; 24 BxR+, K-R1; 25 Q-B8+, Q-N1; 26 Q-Q6, N-B5; with an unclear situation. 26 Q-R3 would be stronger than Staunton's move.

IV — 18 ..., PxN; 19 Q-Q6, RxN; 20 QxNP, K-N1; 21 Q-Q7+, K-B1; 22 B-N6, after which Staunton gives three possible lines: **(a)** 22 ..., R-B2; which he considers best. 23 QR-Q1, N-B5; 24 Q-R8+, K-K2; 25 Q-N8, NxP;

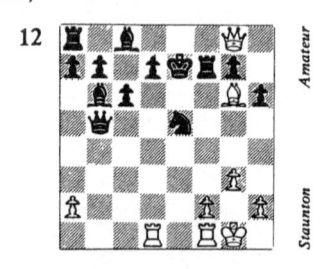

12

26 BxR, NxB; 27 QxP, Q-KR4; 28 QR-K1+, K-Q1; 29 Q-B6+, K-B2; 30 Q-B4+, P-Q3; 31 R-K7+, B-Q2; 32 RxN. **(b)** 22 ..., Q-Q4; 23 P-K6, QxKP; 24 Q-R8+, Q-N1; 25 QR-K1, B-K6; 26 RxB, RxR; 27 PxR+, winning. **(c)** — 22 ..., K-K2; 23 QxP+, K-K3 (Staunton himself gives the improvement K-Q1; 24 P-K6, Q-N4; 25 QR-Q1, P-Q4; with advantage); 24 QR-Q1, QxP; 25 KR-K1, BxP+; 26 K-N2, BxR;

13 *[position diagram — Amateur vs Staunton]*

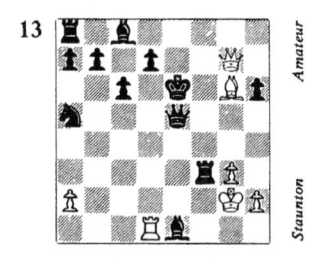

27 Q-N8+, K-K2; 28 Q-K8+, K-B3; 29 Q-B7+, K-N4; 30 P-R4+, K-N5; 31 QxR mate.
V — 18 ..., PxN; 19 Q-Q6, Q-B4; 20 QxNP, K-N1; 21 Q-R7+, K-B2; 22 B-N6+, K-K3; 23 QR-Q1, N-B5; 24 N-Q4+, KxP; 25 KR-K1+, winning. In view of all the possibilities, Black saw fit to decline the offer.

18	K-N1
19 Q-Q6	Q-B4
20 N-K7+	K-R1
21 Q-Q3	P-N3
22 NxP+	

An amusing echo of the earlier position.

22	PxN
23 QxNP	Q-K2
24 QxP+	K-N1
25 N-N5	Q-N2

He still cannot develop by P-Q4 because of 26 B-R7+, K-R1; 27 B-N6+, K-N1; 28 P-K6.

26 B-R7+	K-R1
27 Q-R5	B-Q1
28 B-N6+	K-N1
29 N-R7	B-K2

P-Q4 could now no longer save him.

30 NxR	BxN
31 QR-Q1	

A series of sledgehammer blows now annihilates Black.

31	N-B5
32 KR-K1	P-Q4
33 P-K6	B-Q3
34 R-Q4	N-K4
35 RxN	BxR
36 B-B7+	K-B1
37 R-KN4	Q-B3
38 R-N6	**Resigns**

2

STAUNTON - HARRISON
Casual game, London, c. Oct. 1840
(Staunton gave the odds of his QN)

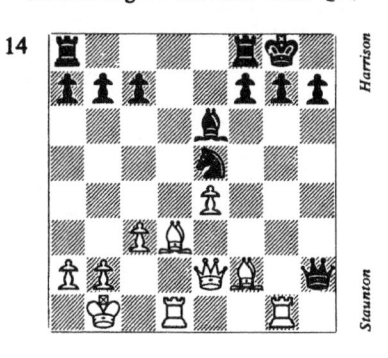

14 *[position diagram — Staunton vs Harrison]*

Staunton has some possibilities for an attack against Black's King, but should they be sufficient for a two pawn deficit? Black's unwise 20th move helps to provide a sparkling answer.

20 ......   NxB?
A positional blunder, in that he exchanges off a powerful blockading piece for a semi-useless Bishop. The move also constitutes a fatal tactical error, and Staunton is quick to spot the refutation.

21 RxP+!   K-R1
Or KxR; 22 B-Q4+.

22 B-Q4!!
Without pausing to recapture the Knight, Staunton delivers a second crushing stroke and Black has no choice but to accept the Queen. A neat see-saw mate then occurs by force.

22 ......   QxQ
23 RxBP+   K-N1
24 R-N7+   K-R1
25 R-N6+   Resigns

Mate cannot long be averted.

3

STAUNTON - POPERT
Match game, London, c. Nov. 1840
Bishop's Opening

1 P-K4   P-K4
2 B-B4

William Hartston is one modern player who does recognise Staunton's real stature. In his notes to one of his own games with this opening he wrote: 'Played by Larsen with success from 1964 until he discovered 1 P-QN3. Philidor rated this opening as the best White can select, while Staunton wrote, 'The move of 2 KB to QB's 4th is perhaps the very best that the first player can adopt.' With Philidor, Staunton and Larsen on my side, who needs theory?'

2 ......   B-B4

This has gone out of fashion. The almost automatic modern choice is N-KB3.

3 P-QB3   P-Q3

T.D.Harding's authoritative manual on this opening also mentions 3 ..., Q-K2 and 3 ..., N-KB3, but White seems to retain a slight edge against both of them.

4 N-B3

By 1847 (in his *Handbook*) Staunton had found the best line to be 4 P-Q4! e.g. 4 ..., PxP; 5 PxP, B-N5+; 6 N-B3, BxN+; 7 PxB, N-K2; 8 Q-R5, O-O; 9 B-KN5, P-KN3; 10 Q-R4, R-K1; 11 BxP+, and wins. Of course Staunton stacked the deck in White's favour by giving Black inferior moves (6 ..., BxN+ is awful), but White in any case is better after 4 P-Q4.

4 ......   N-KB3
5 P-Q4   PxP
6 PxP   B-N5+
7 B-Q2   BxB+
8 QNxB   O-O
9 B-Q3

Directed against P-Q4, or even NxP and P-Q4, exploiting the fork trick idea.

9 ......   N-B3
10 P-QR3   B-N5
11 Q-B2   P-KR3

12 R-QB1   P-Q4

This gives White a permanent positional advantage, but otherwise it was hard to parry the threat of O-O and P-Q5, annexing Black's QBP.

13 P-K5   BxN
14 NxB   N-KR4
15 P-KN3   P-KN3
16 P-QN4

One might have expected the sacrifice BxP, especially from a 19th century player. Doubtless it is quite playable but it leads to nothing definite and Staunton's rejection of the move (and he was probably right to reject it) was typical of his preference for solid moves unless he could see his way clear to a win.

16 ......   Q-Q2

Planning to meet 17 P-N5 with Q-N5; 18 PxN, QxN; 19 O-O, N-B5!; 20 PxN, Q-N5+; drawing.

17 Q-Q2   K-R2
18 O-O

A move to be noted. Late castling (or not castling at all!) is a feature of Staunton's games.

18 ......   QR-K1
19 R-B3

B-N5 looks attractive, but fails against 19 ..., NxKP!; 20 BxQ, NxN+; 21 K-N2, NxQ; etc. The text move threatens B-N5 by lending protection to White's knight.

19 ......   N-Q1
20 N-R4   P-QB3
21 P-B4   P-KB4

At all costs 22 P-B5 had to be prevented but the passed white KP is a useful asset and Black's rigid K-side pawn structure represents a ready target for the line-opening thrust P-KN4.

See Diagram

22 P-N4   N-N2
23 PxP   NxP

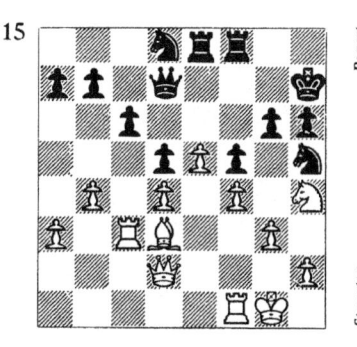

15

Popert

Staunton

24 NxN   PxN
25 K-R1   R-N1
26 R(3)-B1

Planning to break into Black's fortress via the KN-file.

26 ......   Q-KB2
27 Q-QB2

The KBP is a constant source of anxiety for Black. At the moment it requires the defence of two major pieces, which gives White the opportunity to seize the KN-file.

27 ......   R(K)-KB1
28 R-KN1   N-K3
29 RxR   KxR
30 R-N1+   K-R1
31 Q-B2   Q-R4

Given the chance, he had to play R-KN1! Popert's move just loses time.

32 B-K2   Q-B2

And not Q-R6; 33 R-N3, Q-R5; 34 R-N8+, winning Black's Queen.

33 Q-R4   Q-R2
34 B-R5   NxQP
35 R-N3?

Missing a quick win by B-B7! The threat then is Q-B6+, and if 35 ..., RxB; 36 Q-Q8+ is decisive, while 35 ..., QxB loses to 36 QxP+, Q-R2; 37 QxR+.

35 ......   P-N3
36 B-N6?

The previous note still applies.

36 ......   Q-KN2
37 B-B7

Still very strong, but Black now sheds the Queen rather than the King.

37 ......   RxB
38 RxQ   KxR
39 K-N2 and wins.

So says the surviving score, but after 39 ..., N-K3! it's very hard for White to make progress. A better line would be 39 Q-Q8! e.g. 39 ..., N-K3; 40 Q-Q6, NxP; 41 P-K6, which seems to win without difficulty.

4

STAUNTON - POPERT
Match game, London, c. Nov. 1840
Scotch Gambit

When did chessplayers first take account of 'chess theory'? Certainly by 1840, and this game recounts the unfolding of a full-blooded 19th century 'theoretical' duel.

1 P-K4   P-K4
2 N-KB3   N-QB3
3 P-Q4   PxP
4 B-QB4

The popular gambit line of the day. NxP was thought inferior because of 4 ..., Q-R5, and Horwitz only found 5 N-N5 six years later when he introduced it for the first time on 25th March 1846: Horwitz - Staunton, 14th match game. 4 ..., Q-R5; 5 N-N5, QxKP+; 6 B-K2, Q-K4?; 7 P-KB4, Q-QB4; 8 NxP+, K-Q1; 9 NxR, and Black never got anything for his rook. But 4 ..., Q-R5 is still playable and was championed by Steinitz: 5 N-N5, B-N5+; 6 B-Q2, QxKP+; 7 B-K2, K-Q1!; 8 O-O, BxB; 9 NxB, Q-KB5; 10 P-B4, N-B3; 11 N-KB3, N-KN5; 12 P-KN3, Q-B3; 13 N-B3, R-K1 (Vienna - London, Correspondence, 1872-4, in which Steinitz and Potter conducted the Black forces and established an advantage before conceding a draw.)

4 ......   B-N5+

Keres says of this: 'Hardly anyone would strive to win a pawn in this fashion nowadays; 4 ..., N-B3! is the move.' In other words he recommends transposing to the Two Knights Defence, as in Game 1. The text went out of favour very soon after this match and was replaced by B-B4.

5 P-B3!   PxP
6 O-O!   P-B7

The best chance of slowing down White's initiative. If instead 6 ..., PxP? then 7 BxP, N-B3; 8 P-QR3, B-B4; 9 N-N5, O-O; 10 NxBP, RxN; 11 BxR+, KxB; 12 P-K5, with advantage.

7 QxP   P-Q3
8 P-QR3   B-R4
9 P-QN4   B-N3
10 B-N2

Staunton improved on this in a game against de Rives, Brussels, 1853, which went 10 Q-N3, Q-K2; 11 N-B3, B-K3; 12 N-Q5, Q-Q2; 13 B-N2, KN-K2; 14 BxP, BxN; 15 PxB, N-K4; 16 NxN, PxN; 17 BxR, winning.

10 ......   N-B3
11 P-K5   PxP

12 NxP	NxN
13 BxN	O-O

Up to this point the players have been following the current 'book'. Staunton and Popert advanced the theory of the day concerning this line in a number of games from their match.

14 N-B3	N-N5
15 B-KN3	Q-N4
16 QR-K1	

Threatening P-R3, which if played at once would allow N-K6!

16	B-KB4
17 Q-N3	

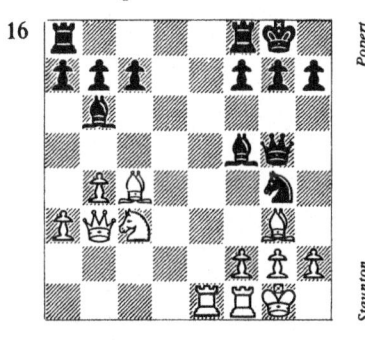

This position was reached three times in the match. One game went 17 ..., P-B3; 18 P-QR4, QR-Q1; 19 N-K2, P-QR3; 20 P-N5, RPxP; 21 PxP, B-R4; 22 R-R1, PxP; 23 QxP, P-QN3; 24 QR-Q1, P-R3; 25 RxR, RxR; 26 B-B4, Q-N3; 27 N-Q4, B-Q2; 28 Q-N3, Q-KB3; 29 N-K2, B-K3; 30 BxB, QxKB; 31 QxQ, PxQ; with a draw on move 59.

In a later game Staunton continued (after 17 ..., P-B3) with the considerably more risky 18 B-Q6. There followed: 18 ..., NxBP; 19 BxR, B-R6; 20 BxP+, KxB? (K-R1!; 21 B-Q5, N-K5+); 21 B-Q5, PxB; 22 QxP, Q-B3; 23 PxB, NxP+; 24 K-N2, N-B7; 25 N-K4, Q-N3+; 26 Q-KN5, Q-QB3; 27 RxN+, BxR; 28 KxB, K-N1; and White won.

On the whole, given that the weakness of Black's Q3 appears not to be serious, 17 ..., P-B3 looks like the best buy for Black. Popert's choice of move in this game leads to unmitigated disaster.

17	N-B3
18 R-K7!	B-N3
19 BxP	N-N5

This sign of hesitation is a clear indication of Black's problems. Possibly he overlooked White's reply, but in any case his position does not inspire much confidence.

20 N-Q5	BxB
21 RxB	QR-K1
22 Q-N3	P-KR3
23 P-B4!	Q-B4
24 N-K7+	

Forcing a decisive material gain. The remainder is in the nature of mopping up.

24	RxN
25 RxR	Q-B3
26 QxN	QxR
27 QxB	Q-K6+
28 K-R1	QxRP
29 Q-K4	Q-QB6
30 P-R3	R-B1
31 B-Q3	R-Q1
32 R-B3	P-KN3
33 B-B4	R-Q8+
34 K-R2	Q-K8?
35 QxP+	Resigns

5

ZYTOGORSKI - STAUNTON
Match game, London, c. April 1841.
Odds of Pawn and Two (Remove Black's KBP)

In a way this game is absurdly lightweight, but it does have the merit of being, perhaps, the first 'Greek Gift' sacrifice on record. Its value is enhanced by the appearance of the motif in a disguised form.

1 P-K4	———
2 P-Q4	P-K3
3 B-Q3	P-B4
4 PxP	Q-R4+
5 N-B3	QxBP

BxP looks more natural. Compare Game 29.

6 B-K3	Q-QR4
7 N-K2	B-Q3
8 O-O	N-KB3
9 P-QR3?	

Preparing for suicide. After P-KR3 White stands clearly better.

| 9 ...... | O-O |

Cunningly ignoring White's intentions.

10 P-QN4?

This sets the seal on his own defeat. Zytogorski was obviously unaware of the little combination conceived by Staunton which has now become the stock-in-trade of all strong players.

| 10 ...... | BxP+! |

See Diagram

The Argive Prelate strikes. This is a good example of a combinational idea that recurs frequently and can therefore be learnt. White's King is stripped of his defences and mate is inevitable.

| 11 KxB | Q-R4+ |

The normal sacrificial mechanism operates while the Queen is on her original square (1 ..., BxP+; 2 KxB, N-N5+; 3 K-N1, Q-R5 etc.). With Staunton's Queen lurking far away on the opposite wing, Zytogorski probably never dreamt that the Black Amazon could switch fronts so rapidly and head a victorious onslaught against the White monarch.

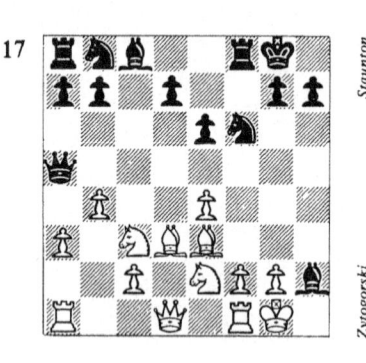

12 K-N1

Or 12 K-N3, Q-N5+; 13 K-R2, Q-R5+; 14 K-N1, N-N5 as in the game.

| 12 ...... | N-N5 |
| | **Resigns** |

A neat smothered mate occurs after 13 R-K1, Q-R7+; 14 K-B1, NxB mate.

6

STANLEY - STAUNTON
Match game, London, December 1841
(Staunton gave the odds of Pawn and Two)

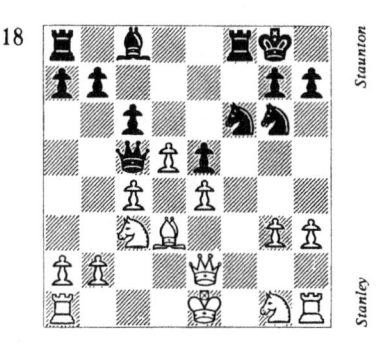

14 ...... N-R4!

A coup which emphasises White's dark square weakness and highlights the soft spot on his KN3.

15 QxN

Q-N2 loses to Q-K6+, so White is obliged to permit the full force of Black's intended idea.

15 ......   Q-B7+
16 K-Q1   QxQNP
17 Q-K2

This loses, but if R-B1, then Q-N7! picks off the other rook.

17 ......   QxR+
18 K-B2   P-N4

Opening more lines against White's King.

19 PxNP   PxNP
20 Q-N2   P-N5
21 KN-K2   R-B7!

A neat simplification after which Black should experience few obstacles in converting his superiority into victory.

22 QxR   QxR
23 N-N5   B-R3
24 Q-KB5   B-B1
25 Q-N5

If White had retreated his Queen to B2, Black would obviously have chosen a different square for his QB.

25 ......   B-Q2
26 N-B7   R-KB1
27 N-K6   R-B1+
28 K-Q2   QxRP
29 B-R6   BxN
30 PxB   QxKP

Black should retain sufficient advantage even after the return of the exchange.

31 BxR   QxB
32 Q-K3   P-QR4?

Uncharacteristically impatient. He should play Q-QN1, not only defending all the pawns but reinforcing the potentially passed QNP.

33 Q-N3+   K-R1
34 Q-Q5   P-R5
35 Q-R5

For after 35 Q-N5, Black has nothing better than P-N6; 36 PxP, PxP; 37 QxP, P-R3 followed by Q-N5 or Q-R6, when he still has winning chances, but it will take a long, long time.

35 ......   P-N6
36 PxP   PxP
37 Q-N4   Q-B7+
38 K-K3   P-R3
Resigns

7

STAUNTON - COCHRANE
Casual game, London, 1842.
Evans Gambit

1 P-K4	P-K4
2 N-KB3	N-QB3
3 B-B4	B-B4
4 P-QN4	

The characteristic move of the Evans Gambit, which was at this time probably the most popular of all openings, at least in English chess circles. For the pawn White obtains open lines and time for developing an attack against the opposing King. Capt. Evans invented his gambit in 1827 after Cochrane had gone to India, but Cochrane was certainly aware of the opening's intricacies.

4	BxP
5 P-B3	B-R4
6 O-O!?	

An inaccurate move, albeit one always played by Tchigorin. Anderssen and Morphy, and most 20th century exponents of the Evans, preferred 6 P-Q4, which reduces Black's defensive options.

6 ...... B-N3!

Black anticipates the discovery of Lasker's Defence by 50 years. Now if 7 P-Q4, P-Q3; 8 PxP, PxP! White can regain his pawn after 9 QxQ+ (Tchigorin - Pillsbury, London 1899), or 9 Q-N3, Q-B3; 10 B-KN5, Q-N3; 11 B-Q5, KN-K2 but either way an ending results where Black's two bishops can take advantage of White's Q-side pawn weaknesses.

7 B-R3!?

White should none the less play 7 P-Q4, since with care he can maintain the balance. The move played commits him prematurely.

7	P-Q3
8 P-Q4	PxP!?

A sound line for Black is 8 ..., Q-B3! since White has denied himself the thematic reply B-KN5. Then 9 B-N5, B-Q2; 10 QN-Q2, KN-K2 leaves him with no genuine compensation for his pawn.

9 PxP

Now by transposition we have reached a version of the 'Normal Position', in which White has played the erratic 9 B-R3 instead of the superior 9 P-Q5 or 9 N-B3.

9 ...... N-B3?

A common 19th century error in similar Evans positions (e.g. with N-QB3 instead of B-R3 for White). After the text White gains an extra tempo, opens lines and his 7th move is suddenly justified. Black should have played KN-K2 so as to answer 10 P-K5 with P-Q4.

10 P-K5! PxP?

A further mistake after which Black is doomed. Only N-KN5 offered chances, although White stands well with 11 P-KR3, N-R3; 12 PxP, PxP; 13 R-K1+, N-K2; 14 N-B3.

11 Q-N3 Q-Q2

The only conceivable defence, but it is prettily refuted.

12 PxP N-QR4

White ignores this demonstration and pursues his attacking theme with single-minded vigour.

13 PxN!	NxQ
14 R-K1+	K-Q1
15 B-K7+	K-K1

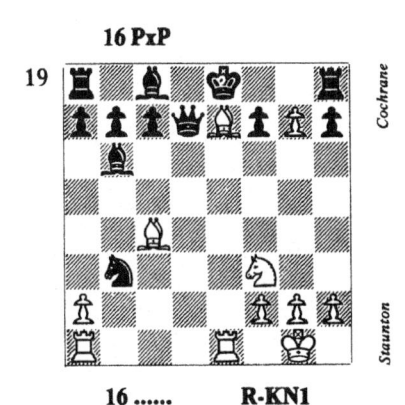

16 PxP		17 B-B6+	Q-K3
		18 BxQ	BxB
		19 PxN	Resigns

Staunton's beautiful Queen sacrifice secured the gain of a piece in every variation. The game is typical of Staunton's style in that he expertly perceived a sacrificial variation which led to an analytically verifiable advantage.

We are indebted to T.D.Harding's encyclopaedic knowledge of 19th century opening theory for help with this and the other Evans Gambits.

16 ...... R-KN1

8

STAUNTON - COCHRANE
Casual game, London, 1842

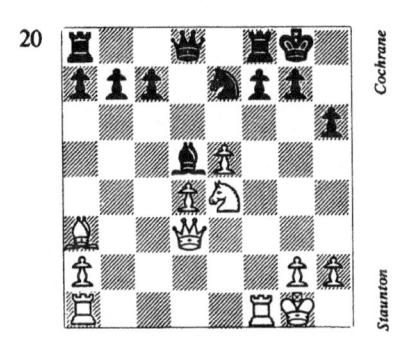

A further example of Staunton's tactical skill in situations where the winning sequence can be verified analytically. This position also arose from an Evans Gambit.

18 N-B6+

This offer must be accepted, for if 18 ..., K-R1?; 19 Q-R7 mate.

18	PxN
19 BxN	QxB

Also obligatory.

20 Q-N3+	K-R2
21 PxP	

The point. Mate and the Queen are threatened, so White secures a decisive gain of material.

21	R-KN1
22 PxQ	RxQ
23 PxR	R-K1
24 QR-K1	B-K3
25 R-K5	Resigns

9

COCHRANE - STAUNTON
Casual game, London, 1842
Bishop's Opening

In spite of its undistinguished opening phase, this game is one among the many that certainly refutes the commonly held misconception that Staunton was lacking in tactical imagination.

1 P-K4	P-K4
2 B-B4	N-KB3
3 P-Q4!?	

N-QB3 or P-Q3 are superior positional continuations.

3 ...... P-B3?!

An essentially dubious idea, although it was the current 'book' move. Black should play PxP, when there are three main variations: (i) 4 P-K5 (Ponziani), P-Q4!; 5 B-N3, N-K5; 6 N-K2, B-QB4; 7 P-KB3, N-N4; as was later suggested by Staunton. (ii) 4 N-KB3 (Urusov), B-B4!? with some advantage to White after 5 P-K5, P-Q4; 6 PxN, PxB. Alternatively there is either 4 ..., P-Q4; 5 PxP with an unclear game, or 4 ..., N-QB3 leading to the Two Knights Defence. (iii) 4 QxP, N-B3 gives a line in the Centre Game.

4 N-KB3

More testing is 4 PxP, NxP (better than 4 ..., Q-R4+; 5 N-B3, NxP; 6 BxP+ as in Marshall - Forsberg, New York, 1925); 5 Q-B3, P-Q4; 6 PxP e.p., NxQP; 7 B-N3 with the better game for White. Black's 3rd move is now only a liability.

4 ...... NxP

Interesting play could follow 4 ..., P-Q4; 5 KPxP, P-K5; 6 N-K5, PxP; 7 B-N5+, B-Q2; 8 Q-K2 and then either (a) 8 ..., Q-R4+?!; 9 N-B3, B-QN5; 10 B-Q2, BxB; 11 QxB+, QxQ; 12 NxQ, BxB+; 13 KxB and the White knights are dominating, or (b) 8 ..., B-K2 (B-Q3!?); 9 O-O, O-O;

10 N-B3, P-QR3 (N-B3!?); 11 BxB, QNxB; 12 B-B4, B-N5; 13 N-Q1! (intending N-K3-B5), NxN; 14 PxN with central pressure.

5 PxP	P-Q4
6 PxP e.p.	NxQP
7 B-K2	

Innocuous. If White wants an opening advantage he must try 7 B-N3, Q-K2+; 8 Q-K2 (not B-K3, N-B4; 9 O-O, NxB; 10 PxN, B-K3!), QxQ+; 9 KxQ, although in view of symmetry his edge is only slight. In another game Cochrane followed the current 'book' more precisely with 7 B-Q3 and eventually won after B-K2; 8 O-O, O-O; 9 B-KB4, B-N5; 10 N-B3, P-QN4?; 11 R-K1, K-R1; 12 Q-K2, B-K3; 13 BxN, BxB; 14 QR-Q1, Q-B2; 15 BxRP.

7	B-K2
8 O-O	O-O
9 B-KB4	B-N5?
10 R-K1	B-K3

Black has wasted a tempo, so White would stand quite well if he continued normally with his development. Instead he returns the tempo at once.

11 B-Q3?

Introducing an artificial attacking idea. The unpretentious N-B3 was correct, planning Q-Q2 followed by QR-Q1, with some advantage at least.

11	P-KR3
12 N-K5	N-Q2
13 N-N6?	

A typical Cochrane ingenuity, with the threat of 14 NxB, QxN; 15 BxN,

QxB; 16 B-R7+, but in fact NxN was necessary. Staunton has seen further and he now springs his trap.

13	PxN
14 BxN	BxB
15 RxB	BxP+!

A bolt from the blue for Cochrane. It is not until his 23rd move that the point of Staunton's combination is revealed.

16 KxB

If K-B1, Staunton intended 16 ..., RxP+; 17 KxR, Q-R5+; 18 K-K2, Q-N5+; 19 K-Q2, B-B5+; etc.

16	Q-R5+
17 K-N1	QxP+
18 K-R1	R-B5

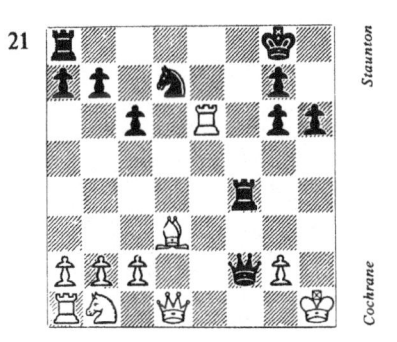

21

Staunton

Cochrane

White has only one way to parry the mate.

19 R-K4	Q-R5+
20 K-N1	RxR
21 BxR	QxB
22 QxN	Q-K8+
23 K-R2	Q-K4+!

The long concealed point.

| 24 K-R1 | QxP |
| | **Resigns** |

Staunton's 15th move inaugurated a fine piece of calculation with a powerful sting in its tail. White emerges from the complications the exchange and several pawns to the bad.

H.Staunton

10

COCHRANE - STAUNTON
Casual game, London, 1842.
Bishop's Opening

1 P-K4	P-K4
2 B-B4	B-B4
3 P-Q4	BxP
4 N-KB3	N-QB3!

In a previous game Staunton tried the weaker Q-B3 and was attractively beaten after 5 O-O, B-N3; 6 N-B3, P-B3; 7 B-KN5, Q-N3; 8 NxP!, QxB; 9 NxBP, Q-QB4; 10 B-N3, P-Q4; 11 NxR, N-B3; 12 PxP, PxP; 13 NxP, QN-Q2; 14 Q-K2+, K-B1; 15 QR-K1 P-QR3?; 16 NxN, NxN; 17 N-B7, B-Q2; 18 N-N5, R-K1; 19 QxR+!, NxQ (BxQ; 20 N-K6+); 20 NxP mate. Anyone may make a mistake once, but only a complete idiot makes the same mistake a second time. Staunton is far from idiotic and now finds a much better line.

5 O-O	N-B3
6 NxB	NxN
7 P-B4	P-Q3
8 PxP	PxP
9 B-KN5	B-K3!
10 BxB	NxB
11 QxQ+	RxQ
12 BxN	PxB
13 RxP	N-B5!

Classic refutation of gambit play by Staunton, who happily returns his pawn for an endgame advantage.

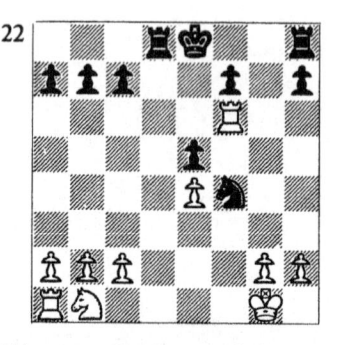

22

This sort of play reminds one of Lasker (e.g. his defence to the Evans Gambit) rather than the miserly Steinitz who always clung to his spoils and sometimes came unstuck because of it!

14 N-B3	R-Q7
15 R-Q1	

P-KN3 is forced even though it is a rotten move.

15	RxP+
16 K-R1	KR-N1
17 R-B5	P-KB3!

Neatly protecting his King from check.

18 RxP	N-R6
19 R(6)-B1	R-N8+!
20 RxR	N-B7 **mate**

A fine revenge for the earlier loss quoted in the note to move 4.

11

STAUNTON - AMATEUR
Casual game, London, c. Dec. 1842
(Staunton gave the odds of his Queen's rook)

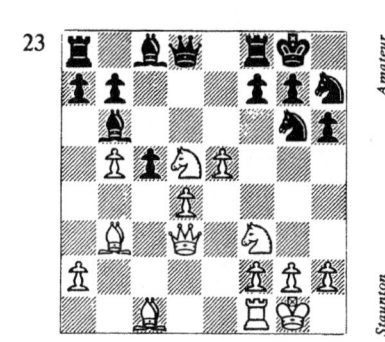

Black has just played 14 ..., P-B4? overlooking White's threat. Staunton duly executes his dark design.

15 QxN! PxQ
16 N-K7+ K-R1
18 NxP mate

Black could have bypassed this finale with 15 ..., K-R1!; but in that case White would have retained more than adequate positional compensation for his slight material deficit — the exchange for a pawn.

12

COCHRANE - STAUNTON
Match game, London, Feb. 1843
Sicilian Defence

The brilliance of Cochrane at his best was fully equal to the splendour of Labourdonnais or McDonnell, as exemplified in a game in the Biography at the start of this book. But eventually Staunton succeeded in taming him, and in their later encounters one can witness the early stirrings of the prophylactic style, later to be formulated by Nimzowitsch. In the following game Staunton thwarts all of Cochrane's efforts to implement an attack on the KB file and by the time Cochrane blunders on move 25, his position has already foundered on Staunton's iron-hard, yet imaginative, defence.

1 P-K4 P-QB4

It was about this time that Staunton began to adopt the Sicilian Defence for important games. Oddly enough, after his day it went out of fashion for almost ninety years and never attained a comparable height of popularity amongst the leading exponents of the game until the dynamic Russian revival of the defence in the middle of the 20th century. The Sicilian received very little attention from Morphy, Steinitz, Tchigorin and Tarrasch, and even so modern a player as Capablanca viewed it with distaste, declaring Black's position to be 'full of holes'. The virtually inevitable weakening of Black's QP rendered it suspect in the eyes of classically orientated players.

Yet Staunton, like the Russians, felt that Black's compensating dynamic chances more than made up for the structural weaknesses Black might have to weather.

2 P-Q4   PxP
3 QxP

Not good, since White gratuitously wastes tempi with the Queen. Cochrane was one of the first to play P-Q4 against the Sicilian, but Staunton it was who saw that an idea tried out by McDonnell was correct and firmly introduced the recapture with the knight after N-KB3.

3 ......   N-QB3
4 Q-Q1   N-B3

In another game from the match Staunton played P-K4 here and won brilliantly: 5 B-QB4, N-B3; 6 N-KB3, B-B4; 7 O-O, O-O; 8 N-B3, P-KR3; 9 P-QR3, P-R3; 10 B-Q5?, P-Q3; 11 BxN (an erroneous plan), PxB; 12 N-K1, N-N5; 13 P-R3, N-B3; 14 K-R1, N-R2; 15 N-Q3, B-R2; 16 P-B4, Q-R5; 17 Q-B3, P-KB4; 18 PxBP, BxP; 19 P-KN4, N-N4!; 20 Q-N2 (PxN, BxNP! wins), NxP; 21 Q-R2, QxP; 22 Q-N2, Q-R5; 23 Q-R2, P-K5; 24 N-K1, B-N8; 25 RxB, N-B7+; 26 K-N2, B-R6+; Resigns.

5 B-Q3   P-K4

Not the only plan of course, but Staunton, when he started playing this defence, favoured this move as a method of staking a claim in the centre and bringing out his KB onto an aggressive square (QB4). For the same idea in more sophisticated form see Game 56. Alternatives here were P-Q3 and P-KN3, or even P-Q4 which gives a free open game.

6 N-KB3   B-B4
7 O-O   P-Q3
8 P-KR3

P-B3 looks best, but the line played represented the theory of the day and was repeated in several games of the match. Obviously both players were satisfied with their prospects in this position. On another occasion Cochrane chose B-KN5 when there followed 8 ..., B-KN5; 9 N-B3, N-Q5; 10 N-Q5, BxN; 11 PxB, P-KR3; 12 NxN+, PxN; 13 B-R4, Q-Q2; 14 P-B3, N-K3.

8 ......   P-KR3
9 N-B3   O-O
10 N-R2

A cumbersome method of playing for P-KB4, which Staunton expertly parries.

10 ......   N-Q5
11 K-R1   N-K3

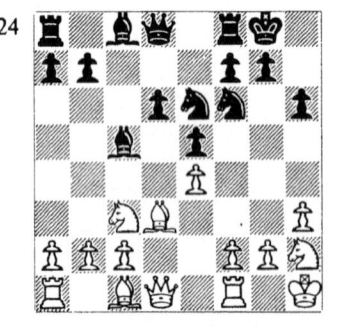

24

A subtle manoeuvre. If White insists on playing P-KB4 (which he does), then Black will gain the Bishop pair, isolate White's KP and establish fluent control of many important central dark squares.

12 P-B4

No modern master would commit this positional error. The most promising course was probably B-QB4, activating the KB.

12 ......   PxP
13 BxP   NxB
14 RxN   B-K3
15 Q-K2   B-Q5

Transferring this piece to a square whence it exerts a powerful influence on both wings.

16 QR-KB1

If N-B3, then 16 ..., BxN; 17 PxB, N-Q2 aiming for K4, is very good for Black. The text could be very dangerous for Black if he defended incautiously.

16 ......   B-K4
17 R(4)-B2   R-B1

Even here BxQN; 18 PxB, N-Q2 would be excellent for Black, but the active textmove is more ambitious.

18 P-R3

Evincing an anxiety for his Q-side pawns, but also setting a trap which Staunton avoids.

18 ......   R-B4!

A wonderful defensive idea. Black actually intends to switch this unit into action on the K-side via the dark squares, beating White at his own game. But not 18 ..., BxN; 19 PxB, RxP? (N-Q2 would still be all right); 20 RxN!, PxR; 21 N-N4, K-R2; 22 Q-Q2 and wins. 22 P-K5+, would also be very strong.

19 N-Q1   B-Q5

Making way for the Rook.

20 R-B3   R-KN4
21 P-B3   B-K4
22 P-KN4

To prevent N-R4-N6 and probably hoping to corner Black's Rook, but now comes the climax of Staunton's conception which smashes holes in White's K-side.

22 ......   P-KR4!

25

Hereafter White cannot defend his KNP, while if 23 PxP, then NxRP and N-N6+ cannot be prevented in any satisfactory manner.

23 Q-K3   PxP!
24 QxR   PxR
25 RxP?

Losing at once. If White wanted to recapture the advanced Black KBP, it had to be with the Knight, e.g. 25 NxP, N-Q2 (BxRP; 26 R-KN1 gives White unnecessary chances); 26 QxQ, RxQ; 27 NxB, PxN; 28 N-B2, N-B4 but then Black's positional advantage is overwhelming; White's pawns are weak and his pieces miserably placed in comparison with his opponent's.

25 ......   BxN

A simple refutation.

26 RxN   B-K4
27 R-B5   BxR
28 QxB   Q-R5
         Resigns

13

COCHRANE - STAUNTON
Casual game, London, March 1843
Odds of Pawn and Move (Remove Black's KBP)

A game that could easily pass for one by Nimzowitsch, both in the opening, in which Staunton uses a Nimzowitschian idea to cope with the absence of his KBP, and also in the subsequent strategy.

1 P-K4	N-QB3
2 P-Q4	P-Q4
3 P-K5	

Too static. With Black's KBP missing White should try the more energetic N-QB3, since the text grants Black a welcome respite to consolidate his position. We must not forget that Black not only had to overcome a material disadvantage at these odds, but was also faced with the problem of surviving the opening moves minus the natural protector of his King. In view of this it was hardly wise for White to construct a blocked pawn chain at such an early stage.

3	B-B4
4 P-QB3	P-K3
5 N-B3	KN-K2
6 B-Q3	BxB
7 QxB	

So far Black's play (anachronistically speaking) has been pure Nimzowitsch but now Nimzowitsch would have fortified the light squares on the K-side by P-KR4 and N-B4. Staunton cannot follow such a line without a KBP because of the resulting weakness of his KN3.

7	N-N3
8 N-N5	

Starting a vain attack on Black's KP, which turns into a dubious hunt for the KRP. More sensible would have been B-N5. Staunton's own comments on odds play, quoted in the introductory portion of the book, make pertinent reading here.

8	Q-Q2
9 Q-R3	N-Q1
10 O-O	B-K2
11 NxRP?	

Quite wrong. This irrelevant capture leaves White's Knight in difficulties and the energy expended in extricating the poor beast gives Black the opportunity for a powerful counter-attack along the files White has conveniently opened. Had White had his eye only on the KRP, and not also on the KP, he would have made this capture on the 9th move, but he would still have opened files for his opponent.

| 11 ...... | N-B2! |

And not the precipitate N-B1 on account of 12 N-B6+.

12 Q-R5	N-R5
13 P-KN3	

There is no other remedy against the threat of P-KN3.

13	P-KN3
14 Q-N4	RxN
15 PxN	BxP
16 QxP?	

Suicidal. Black now obtains a decisive attack. White had to ferry pieces across to the defence of his King (e.g. by N-Q2-B3) while striving to keep the Q-side files firmly blocked.

16	R-R1
17 P-KB4	O-O-O

Black's attack now plays itself.

18 K-R1	QR-N1
19 Q-B2	N-R3

20 N-Q2	N-N5
21 N-B3	B-N6

26

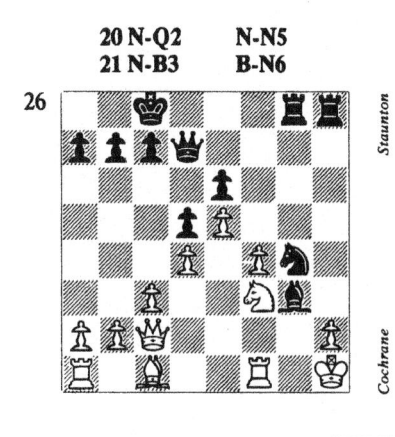

Cochrane — Staunton

White could have resigned already without risking anything.

22 R-KN1	N-B7+
23 K-N2	BxRP+
24 KxN	BxR+
25 K-B1	

Or 25 NxB, R-R7+.

25	R-R8
26 N-N5	Q-N4+
27 P-B4	PxP
28 P-R4	BxP+
29 K-N2	Q-Q4+
Resigns	

14

STAUNTON - SAINT-AMANT
4th match game, London, 2nd May 1843
Giuoco Piano

1 P-K4	P-K4
2 N-KB3	N-QB3
3 B-B4	B-B4
4 P-B3	Q-K2

The 'strong-point' defence but Black misinterprets it.

| 5 P-Q4 | PxP? |

Missing the point. B-N3! is the thematic move.

6 O-O	N-K4
7 NxN	QxN
8 P-B4	PxP+
9 K-R1	

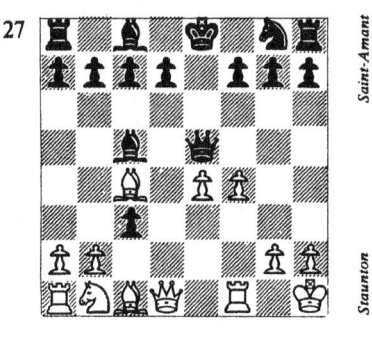

27

Saint-Amant — Staunton

9 ...... Q-Q5!

If PxP; 10 PxQ, PxR/Q; 11 Q-Q5 wins. E.g. 11 ..., N-R3; 12 BxN, O-O; 13 RxP, QxN+; 14 R-B1+ or 11 ..., Q-Q5; 12 QxBP+, K-Q1; 13 B-N5+, N-K2; 14 Q-B8+!, RxQ; 15 RxR mate. Not variations one would associate with the dull plodder Staunton is held to be by his detractors. In one sense it is a pity that Saint-Amant was too bright to fall for such things; otherwise Staunton's reputation as a combinative player might equal that of McDonnell.

10 Q-N3	N-R3
11 NxP	O-O

White has excellent compensation for the pawn.

| 12 P-KR3 | P-B3 |

Trying to free himself with P-Q4 but Staunton doesn't give him the chance.

13 P-B5	Q-B3
14 P-K5!	Q-R5

Staunton conducts the attack with magnificent elan. If QxKP; 15 BxN, PxB; 16 QR-K1 is overwhelming.

15 BxN	QxQB
16 N-K4	B-Q5
17 N-Q6	

Paralysing the Black Q-wing. From now on Saint-Amant is handicapped by the non-combatant role of half his army.

17	Q-R4
18 BxP+	RxB
19 P-N4	

Bringing about a decisive deflection of Black's Queen from the crucial KB2 square. Saint-Amant now plays, rather forlornly, to obtain two pieces for his Queen with struggling possibilities. Any move of Black's Queen now, such as Q-R3 or Q-N4, is ruled out by 20 QxR+, and mates.

19	BxKP
20 QR-K1!?	

Obviously PxQ wins, but if anything the text is even more accurate since Black's Queen cannot escape. It's hard to say whether the text is the move of a genuine master or an unnecessary refinement — hence the !?

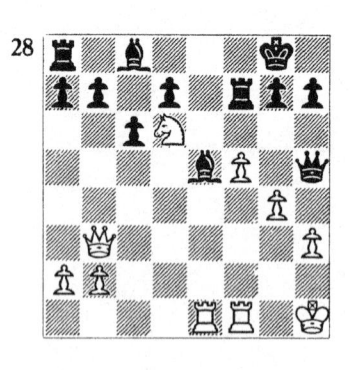

20	QxP+
21 QxQ	BxN
22 R-K8+	B-B1
23 R(1)-K1	P-Q4
24 R-Q8	R-Q2
25 R(1)-K8	RxR
26 RxR	P-QN3
27 Q-K3	B-N2
28 RxR	BxR
29 Q-K6+	K-R1
30 Q-B7	Resigns

15

SAINT-AMANT - STAUNTON
1st match game, Paris, 14th Nov. 1843
Sicilian Defence

The Champions of England and France meet in the Great Hall of the Cafe de la Regence in the first game of what is virtually a match for the Championship of the World. The French Champion, seated beneath the busts of his illustrious Gallic predecessors Philidor and de Labourdonnais, selects as his second move the method of combating the Sicilian which was made fashionable by the Labourdonnais - McDonnell matches nine years previously, although on that occasion it was the Frenchman who favoured the Sicilian Defence and his Irish antagonist who adopted the thrust of the KBP.

1 P-K4   P-QB4
2 P-KB4   P-K3
3 N-KB3   N-QB3
4 P-B3

Too cumbersome, although regarded as the 'theoretical' continuation at the time. Best is B-N5! — e.g. 4 B-N5, KN-K2; 5 O-O, P-QR3; 6 B-K2, P-KN3; 7 P-Q3, B-N2; 8 P-B3, O-O; 9 B-K3, P-Q3; 10 P-Q4 (Larsen - Kavalek, Las Palmas, 1974).

4 ......   P-Q4
5 P-K5

Making it a version of the French Defence.

5 ......   N-R3

One of the McDonnell - Labourdonnais games went 5 ..., P-B4; 6 B-Q3, B-K2; 7 B-B2, Q-N3; 8 O-O, N-R3; 9 K-R1, O-O; 10 P-Q4, B-Q2; 11 P-QR3, P-R4; 12 P-R3, B-K1; 13 P-QN3, PxP; 14 PxP, B-R4; 15 B-K3, QR-B1; 16 R-R2, K-R1; 17 Q-Q2, Q-B2; 18 N-R2, B-R5; 19 R-N1, B-N6; 20 N-B1, B-R5; 21 Q-Q3, B-N3; 22 QN-Q2, B-K2; 23 Q-K2, Q-Q2; 24 P-KN4 and White eventually won with a K-side pawn avalanche. This extract gives a good insight into the broad strategic intention behind White's second move. Another game between the same opponents varied with 5 ..., P-B3!?; 6 N-R3, N-R3; 7 N-B2, Q-N3; 8 P-Q4, B-Q2; 9 N-K3, QBPxP 10 BPxP, B-N5+; 11 K-B2, O-O; 12 K-N3, PxP; 13 BPxP, QR-B1; 14 P-KR4, RxN+!; 15 PxR, NxQP; 16 B-Q3, R-B1; 17 P-B4, B-B4; 18 R-KB1, B-N4; 19 BxB, QxB when Black had more than enough compensation for the exchange in terms of central control, and went on to win in 35 moves. The variation cropped up again in the 5th game of this match, when Staunton improved with the 'last word' — 5 ..., Q-N3.

6 N-R3

A logical enough idea. On QB2 the Knight will bolster up his QP.

6 ......   B-K2
7 N-B2   P-B4

P-B3 also merited consideration, but Staunton had a preference for moves which stifled his opponents' possibilities of expansion. For that purpose P-B4 is ideal, since it rules out any hostile advance on the K-side which does not involve the most elaborate and painstaking preparation. Such moves in Staunton's games show quite clearly that he was a Master (few and far between in those days) who had appreciated Philidor's rudimentary feeling about pawns that was not succinctly formulated until Nimzowitsch came along. 'The positional rule that the entire struggle, in its essence, amounts to a struggle between two forces, namely the pawns' tendency to advance (lust to expand) on the one hand and the tendency to blockade the pawns on the other' (A.Nimzowitsch in *How I became a Grandmaster*).

8 P-Q4	O-O
9 B-K2	B-Q2
10 O-O	R-B1
11 K-R1	PxP
12 PxP	N-B2
13 R-KN1	K-R1
14 P-KN4?	

Saint-Amant loses this game primarily through impatience! Staunton's men are superbly positioned to challenge this premature breakthrough and they now leap out to seize all the key squares in the vicinity of White's King. It was quite unrealistic of White to believe that P-KN4 will be playable while on the one hand he lacks the co-operation of his Q-side pieces and on the other cannot recapture on KN4 with his KRP, thus allowing the vital square KB5 to fall into enemy hands. McDonnell in a similar situation, as seen in the note to move 5, did not dispense with P-KR3, nor did he advance P-KN4 until he had created inner lines of communication for his Q-side pieces to make contact with his K-side aggression.

14	PxP
15 RxP	N-R3
16 R-N3	B-K1!
17 B-Q3	B-R4

See Diagram

Black's advantage is already of near decisive proportions, and this can be directly traced back to White's lemming-like 14th move.

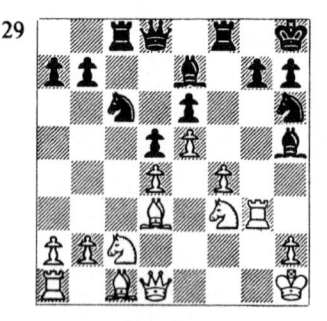

18 Q-N1	B-R5
19 NxB	QxN
20 N-K1	

Naturally not 20 RxP?, B-B6+.

20 ...... N-QN5

Unmasking a further channel for invasion of the White position. Staunton's pieces could hardly be occupying more effective squares.

21 B-Q2

On 21 B-B1, Staunton gives the pleasant variation: 21 ..., RxB!; 22 RxR, QxP; 23 N-Q3, NxN; 24 BxN, B-B6+; 25 R-N2, BxR+; 26 QxB, QxR+ winning. In view of this line White must surrender his KB, the last custodian of his wretchedly weak light squares.

21	NxB
22 RxN	B-N3
23 Q-N3	Q-R4
24 R-N3	Q-K7
25 Q-K3	Q-B8+
26 Q-N1	B-K5+

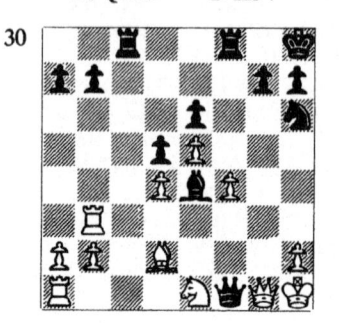

The evil consequences of White's suicidal 14 P-KN4 have been glaringly exposed by Staunton's consistent conquest of the light squares. White could now have resigned but dragged on his futile resistance for a further seven moves.

27 R-B3	BxR+
28 NxB	QxN+
29 Q-N2	QxQ+
30 KxQ	R-B7
31 R-Q1	RxBP
32 K-N3	RxQP
33 BxN	RxR
Resigns	

16

STAUNTON - SAINT-AMANT
4th match game, Paris, 19th Nov. 1843
Benoni Defence

1 P-Q4   P-QB4

In our own time the height of fashion.

2 P-Q5

Staunton rightly accepts the 'Benoni Challenge'.

2 .....   P-B4?

This is too loosening; N-KB3! is the move. Saint-Amant has been condemned for playing a kind of Nincompoop Opening in this game, but the strategic idea of employing the two BPs to watch the centre is a perfectly reasonable one. It is better, however, when given more preparation or employed when White, since he would then have a move in hand. In the Southern Counties Junior Team Jamboree in London in 1964 Hartston, as Black against Whiteley, followed Saint-Amant's opening with 1 P-Q4, P-QB4; 2 P-Q5, P-B4; 3 P-KN3, N-KB3; 4 B-N2, P-Q3; 5 P-QB4, P-KN3; 6 N-QB3, B-N2; 7 N-R3, N-R3; 8 O-O, N-B2; 9 P-K4, PxP; 10 N-KN5, P-QN4; 11 PxP, P-K3; 12 PxP, P-Q4; 13 N-B7, and White won. Basman did better by employing the idea as White in the 4th game of his 1974 match with Hartston, which began 1 P-KB4, P-KN3; 2 P-B4, P-QB3; 3 N-KB3, P-Q4; 4 P-K3, B-N2; 5 B-K2, N-B3; 6 O-O, O-O; 7 N-B3, QN-Q2; 8 PxP, NxP; 9 P-Q4, QN-B3; 10 N-K5, P-K3; 11 B-B3, and though White's position looks good, he only managed to draw. At Hastings 1973-4 Basman used the same idea with more preparation against the former World Champion, Tal, with 1 P-KB4, P-Q3; 2 N-KB3, P-KN3; 3 P-KN3, B-N2; 4 B-N2, N-KB3; 5 P-B4, and obtained a considerable advantage, only to let the game slide into a draw.

3 N-QB3   P-Q3
4 P-K4!   PxP
5 NxP   P-K4

Black has a terrible position whether he plays this or not. If the Black KP remains at K2 it will soon become an unpleasant weakness on an open file; if it advances to K4 Black's KB becomes a useless piece and White is presented with a beautiful blockading square for his knight on K4.

6 B-KN5

No doubt hoping that Black will try and exchange off his bad KB by B-K2, when he intends 7 B-N5+, K-B1 (not N or B-Q2; 8 NxP+); 8 B-Q2. Though Black sees the danger, he is forced into a somewhat pointless excursion with his Queen.

6	Q-R4+
7 P-B3	B-B4
8 N-N3	B-N3
9 B-Q3!	

Very good. The exchange of light-squared bishops enhances White's control of the invaluable square K4.

9	BxB
10 QxB	P-KN3
11 KN-K2	B-K2
12 N-K4	Q-N3
13 O-O	N-Q2
14 BxB	

A dubious exchange, eliminating Black's worst piece. Clearly Staunton wanted to occupy his K6 without delay, but in his desire to avoid the loss of time involved in the better 14 B-Q2!, and only then P-KB4, he mistakenly sacrifices his positional advantage, thus jeopardising his chances of victory.

14	NxB
15 N-N5	P-KR3
16 N-K6	N-KB1

Repelling the boarders. For the next five moves Saint-Amant defends most accurately.

| 17 NxN | RxN |
| 18 P-QN4 | |

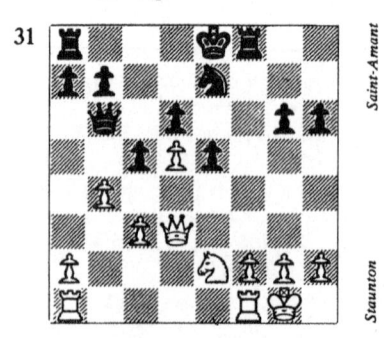

31

Saint-Amant

Staunton

There is a striking contrast in this match between Staunton's careful and painstaking conduct of play with the Black pieces and the volatile energy he displays when in possession of the first move. With this thrust he opens up an offensive on a hitherto dormant front.

| 18 ...... | PxP |
| 19 PxP | K-B2! |

Naturally not QxP; 20 QR-N1, with decisive penetration of the hostile lines of defence.

| 20 K-R1 | K-N2 |
| 21 P-B4 | QR-Q1 |

Here, or on his next turn, Black had to try N-B4!, which would probably have enabled him to hold the position.

| 22 QR-Q1 | P-KR4? |

Quite pointless.

| 23 Q-QB3 | Q-N4 |
| 24 Q-Q2 | |

Black's last move set a neat trap, but Staunton sees through it. On 24 PxP?, White loses to 24 ..., RxR+! (QxN?; 25 PxP+, K-N1; 26 KR-K1!, NxP; 27 Q-QN3); 25 RxR, QxN; 26 PxP+, K-N1; 27 R-K1, R-KB1!; with a back rank mate.

| 24 ...... | R-B4? |

Not good. He should still have tried N-B4. Staunton mentioned NxP; 25 QxN, QxN; but then 26 KR-K1!, leaves White with a substantial plus — e.g. 26 ..., Q-R3; 27 PxP, PxP; 28 QxP+, and White dominates the centre.

| 25 N-N3 | R-B3 |

After this he is definitely lost. RxP was the last slim chance.

26 PxP	RxR+
27 RxR	PxP
28 Q-N5	

Decisive. Black's weakened position (P-KR4?) cannot withstand the multiplicity of threats.

| 28 ...... | R-Q2 |
| 29 QxKP+ | K-R3 |

and White mates in 4.
A brisk conclusion by Staunton.

Pierre de Saint-Amant

17

SAINT-AMANT - STAUNTON
5th match game, Paris, 21st Nov. 1843
Sicilian Defence

Reuben Fine includes the following game in one of his books as a grudging tribute to Staunton's prowess, adding: 'Because of his style Staunton's play is not very impressive to our eyes' and damning the game before he starts with: 'The best game of his I have been able to find'.

These statements by Fine are typical of the slights that have been heaped upon Staunton by the undiscerning, and it will be observed from the notes to the game that at critical points it was Staunton who saw more than Fine, even though the latter was operating with the benefit of hindsight and an extra hundred years of accumulated chess wisdom and technique! The accuracy of Staunton's vision compared with Fine's lends concrete testimony to Bobby Fischer's acknowledgement of the Old Master's merit when he included him in his list of the world's ten best.

1 P-K4	**P-QB4**
2 P-KB4	**P-K3**
3 N-KB3	**N-QB3**
4 P-B3	**P-Q4**
5 P-K5	**Q-N3**

Staunton's theoretical novelty. From now on the sensitivity of White's Q4 forms the thematic basis of Black's strategic offensive. This development of the Queen originated with Philidor, who however played it later. A simultaneous blindfold game Atwood - Philidor, played on 22nd March 1794, went: 1 P-K4, P-QB4; 2 P-KB4, P-K3; 3 N-KB3, N-QB3; 4 P-B3, P-Q4; 5 P-K5, P-KB4; 6 P-Q4, N-KR3; 7 P-QR3, N-B2; 8 B-K3, Q-N3.

6 B-Q3

This looks weird but the bishop will go to QB2 to allow White's P-Q4.

6	**B-Q2**
7 B-B2	**R-B1**
8 O-O	**N-R3**
9 P-KR3	**B-K2**
10 K-R2	

While it is quite logical to remove the King from the diagonal as a preparation for P-Q4, White's manoeuvres are tainted with a certain artificiality which gives grounds for criticism of his entire opening plan.

10 ......   P-B4

Characteristic Stauntonian prophylaxis. Compare also Game 15.

11 P-R3	**P-R4**
12 P-QR4	

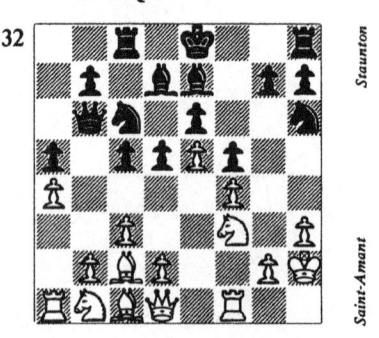

32

To moves 11 and 12 Fine has the sarcastic and derogatory note: 'If the subtleties of some of these moves escape the reader he need not be too surprised. They escape me too.' This is a comment on Fine rather than on the moves. The point of 11 P-R3 is crystal clear: first, to prepare for

P-Q4 without allowing the reply PxP; PxP, N-QN5; and secondly, in some circumstances to allow White to play P-QN4. Black's 11 ..., P-R4 is designed to prevent P-QN4 (restraint), while White's 12 P-QR4 very sensibly takes control of the weakened QN5 square. As Tartakover (writing before Fine!) put it: 'He now hopes to utilise the liberated square at QN5,' a comment which is given added point when one reaches White's 15th move. Two examples will show that such manoeuvres are recognised as commonplace strategic devices in modern chess. 1 P-Q4, N-KB3; 2 P-QB4, P-KN3; 3 P-KN3, B-N2; 4 B-N2, O-O; 5 N-QB3, P-Q3; 6 P-K3, QN-Q2; 7 KN-K2, **P-QR3**; 8 P-N3, R-N1; 9 **P-QR4, P-QR4**; 10 B-QR3, P-B3; 11 O-O, Q-B2; 12 Q-Q2, KR-K1; 13 QR-B1, R-R1; 14 KR-Q1, **N-N1**; 15 P-R3, **N-R3**; 16 K-R2, P-R4; 17 P-B4, **N-QN5** (Petrosian - Spassky, 24th game, World Championship match, Moscow, 1966). Or again 1 P-Q4, N-KB3; 2 P-QB4, P-KN3; 3 N-QB3, B-N2; 4 P-K4, P-Q3; 5 B-K3, P-B3; 6 P-B3, **P-QR3**; 7 **P-QR4, P-QR4!**; 8 KN-K2, **N-R3**; 9 N-B1, N-Q2; 10 N-N3, P-K4 (Korchnoi - R.Byrne, Hastings, 1971-2). Both these games, involving four outstanding modern Grandmasters, all of whom competed in the 1974 Candidates' Tournament, were eventually drawn.

12 ...... N-B2
13 P-Q4

At last White must make this advance since Black was already threatening to gain a K-side initiative with P-KN4. It is remarkable to see the way in which Staunton cleverly delays castling to extract the maximum advantage from the potential mobility of his K-side pawns. We can see from this that Staunton was well aware of the truth of the Steinitzian dictum long before it was uttered: with the centre closed it is possible to strike on the wings.

13 ...... P-R3
14 R-K1!

To meet 14 ..., P-N4?; with 15 BxP!, PxB; 16 P-K6, disrupting Black's centre.

14 ...... P-N3
15 N-R3 PxP
16 NxP

Not wishing to allow 16 PxP, N-N5.

16 ...... NxN
17 PxN

'Clearly not 17 QxN, QxQ; 18 PxQ, BxN; winning a piece. The weakness of the point Q4 now becomes chronic' (Tartakover).

17 ...... P-N4

Tartakover again: 'Without delay Black now starts a war of movement on the K-side, where he is master.'

18 N-N5

BxP is no longer on since Black has lent additional lateral protection to his K3. The text gains some counterplay but also leaves White with another vulnerable point to defend in any heavy piece ending.

18 ...... BxN
19 PxB R-B5?

Not QxNP??; 20 B-R4. But 19 ..., PxP; would have saved a tempo.

20 B-Q3 R-QB1

Staunton had overlooked the simple tactical point 20 ..., RxP; 21 B-K3. Uncharacteristic carelessness on his part since White has now found it possible to protect his QNP with gain of time.

21 B-K2 PxP
22 R-B1 N-N4

Black still has a formidable initiative in spite of his 19th move.

23 BxP N-K5
24 R-B1 RxR

25 QxR   K-Q2!

Black's knight dominates the centre and White is saddled with an assortment of weak pawns. The resolute text gives White something else to worry about: the defence of his King's position.

26 Q-K3

Not 26 BxP?, QxQP; and White's centre collapses.

26 ......   B-N4!
27 B-Q3

It is a good idea to remove Black's unpleasant knight, even if the intended capture does deprive the White QNP of its natural protection.

27 ......   R-KN1
28 BxN   QPxB
29 BxB

Of course White would prefer to avoid this exchange which gives Black an impressive array of pawns, but if 29 Q-QN3, BxB; 30 RxB, QxQP; 31 RxBP, Q-Q7; 32 R-B7+, K-Q1; and Black wins. Equally 29 Q-K2 loses to BxB and QxQP.

29 ......   PxB
30 Q-QN3   P-N5

See Diagram

This advance appears hazardous, but if Black wishes to continue his offensive he has no choice but to enter upon this tense, knife-edge variation.

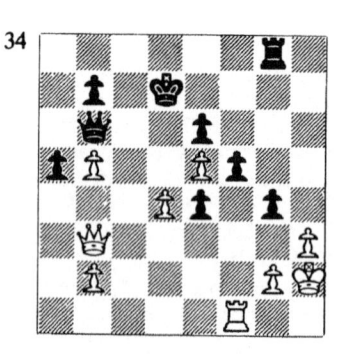

Consolidation by K-B1, for example, is ruled out by White's threats of RxP and P-Q5. Now after 31 P-Q5, which is the obvious counterchance, Black must play 31 ..., Q-Q5; 32 PxP+, K-K2; with good winning prospects, based on the isolation of White's King from the centre e.g. 33 RxP, P-N6+; 34 K-R1, R-QB1!; 35 R-B1 (QxP?, R-B8+; and Q-N8 mate), P-K6; with advantage in spite of his two pawns deficit. Or 33 Q-R3+, Q-N5; 34 QxQ+, PxQ; 35 RxP, P-N6+; 36 K-N1, KxP; 37 R-B1, KxP; and Black's passed KP is a major force. Ironically, in all of these lines White's pieces seem to be incapable of landing a direct hit on Black's apparently exposed King, while White's King, tucked away in a corner, often drifts into mortal danger from back rank threats.

31 R-Q1

To this move, over which White cogitated for 35 minutes, Fine comments: 'Overcautious. With 31 RxP!, he should have been able to draw anyhow.' However, he neglects to analyse the obvious reply 31 ..., QxQP!; after which a tense situation arises. White dare not play 32 PxP?, R-R1+; 33 K-N3, PxR; and wins, nor 32 R-B1, QxP+; 33 K-N1, PxP; 34 QxP, Q-Q5+; with advantage. His best bet would be 32 R-B7+!, K-Q1; 33 K-R1, and now either 33 ..., PxP;

34 QxRP, QxNP; 35 RxP, Q-R8+; 36 K-R2, QxP+; or 33 ..., QxKP; 34 Q-Q1+, Q-Q4; 35 QxQ+, PxQ; 36 RxP, K-B1; still with some advantage to Black in each variation.

| 31 ...... | PxP |
| 32 QxP | Q-Q1 |

Transferring the attack to the KR-file. Staunton conducts the finale with admirable finesse.

| 33 P-Q5 | K-B1! |

Not R-R1?; 34 PxP+, K-B2; 35 P-N6+, winning.

34 Q-B3+

Saving his Queen with tempo, but the drawback to this move is that a valuable defender is deflected from the King's field.

34	K-N1
35 P-Q6	P-B5
36 Q-B5	

Hoping to get in P-N6 and Q-B7+, but Staunton does not give him sufficient time. 36 R-QB1 has been variously recommended as a saving resource (it threatens the Queen swap with Q-B7+) but against that Black has the elegant manoeuvre R-R1+; 37 K-N1, R-R2!; eliminating Queen checks on his QB2, except at the cost of a lost King and pawn ending, and preparing for P-B6 or P-K6 or even Q-R1 and R-R8+.

| 36 ...... | P-K6 |

See Diagram

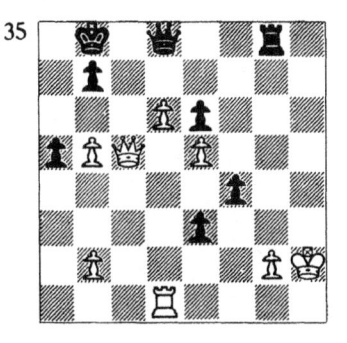

35

The decisive final attack against White's King.

37 Q-B2

Black threatened Q-R5+ -B7+ xNP mate.

| 37 ...... | Q-R5+ |
| 38 K-N1 | R-QB1! |

Not the over-eager R-R1?; 39 Q-B7+!, and White wins.

39 Q-K2

39 P-Q7, RxQ; 40 P-Q8/Q+, QxQ; 41 RxQ+, K-B2 is a lost rook and pawn ending.

| 39 ...... | R-R1 |
| | **Resigns** |

This game, which lasted for no less than nine and a half hours, was a monumental achievement on Staunton's part. At the very least it is a much better game than Fine would have us believe. In fact it is a masterpiece of grand strategy carried out by Staunton in a manner years ahead of his time.

18

SAINT-AMANT - STAUNTON
7th match game, Paris, 25th Nov. 1843
Queen's Gambit Declined

1 P-Q4	P-K3
2 P-QB4	P-Q4
3 P-K3	P-QB4
4 N-QB3	N-KB3
5 N-B3	N-B3
6 B-Q3	

Not particularly refined, but it was an opening still designated as Irregular at the time. Black could now play 6 ..., PxBP gaining a tempo in modern fashion. 6 PxQP or 6 P-QR3 were therefore to be preferred.

6 ......   P-QR3

Neither side conducts the opening in the most accurate fashion. After this omission on Black's part Saint-Amant should still have captured on Q5.

7 O-O	B-Q3
8 P-QR3	

Once again missing his chance of PxQP.

8 ......   P-QN3!

The mark of approval is for the idea rather than the strength of the move since PxBP; 9 BxBP, P-QN4 would still have granted Black a very comfortable game. This is the first example of a fianchetto which we have so far seen in this match and which Staunton employed with such effect against the Frenchman, who was clearly unfamiliar with the concept. Staunton was the first master to appreciate the strength of the fianchettoed bishop and he had initially confronted Saint-Amant with this ploy in the 6th match game, when he had the White pieces: 1 P-QB4 (the first example of this move which, with later games, gave the name English to this opening), P-QB4; 2 N-QB3, P-B4; 3 P-K4, P-Q3; 4 B-Q3, P-K3; 5 PxP, PxP; 6 N-R3, N-KB3; 7 P-QN3, P-KN3; 8 O-O, B-K2?; 9 B-N2, O-O; 10 N-B4, N-B3; 11 N(3)-Q5, NxN; 12 NxN, B-K3; 13 NxB+, QxN; 14 Q-K2, Q-KB2; 15 QR-K1, with advantage. The unopposed power of White's QB is striking.

9 R-K1

An insipid move, in that White cannot seriously contemplate playing for P-K4 given the fluid nature of the centre.

9	O-O
10 P-R3	

White is patently at a loss for a plan, in marked contrast to Staunton.

10	Q-B2
11 P-QN3	

Flattering imitation without the underlying strategic conception. He must only have thought he was supporting his QBP.

11 ......   N-K2

Preparatory to B-N2, taking control of his K5.

12 B-Q2

Very feeble; B-N2 was the move. Staunton remarked that Saint-Amant in subsequent games at length discovered the superiority of his adversary's tactics and wisely adopted that plan of operation himself.

12	B-N2
13 PxQP	KPxP

Black can now look forward to eventual occupation of the outpost on K5. This gives him a definite advan-

tage since White enjoys influence over no correspondingly strong central square.
14 K-R1
A very weak, drifting move which deprives his KBP of much-needed support.
14 ...... QR-K1
Staunton consistently masses his pieces in order to bring them into contact with the key square K5. Nimzowitsch may have diagnosed 'overprotection' (and coined the word) but he didn't *invent* the idea!
15 R-R2
White already stands much worse, but after this further artificial move his game crumples. By this stage, however, it is hard to suggest a reasonable alternative — maybe K-N1!
15 ...... N-K5
With the dual threat of NxP+ and PxP. White's hand is forced.

16 BxN	PxB
17 N-KN1	PxP
18 PxP	N-B4

See Diagram

The pieces grouped together in touch with the key square now burst into devastating life.
19 QN-K2 P-K6!
Unmasking the full force of the fianchettoed bishop.
20 PxP RxP!
The rook is immune. If 21 BxR?, NxB; 22 Q-B1, BxP mate.
21 Q-B1 QxQ

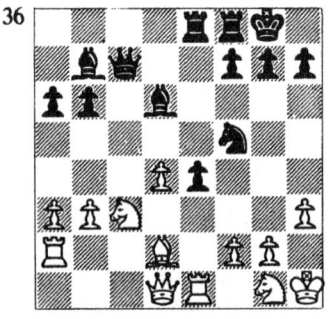

36

Also very good was N-R5 (22 QxQ?, BxP mate). Staunton even considered BxP+, but in his own words 'the surest line of play, in such a match, is the best.'

22 RxQ	RxP
23 R-B3	RxR
24 BxR	N-R5
25 N-B3	

Not 25 N-B1, R-B1.

25	NxN
26 PxN	BxP+
27 K-N1	R-K1
28 K-B2	BxN
29 RxB	RxR+
30 KxR	BxP
31 K-Q3	P-R3
32 K-K4	P-QN4
33 K-Q5	P-N5
Resigns	

A miserable performance by Saint-Amant but a compensatingly energetic demonstration by Staunton (and one that could hardly be bettered) of the aggressive potential of the fianchettoed bishop.

19

STAUNTON - SAINT-AMANT
8th match game, Paris, 26th Nov. 1843
Sicilian Defence

1 P-K4	P-QB4
2 N-KB3	P-K3
3 P-Q4	PxP
4 NxP	N-QB3

Thus far a recognisably 'modern' version of the Sicilian, but Staunton's next move is a cumbersome retreat which impedes the advance of his KBP. N-N5 or N-QB3 are now the accepted alternatives.

5 N-KB3? B-B4

As we have seen from Staunton's games with Cochrane, this development of Black's KB represented a commonplace interpretation of the Sicilian in 'pre-Classical' times. Staunton himself later devised the development of the piece in fianchetto. With the advent of Steinitz and the theory of weak squares such a daring deployment of the KB as the text fell completely into desuetude, but modern players, conscious of concealed dynamic possibilities, have resurrected this move and elaborated it into a fully viable system. For a more detailed discussion of this whole variation see Game 56.

6 B-Q3	KN-K2
7 N-B3	P-QR3
8 O-O	N-N3
9 K-R1	P-B3

Hitherto Black has built up his position in a strikingly modern vein but now he begins to go astray. Q-B2 was in order, or even an immediate expansion via P-N4.

10 N-K1

Staunton's strategy is simple but effective. He plans the manoeuvre P-B4, R-B3-R3, culminating in Q-R5.

10	O-O
11 P-B4	QN-K2

The French champion seems obsessed with defence and neglects the development of his remaining forces. Such timidity justifies Staunton's rather unsubtle attack.

12 R-B3	P-Q3
13 R-R3	P-B4
14 PxP	QNxP
15 Q-R5	K-B2

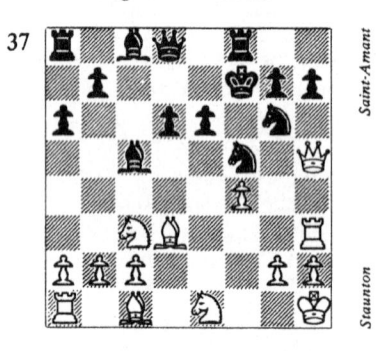

37

If B-Q2; 16 QxP+, K-B2; 17 R-R6, NxR; 18 BxN+, K-K2; 19 QxP+, N-B2; 20 P-B5. That the pitiful text is the only move to hold the KRP is a tragic commentary on his earlier play. Saint-Amant consumed 45 minutes over the move. White's attack now plays itself.

16 N-B3	R-R1
17 P-KN4	N(4)-K2
18 P-B5	

Forcing material gain. Black's position is already quite beyond repair.

18	PxP
19 PxP	K-B1
20 PxN	

Even stronger is 20 B-KN5, N-K4; 21

NxN, PxN; 22 P-B6! But Staunton's choice is certainly adequate for victory.

20	BxR
21 QxQB	Q-B1
22 Q-R4	Q-K3
23 N-KN5	Q-K4
24 B-KB4	N-B4
25 BxQ	NxQ
26 R-KB1+	K-K1
27 BxNP	K-Q2
28 BxR	

Here Black could have abandoned the struggle, but he clung on for a further eight moves. For the record they were:

28	RxB
29 R-B7+	K-B3
30 B-K4+	P-Q4
31 BxP+	K-Q3
32 P-N7	R-K1
33 R-B1	B-Q5
34 P-N8/Q	RxQ
35 BxR	P-R3
36 N(5)-K4+	Resigns

20

SAINT-AMANT - STAUNTON
9th match game, Paris, 28th Nov. 1843
Queen's Gambit Declined

1 P-Q4	P-K3
2 P-QB4	P-Q4
3 N-QB3	N-KB3
4 N-B3	P-B4
5 P-K3	N-B3
6 P-QR3	P-QN3
7 B-Q3	B-Q3
8 BPxP	KPxP
9 B-N5	

Giving away a tempo.

9	B-N2
10 PxP	BxBP

Reaching what soon becomes a typical isolated QP position, readily recognisable from modern play.

11 P-QN4	B-Q3
12 B-N2	

Naturally not 12 NxP, NxN; 13 QxN, BxP+.

12	O-O
13 N-K2	

Very good. Saint-Amant prepares to plant a blockading knight on Q4.

13	Q-K2
14 O-O	QR-Q1
15 R-B1	N-K4
16 N(2)-Q4	NxN+
17 QxN	Q-K4
18 P-N3	N-K5

A position which could easily come from a modern game.

19 Q-K2	Q-N4
20 P-B4	

From this point White wavers. Instead of building up single-minded pressure against the QP he hovers between this logical plan and the idea of creating tactical chances on the K-side, which is not at all consonant with the demands of the position. The advance of the KBP lends Black definite counterchances.

20	Q-N3
21 R-QB2	B-B1
22 P-B5	Q-R3
23 B-Q3	

To answer 23 ..., BxKNP with 24 BxN.

| 23 ...... | KR-K1 |
| 24 B-B1 | |

Now the threat was NxP; 25 PxN, RxP.

| 24 ...... | B-Q2 |
| 25 Q-B3 | B-R5! |

Capturing the important QB-file.

26 R-KN2	R-QB1
27 R-K1	N-N4
28 QxP	N-R6+
29 K-B1	

If 29 K-R1, RxB; 30 RxR, QxP (Staunton).

29	B-K4
30 R(2)-K2	BxN
31 QxB	KR-Q1
32 P-N5!?	

38

An inspired tactical idea. He threatens Black's B and prepares to meet 32 ..., RxQ with 33 PxR, menacing Black's Queen and also R-K8+. If 32 ..., RxQ; 33 PxR, Q-Q3; 34 R-K8+, RxR; 35 RxR+, Q-B1; 36 RxQ+, KxR; 37 K-N2 winning. Staunton called the move 'a desperate but masterly resource.'

| 32 ...... | Q-R4? |

Staunton is so thrown off balance that he overlooks B-Q8!, which by dislocating White's column of rooks on the K-file would have given him his win, e.g. 32 ..., B-Q8; 33 RxB, RxQ; 34 PxR, Q-R4; 35 B-K3, Q-B6+; 36 K-K1, R-K1; 37 K-Q2, N-B7 (Dr. O.S.Bernstein).

| 33 P-N4! | RxQ?? |

Shattered now by the realisation that he has missed his win, Staunton progresses to a gross blunder. After Q-R5; 34 QxB, RxKB he would have none the worst of it. Afterwards Staunton, who was then leading 7 - 0 with one draw, remarked that had he won this game, as he should have done, Saint-Amant in all probability would have resigned the match.

| 34 PxR | P-B3 |
| 35 PxQ | **Resigns** |

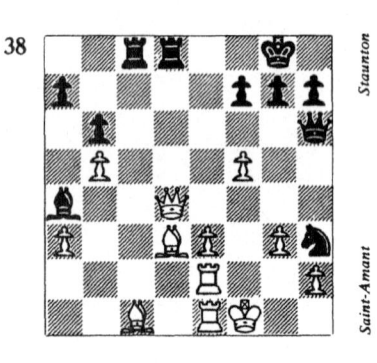

21

SAINT-AMANT - STAUNTON
13th match game, Paris, 6th Dec. 1843
Queen's Gambit Declined

It often happens that the loser of a series against a particular opponent receives the consolation of playing the most brilliant game. Thus it was in this match. Staunton won the series decisively but the honour of the most dashing victory must surely be awarded to the Frenchman for this game.

1 P-Q4	P-K3
2 P-QB4	P-Q4
3 P-K3	

There is nothing wrong with this move other than restriction of White's options. The most feasible course here is N-QB3, retaining the possibility of B-KN5, exerting more pressure against Black's QP. But at this time it was thought that a satisfactory answer for Black lay in Q-QN3 after P-QB4. Only in the 15th game of the match, when White had already played P-QB5 preventing such a defence, did Saint-Amant venture on B-KN5. The first appearance of the move, according to W.Cook in *The Evolution of the Chess Openings*, was in 1848 in a game Mayet - Harrwitz, which went: 1 P-Q4, P-Q4; 2 P-QB4, P-K3; 3 N-QB3, N-KB3; 4 B-N5, QN-Q2; 5 PxP, PxP; 6 NxP, NxN; 7 BxQ, B-N5+; 8 Q-Q2, KxB!; 9 P-K4, R-K1; 10 P-B3, P-KB4; 11 B-Q3, N-B5!; 12 K-Q1, BxQ; 13 KxB, NxP and wins.

3	N-KB3
4 N-QB3	P-B4
5 N-B3	N-B3
6 P-QR3	B-K2
7 B-Q3	O-O
8 O-O	P-QN3
9 P-QN3	B-N2

Anticipating by half a century the 'normal position' from Tarrasch's Defence to the Queen's Gambit (1 P-Q4, P-Q4; 2 P-QB4, P-K3; 3 N-QB3, P-QB4).

10 BPxP	KPxP

It looks more sensible to recapture with pieces on Q4 in order to maintain an open diagonal for the QB, e.g.: 10 ..., KNxP; 11 NxN, QxN; 12 P-K4, Q-Q2; 13 P-Q5, PxP; 14 PxP, N-R4; 15 P-QN4, PxP; 16 PxP, BxNP; 17 BxP+, KxB; 18 N-N5+, K-N1; 19 Q-R5, Q-B4! But White does better by 12 PxP, keeping an infinitesimal edge after 12 ..., BxP; 13 P-QN4 followed by Q-B2 (with traps against Black's KRP) and B-N2. In any case there is little wrong with Staunton's actual choice, and he himself had no doubts that it was to be preferred to a piece recapture because of the 'outpost' possibilities on K5.

11 B-N2	PxP
12 PxP	B-Q3
13 R-K1	P-QR3
14 QR-B1	R-B1
15 R-B2	

From the opening White had gained precisely one move, but in such a symmetrical position this is insufficient for a genuine advantage if White continues quietly. So instead of the tame text Alexander recommended the sharp attempt 15 B-B5, R-B2; 16 N-K5, R-K2; 17 N-R4, when KR-K1! (pinning the advanced

Knight) is the only move for Black.

| 15 ...... | R-B2 |
| 16 QR-K2 | Q-B1? |

Essential was R-K2, challenging the open file. Occupation of the QB-file is no compensation.

17 P-R3

Missing a good chance: 17 N-QR4!, P-QN4; 18 N-B5, and White's Knight has attained a dominating position. Over the next couple of moves both players remain oblivious to this opportunity.

| 17 ...... | N-Q1 |

Better P-QN4 to blot out White's Knight from his QB4.

18 Q-Q2?

Once again he had 18 N-QR4!, P-QN4; 19 N-B5, BxN; 20 PxB, RxP; 21 N-N5!, and White stands better.

18	P-QN4!
19 P-QN4	N-K3
20 B-B5	N-K5
21 NxN	PxN
22 P-Q5!	

And not 22 BxP?, BxB; 23 RxB, R-B7 with advantage to Black.

| 22 ...... | PxN? |

Staunton himself pointed out a vital improvement for Black at this moment with B-B5!, when a likely continuation was 23 Q-Q1, PxN; 24 RxN, Q-Q1; 25 R(6)-K4, Q-N4; 26 QxP, QxB; 27 RxB, QxP with equality. After the error Saint-Amant concludes well with a brisk and attractive attack.

23 RxN!

Obviously this cannot be captured.

| 23 ...... | Q-Q1 |
| 24 B-B6! | |

See Diagram

An elegant way of breaking up

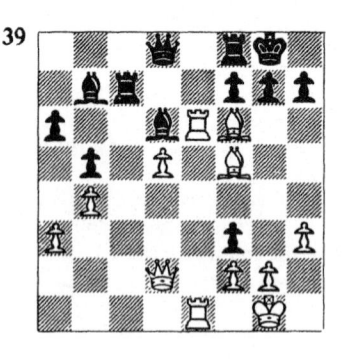

39

Black's King's defences.

| 24 ...... | PxB |
| 25 RxB | K-N2 |

Or QxR; 26 Q-R6.

| 26 RxQ | RxR |
| 27 B-K4 | |

Of course Black is hopelessly lost, but Staunton was no addict of 'premature' resignation.

27	PxP
28 Q-B4	R-B5
29 Q-N4+	K-B1
30 Q-R5	K-K2
31 P-Q6+	KxP
32 BxB	K-B2
33 BxRP	**Resigns**

Saint-Amant's supporters hailed the spirited final combination as an attack in the style of Labourdonnais, and what greater praise could they have lavished upon their hero's achievement against the English Champion ?

Most versions of the score in English erroneously give 13 ..., P-KR3 instead of 13 ..., P-QR3, but there appears to be some doubt then as to whether Black's 18th move was P-R3 or P-QN4. The version of the score chosen here is the one that appears to have the greatest claim to validity.

22

SAINT-AMANT - STAUNTON
15th match game, Paris, 9th Dec. 1843
Queen's Gambit Declined

1 P-Q4	P-Q4
2 P-QB4	P-K3
3 N-QB3	N-KB3
4 N-B3	P-QR3
5 P-B5	

If the last couple of moves look somewhat odd, they should not do so, for parallels can be found in the most impeccable 20th century sources. Alekhine - Rubinstein, The Hague, 1921, went 1 P-Q4, P-Q4; 2 N-KB3, P-K3; 3 P-B4, **P-QR3**; 4 **P-B5**, N-QB3; 5 B-B4, KN-K2; 6 N-B3, N-N3; 7 B-K3, P-N3; 8 PxP, PxP; 9 P-KR4! with a good game for White. Nimzowitsch - J.Bernstein, Carlsbad, 1923, opened with 1 N-KB3, N-KB3; 2 P-Q4, P-Q4; 3 P-B4, P-K3; 4 N-B3, B-K2; 5 P-K3, O-O; 6 P-QR3, **P-QR3**; 7 **P-B5!**, P-B3; 8 P-QN4, QN-Q2; 9 B-N2, Q-B2; 10 Q-B2, P-K4; 11 O-O-O, P-K5; 12 N-KR4, N-N1; 13 P-N3, N-K1; 14 N-N2, P-B4; 15 P-KR4, also with a fine position for White. And finally, Portisch - Petrosian, 10th Candidates' match game, Mallorca, 1974, started with 1 P-Q4, P-Q4; 2 P-QB4, P-K3; 3 N-QB3, B-K2; 4 N-B3, N-KB3; 5 B-N5, O-O; 6 P-K3, QN-Q2; 7 R-B1, **P-QR3**; 8 **P-B5**, P-B3; 9 B-Q3, P-QN3; 10 PxP, P-B4; 11 O-O, P-B5; 12 B-B2, NxP; 13 N-K5, B-N2; 14 P-B4, with a winning attack. In each case White answered Black's P-QR3 with P-QB5 and secured the better game.

5	B-K2
6 B-N5	O-O
7 P-K3	P-QN3
8 P-QN4	

Supporting the pawn-chain is quite satisfactory since 8 ..., P-QR4; 9 P-QR3 achieves little for Black. A playable alternative was 8 PxP, PxP; 9 B-Q3, followed by N-K5, as chosen in a similar position by Portisch in the game quoted above.

8	B-N2
9 BxN	

White obviously wanted to eliminate the possibility of N-K5 with Black counterplay in the centre. In the closed position which now arises Black's bishops are no great asset, so one can hardly criticise Saint-Amant's choice for his 9th move.

9	BxB
10 B-Q3	P-QR4
11 P-QR3	N-Q2

Threatening to exploit the exposure of White's QN by capturing twice on his QB4. This menace persuades White to liquidate the Q-side tension.

12 BPxP	BPxP
13 O-O	Q-K2

As Staunton himself pointed out, the thematic freeing move of P-K4 is not on: 13 ..., P-K4?; 14 QPxP, NxP; 15 NxN, BxN; 16 BxP+ (Q-R5?, P-B4; 17 BxP, RxB; 18 QxR, BxN), KxB; 17 Q-R5+.

14 Q-N3	PxP
15 PxP	KR-B1
16 B-N5	

See Diagram overleaf

White has relinquished his spatial plus on the Q-side (12 BPxP) but Black remains tied up in that sector; his QB is not a very glorious piece and

40

Staunton / Saint-Amant

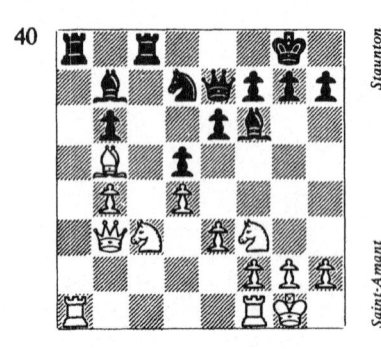

his QNP could become weak in the future. However, Black's pieces are well co-ordinated and he does possess the long-range insurance of the bishop pair. In other words, the position that has arisen from the opening is balanced and the decision will fall to the more skilful manoeuvrer in subsequent play.

16 ......   N-B1!

Very good. White was threatening N-QR4 and BxN. Now 17 N-QR4 achieves nothing after Q-Q1.

17 KR-B1   N-N3
18 B-K2   Q-Q1
19 N-QN5   B-K2

Eyeing White's QNP.

20 N-K1?

Saint-Amant begins to falter. He should have retracted his previous move with N-B3, preparing to station this piece on QR4, if necessary, in conjunction with P-QN5, to safeguard the QNP. The text inaugurates an illogical plan of aggression on the K-side, where he can boast of no advantage whatsoever.

20 ......   B-R3

'Pinning' White's QN. If it retreats, allowing an exchange of light-squared bishops, Black will capture his vital QB5 square.

21 P-B4

Pursuing his incorrect idea, but it only encourages Staunton to place his knight on the ideal square KB4, whence it menaces White's fragile and backward KP.

21 ......   N-R5!
22 K-B2   N-B4
23 N-KB3   BxN!

Absolutely the correct moment to cash in the advantage of the bishop pair. This exchange is the key move of a sequence designed to seize control of his QB5. Staunton has correctly appreciated that the presence of 'opposite colour' bishops is of no avail to his opponent, since White's KB enjoys a most restricted sphere of activity.

24 QRxR   RxR(R1)
25 BxB   N-Q3
26 B-Q3   P-QN4
27 N-K5   N-B5

Positionally decisive. If White exchanges minor pieces on his QB4, Black will obtain a passed QBP of giant proportions, saddling White with a horribly weak and exposed pawn on the QN-file. White's corresponding outpost on the K-file is of little value, since Black can always neutralise its efficacy with P-B3. In fact, Saint-Amant recognises this fact and exchanges his knight for Black's KB without waiting to be asked, in the hope of minimising the pressure against his QNP.

28 N-B6   Q-Q3
29 NxB+   QxN

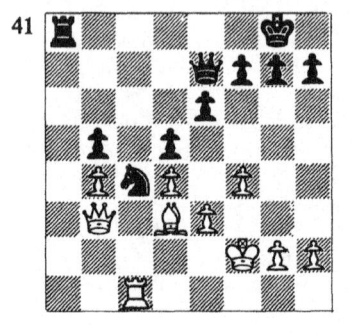

41

Staunton / Saint-Amant

30 BxN

Acquiescing in the positional loss outlined in the previous note, but what could he do against the threats of R-R5, R-R6, or even Q-R5+?

30	QPxB
31 Q-N2	R-R5
32 R-QN1	Q-R2
33 Q-B2	P-N3
34 P-R4?	

An unfortunate blunder which sheds a pawn. He should have continued resistance with some passive course such as K-K2, but even then Black's superior mobility would enable him to force a decision in his favour; e.g. 34 K-K2, P-B4 (crippling White's central pawn majority and controlling the useful square K5); 35 K-Q2, Q-R1; 36 K-K1, R-R6; 37 K-B2, R-Q6; 38 R-Q1 (not 38 Q-N2, P-B6; and R-Q7+), RxR; 39 QxR, Q-R6; 40 Q-N1, Q-N6; 41 Q-K1, P-B6.

34	Q-K2!
35 R-KR1	QxP

Achieving a decisive material advantage, after which White could have resigned. The unnecessary prolongation of play in lost positions at that time probably stemmed partly from a sensitivity towards the spectators — often eminent men, but novices at chess. It is certain that Saint-Amant realised perfectly well that his position here was lost, but to resign 'only one pawn down' or even 'only one piece down' might have seemed almost cowardly in the eyes of his doubtless enthusiastic but largely chessically untutored supporters.

36 Q-K4	Q-N7+
37 K-N3	R-R7
38 R-KB1	P-N5
39 Q-N7	P-R4
40 K-R3	P-B6
41 R-KN1	Q-KB7
42 Q-N8+	K-R2
43 Q-KB8	QxKP+
44 P-N3	R-R2
45 R-QR1	QxQP
46 RxR	QxR
47 QxP	Q-N8
48 Q-N7	K-N2
49 Q-K4	Q-B4
50 Q-K1	P-B7
51 Q-R1+	K-R2
52 Q-QB1	Q-B4+
53 K-R2	Q-Q6
54 P-B5	Q-K7+
55 K-R3	Q-Q8
56 PxP+	PxP
Resigns	

An admirable positional game by Staunton.

23

SAINT-AMANT - STAUNTON
21st match game, Paris, 19th and 20th Dec. 1843
Queen's Gambit Declined

This is one of Staunton's most important strategic games. Each of us in turn picked it to illustrate an article on the match — Coles in 1943 for *Chess* to commemorate the centenary, and Keene in 1968 for *Schakhmatny Bulletin* to celebrate the 125th anniversary. As a pendant to Staunton's game we append a modern World Championship game which is so astonishingly similar, particularly coming within a year of Petrosian probably reading Keene's article in the Russian monthly magazine that, though it can only be a coincidence, it goes to confirm the suggestion in the Biography that Petrosian and Staunton, two World Champions, were so 'astrally related' that the former could reproduce a conception of the latter's in similar circumstances 126 years later!

1 P-Q4	P-Q4
2 P-QB4	P-K3

In the 19th game Staunton accepted the gambit (as McDonnell was wont to do against Labourdonnais) but White obtained the upper hand: 2 ..., PxP; 3 P-K3, P-K4; 4 BxP, PxP; 5 PxP, B-Q3?; 6 N-KB3, N-KB3; 7 P-KR3, O-O; 8 O-O, N-B3; 9 B-KN5, B-K2; 10 N-B3, B-KB4; 11 P-R3, N-K5; 12 B-K3, B-B3; 13 R-K1, N-Q3; 14 B-R2, P-KR3; 15 Q-R4, N-K2; 16 QR-Q1, N-N3; 17 B-B1, P-B3; 18 N-K5, and won after 79 moves.

3 P-K3	P-QB4
4 N-QB3	N-KB3
5 N-B3	B-K2
6 B-Q3	P-QN3
7 O-O	

White could have tried PxQP in conjunction with B-N5+.

7	O-O
8 P-QN3	B-N2
9 BPxP	KPxP
10 Q-B2	

The position is very similar to that in their 13th game (Game 21).

10	N-B3
11 P-QR3	P-QR3
12 R-Q1	PxP
13 PxP	P-R3
14 P-QN4	B-Q3
15 R-K1	P-QN4
16 P-R3	R-B1
17 Q-N3	Q-B2
18 B-Q2	Q-N3

Most modern players would be tempted to agree to a draw in such an arid position, but drawn games did not count in this match, so both sides were willing to exhaust all possibilities before concluding peace.

19 B-K3	N-K2
20 QR-B1	N-R4

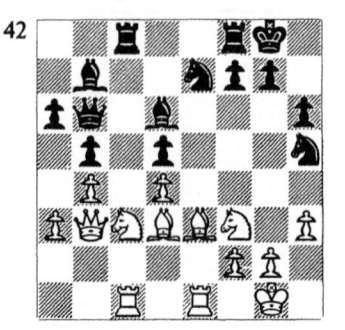

(42) *Staunton / Saint-Amant*

Premature, as Staunton admits in his notes to White's next two moves.

21 Q-Q1

'This is well played, as it effectually prevents Black from maturing the attack on the adverse King, and obliges him to retire his Knight again' (Staunton).

21	N-KB3
22 N-KR4	

'Having driven back the enemy, White in turn commences a well-directed attack himself' (Staunton).

22	R-B2
23 Q-Q2	N-R2

'An obstacle to the sacrifice of his Bishop, which White, doubtless, contemplated, and which would have given him a position fully equivalent for the piece' (Staunton). Now 24 BxRP?, PxB; 25 QxP, B-R7+.

24 Q-B2	N-KB3
25 K-R1	

Eliminating the possibility of Black's B-R7+, and thereby contemplating anew the sacrifice at KR6.

25 ...... N-K1

'This adds greatly to the strength and solidity of the King's stronghold, and enables Black to resume offensive operations in freedom and security' (Staunton).

26 N-B5?	NxN
27 BxN	P-QR4!

Seizing the opportunity for this move since White's KB no longer attacks Black's QNP.

28 Q-N3 PxP

The difficult manoeuvring had been too much of a strain for Saint-Amant and Staunton seizes the initiative which White forfeited with his 26th move.

29 PxP

'At this point, the battle having lasted 8 hours, the combatants adjourned for an hour, to recruit their energies' (Staunton).

29 ...... R-B5

'An excellent move, the brilliant beginning of renewed hostilities, during which the English player never ceased to retain the advantage' (Saint-Amant).

30 N-R2	N-B3
31 B-Q3	Q-B3
32 Q-N2	

Not 32 BxR, QPxB threatening both the mate and the Queen.

32 ...... Q-Q2!

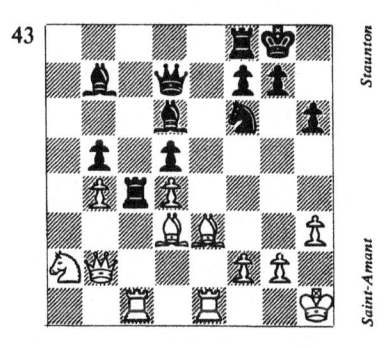

43

A very fine 'outpost' positional exchange sacrifice, probably the first example of its type in the history of chess. It is outstandingly modern in its concept and echoes of this sacrifice have reverberated down to the present day; compare the pendant game, Spassky - Petrosian, which is amazingly similar. It says a lot for Staunton's profound positional understanding that he appreciated to the full the compensating factors for the loss of the exchange: a weak White QNP, control of all key light squares, enhanced power of the fianchettoed bishop and increased mobility for his K-side attack. Possibly White's position can be defended but under pressure from Black's initiative White's chances of defending accurately are slim.

33 K-N1

Saint-Amant's reluctance to accept the offer testifies to the accuracy of Staunton's vision. After 33 BxR,

QPxB he would be threatened with QxP+.

33	N-R4
34 Q-Q2	P-B4
35 P-B4	N-N6
36 BxR	QPxB
37 Q-N2	

Or 37 P-Q5, N-K5; 38 Q-Q4 when Black has several promising continuations: 38 ..., R-R1; 39 R-R1, R-R6 planning R-Q6, or 38 ..., N-B3 and White's QP goes.

37	R-B3
38 N-B3	N-K5
39 R-K2	R-N3
40 R-Q1?	

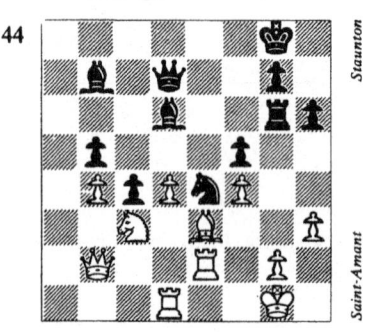

44

Saint-Amant / Staunton

A blunder after which Black regains the exchange with a simple win. However, White's position is precarious in any case, as can be seen from: 40 NxN, BxN; 41 Q-B3, R-N6; 42 R-KB2, Q-K2!; or 40 P-Q5, NxN; 41 QxN, BxQP; 42 R-Q1, Q-N2; 43 R(2)-Q2, B-K5; 44 RxB, RxP+; 45 K-B1, B-Q6+ with a clear advantage for Black in either variation; while if 40 R-KB1, there is either the instant N-N6 or 40 ..., NxN; 41 QxN, Q-K2; 42 R-N2, R-N6 and White collapses. In these lines the weakness of White's QNP is evident.

40	NxN
41 QxN	B-B6
42 R(1)-K1	BxR
43 RxB	Q-K2
44 Q-N2	R-K3

45 K-B2	R-K5

White's pawns fixed on dark squares are an easy prey to the opposition.

46 Q-R2

The QNP cannot be held, but Black is in no hurry.

46	K-B2
47 P-N3	Q-N2

The touch of the master, allowing the QNP to survive so that he can penetrate White's position down the long diagonal.

48 Q-R3	R-K1
49 Q-B3	Q-R8
50 P-R4	P-N4
51 Q-K1	Q-R7+

The pendant game shows a similar infiltration by Black's Queen.

52 K-B1	Q-R6+

45

Saint-Amant / Staunton

53 K-N1	Q-N5
54 RPxP	

'At the solicitation of M. St. Amant's seconds it was now agreed, as the game had been prolonged beyond midnight, that hostilities should be suspended till the following morning' (Staunton). This was the only game of the match not completed in one day.

54	BxBP
55 BxB	QxR
56 QxQ	RxQ
57 PxP	P-B6
58 K-B1	R-K5

Threatening RxB+.

59 B-B1	K-N3

| 60 P-Q5 | P-B7 |
| 61 B-Q2 | RxP |

The poor pawn falls after all.

62 P-Q6	R-Q5
63 K-K2	RxP
64 K-K3	KxP
65 K-K2+	K-N3
66 K-K1	P-N5

Saint-Amant now resigned the game and the match.

Now compare Spassky - Petrosian, 11th World Championship game, Moscow, 1969. — Queen's Indian Defence — 1 P-Q4, N-KB3; 2 P-QB4, P-K3; 3 N-KB3, P-QN3; 4 P-QR3, B-N2; 5 N-B3, P-Q4; 6 P-K3, QN-Q2; 7 PxP, PxP; 8 B-K2, B-Q3; 9 P-QN4, O-O; 10 O-O, P-QR3; 11 Q-N3, Q-K2; 12 R-N1, N-K5; 13 P-QR4, N(2)-B3; 14 P-N5, NxN; 15 QxN, N-K5; 16 Q-B2, KR-B1; 17 B-N2, P-QB3; 18 PxBP, BxBP; 19 Q-N3, Q-Q2; 20 R-R1, P-QN4; 21 P-R5, B-N2; 22 N-K5, Q-Q1; 23 KR-Q1, Q-R5; 24 P-N3, Q-K2; 25 P-B3, N-N4; 26 P-R4, N-K3; 27 P-B4, P-B3; 28 N-B3, N-Q1; 29 K-B2, N-B2; 30 N-Q2, R-B5!;

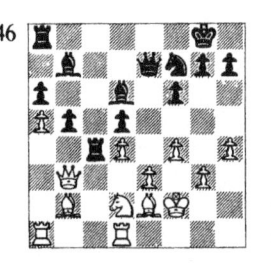

The outpost exchange sacrifice. Here it is in strikingly similar circumstances, although in this case the position is even more in Black's favour.

31 Q-Q3, R-K1; 32 B-KB3, B-N5; 33 B-R3, BxB; 34 RxB, N-Q3; 35 R-K1, P-B4; 36 R(3)-R1, N-K5+; 37 BxN, BPxB; 38 Q-N1, Q-Q2; 39 R-R2, R(K)-QB1; 40 NxR, QPxN; 41 P-Q5, BxP; 42 R-Q1, P-B6; 43 R-B2, Q-R6; 44 R-N1, Q-N5; 45 K-N2, Q-B6+; 46 K-R2, QxKP; 47 P-B5, Q-B4; 48 R-KB1, P-N5; 49 P-B6, P-N6; 50 R(2)-B2, P-B7; 51 Q-B1, P-K6; 52 P-B7+, K-B1; 53 R-B5, P-N7; 54 QxNP, P-B8/Q; 55 QxP+, KxQ; 56 R-N5+, and faced with 56 ..., K-R1, White resigned.

24

STAUNTON - AMATEUR
Casual game, London, 1844
Odds of Queen's Knight (remove White's QN)
Evans Gambit

1 P-K4	P-K4
2 N-KB3	N-QB3
3 B-B4	B-B4
4 P-QN4	BxP
5 P-B3	B-R4
6 O-O	P-Q3
7 P-Q4	BxP?

This superfluous capture is simply asking for trouble — and eventually he gets it! Already a knight ahead Black does not need any more material. He should develop, and hence N-B3 was the correct move both psychologically and practically.

| 8 Q-N3 | BxR |

Black's voracity knows no bounds.

| 9 BxP+ | K-K2 |

After K-B1; 10 B-N5 keeps White's chances alive.

| 10 B-N5+ | N-B3 |

11 RxB   P-KR3

An unsubtle move which permits a serious weakness on his KN3. Black should try N-R4; 12 Q-R3, KxB improving his chances by the elimination of White's KB. He should then be a rook ahead for which White still has insufficient compensation. To that extent one must accord a certain grudging justification to Black's gross handling of the opening.

12 N-R4!!   NxQP

Not PxB?; 13 N-N6+, K-Q2; 14 Q-K6 mate.

13 N-N6+   K-Q2
14 Q-R3+   K-B3
15 R-B1+   K-N3
16 R-N1+   N-N4

Not K-R3; 17 Q-R3 mate. But Black still had a draw after K-B3; 17 R-B1+ which shows how many errors can be made at these large odds before the game swings to the odds giver. However, this is the sort of situation where Staunton often took a chance which would be unjustified against a stronger opponent, so he might have answered K-B3 with the try 17 B-Q5+ hoping for some such line as K-B4; 18 Q-B3 mate, and risking Black finding the more accurate 17 ..., NxB; though even that leaves Black plenty of opportunities for further error. After the move actually chosen by Black, his King is amusingly driven back along the path it has just taken, only to be chased out once again to perish at the furthest limit of his empire — the QR-file.

17 RxN+   KxR

18 Q-N3+

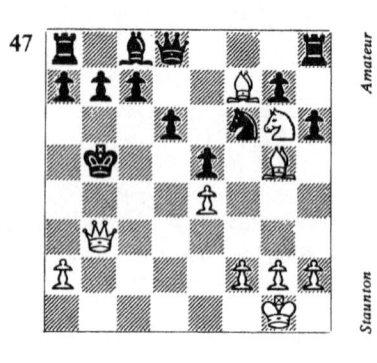

47

The see-saw manoeuvres of the white Queen are most attractive.

18 ......   K-B3

Obviously forced.

19 Q-B4+   K-Q2
20 NxP+!?

A good try, hoping for PxN; 21 Q-K6 mate. But since Black does not oblige it would have been more expeditious to continue 20 Q-K6+, K-B3; 21 NxP+, transposing into the actual game two moves ahead of schedule.

20 ......   K-K2
21 N-N6+   K-Q2
22 Q-K6+   K-B3
23 N-K5+   K-N3
24 Q-N3+   K-R4
25 N-B4+   K-R3
26 Q-R4 mate

Fourteen consecutive checks by White and a Black King journey from K1-K2-Q2-QB3-QN3-QN4-QB3-Q2-K2-Q2-QB3-QN3-QR4-QR3.

Another rebuff to those who decry Staunton's tactical ability.

77

The 1843 Match between Staunton and Saint-Amant, played in Paris at the Cercle des Echecs (Café de la Regence). Sitting, from left to right: Barthes de Marmoriere, Charron, Laemlein, Bryan, Staunton, Calvi, de Saint-Amant, Lecrivain, Sasias, Laroche, Graf de Sobanski and Rousseau. Sitting, from left to right: General Baker, Doazan, Saint-Elme le Duc, General Graf Duchaffault, Devinck, Vuillermet, Ricketts, Dr. Berthel, Norbert Monget, Kieseritsky for Alfred de Musset, Dizi, General Guingret, Deskaubiers, Chamouillet, Lemaitre, Jules Grillenzoni, Francois, Edouard Proux, Barthes and Baron Dumesnil. The busts on the wall represent De Labourdonnais (left) and Philidor (right).

25

STAUNTON - BRISTOL CHESS CLUB
Correspondence, 1844-5
Bird's Opening

Staunton's penchant for prophylaxis appears frequently in his games. This game could pass for one by Nimzowitsch; both the opening and the strategy — exploitation of doubled pawns and play on squares of a certain colour — are entirely Nimzowitschian. There is even a Queen move strongly associated with Nimzowitsch, to wit Q-KN4, which the 20th century master used as a method of cramping Black's K-side both in his own special opening (1 N-KB3, P-Q4; 2 P-QN3) and in his patent variation of the French Defence (1 P-K4, P-K3; 2 P-Q4, P-Q4; 3 P-K5, P-QB4; 4 Q-N4!?). Readers who wish to delve deeper can examine Games 35 and 39 in the English translation of *My System*. But here is a game played over 40 years before Nimzowitsch's birth.

Bird dates the game 1843, but he is a notoriously unreliable authority where dates are concerned. Staunton was not in demand with provincial chess clubs until after he had beaten Saint-Amant, so it can almost certainly be dated after that, especially as the style is that of the more mature Staunton. The conduct of the Black pieces was probably chiefly in the hands of Williams, the club President, and Withers, the Secretary. One suspects that Williams must have learnt a thing or two from Staunton's play here, for his own later style could be said to have been often modelled on White's in this game.

1 P-KB4	P-Q4
2 N-KB3	P-QB4
3 P-K3	N-QB3
4 B-N5!	

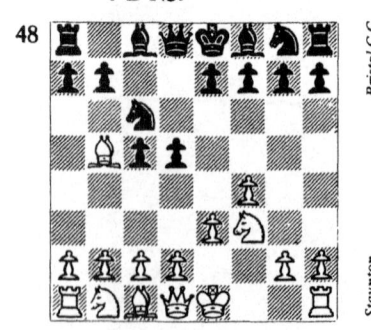

A reversed Nimzo-Indian? We usually regard Nimzowitsch as the Primum Mobile of the strategy of doubling the opponent's QBPs in the interests of reducing his dynamic possibilities, but this little known game by Staunton must force us to revise that opinion. Staunton did not elaborate on his idea with a body of supporting positional theory, as Nimzowitsch did, nor did it attain any mass popularity, but the remarkable thing is that Staunton should have anticipated such a major development of modern chess by over half a century!

  4 ......   P-QR3

The Black partners handle the opening in somewhat unsophisticated fashion. Since White intends BxN+ anyway, it was foolish to encourage the exchange.

5 BxN+	PxB
6 O-O	P-K3
7 P-B4!	

Absolutely regulation nowadays in such positions to blockade the doubled pawns, but in the 1840s this strategy was unknown — except to Staunton! Only after Nimzowitsch's games from the 1920s did such ideas gain universal currency.

7 ......   N-R3

An eccentric square for the knight. It should be developed on KB3 in order to maintain contact with the vulnerable forward QBP by a later N-Q2.

8 Q-K2   B-Q3
9 N-B3   Q-K2
10 P-QN3

Introducing the possibility of N-QR4 and B-QR3, another very modern concept.

10 ......   P-B3
11 P-Q3   O-O
12 P-K4   PxKP

A positional blunder which removes all the flexibility from Black's pawn structure. Just as bad would have been P-Q5; 13 N-QR4, eyeing the front QBP. The only playable move at this point is B-N2!, holding firm in the centre, but such positional necessities were not generally understood until Nimzowitsch explained them in his books *My System* and *Chess Praxis*.

13 PxP   P-K4

Clearly Black wanted to liberate their QB, but the text allows White a free hand on the K-side.

14 P-B5   N-B2
15 N-KR4   B-Q2
16 R-B3   KR-Q1
17 B-K3

There is no need now to develop the bishop on QR3. It fulfils the function of attacking the QBP with equal efficiency from this central post.

17 ......   B-K1
18 QR-KB1 N-N4
19 R-N3   P-R3
20 Q-N4!   R-Q2

There is not much that Black can undertake and White's next move forces a decisive weakening of Black's King's position.

21 N-B3!

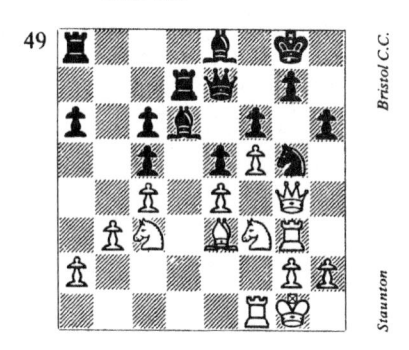

49

Bristol C.C.

Staunton

21 ......   K-B1

Or NxN+; 22 R(1)xN (threatening BxRP), K-R2; 23 BxRP!, KxB (PxB allows mate); 24 R-R3+ winning.

22 NxN   RPxN
23 P-KR4 B-KB2

Equivalent to resignation, but 23 ..., PxP (the only way of warding off immediate material loss) loses as follows: 24 QxP, B-KB2; 25 Q-R8+, B-N1; 26 B-R6!, or 24 QxP, K-N1; 25 R-R3, Q-B1; 26 N-R4, QR-Q1 (otherwise N-N6 picks off a rook); 27 Q-B2 and Black's Q-side collapses. Such combined play on both wings — the attack against Black's King deflecting his pieces from the defence of the Q-side — must strike us as a further highly advanced motif for the first half of the 19th century, when the open game, incorporating such debuts as the Evans and King's Gambits, was rife.

24 PxP   K-K1
25 P-N6   B-KN1
26 R-R3   K-Q1
27 Q-K2

As in the previous note, White now diverts his attention to Black's doubled pawns.

27 ......   K-B2
28 N-R4   R(2)-Q1

29 Q-KB2	K-N2
30 P-KN4	Q-QB2
31 BxP	

Achieving a winning advantage.

31	BxB
32 NxB+	K-B1
33 R-Q3	RxR
34 NxR	Q-Q3
35 R-Q1	K-B2
36 R-Q2	Q-Q5
37 QxQ	PxQ
38 K-B2	R-Q1
39 K-B3	

And Black resigned after a few more moves.

26

MONGREDIEN - STAUNTON
Match game, Liverpool, May 1845
(Staunton gave the odds of Pawn and Two)

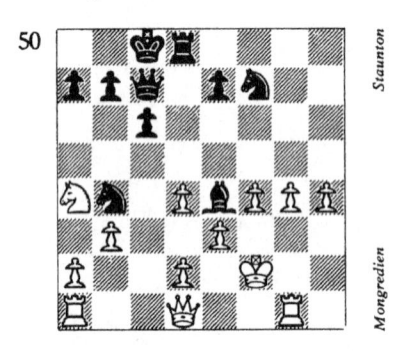

In this picturesque position White's superiority in *pawns* is immense, but Staunton understands perfectly how to turn to account the greater activity of his *pieces*.

21	RxP!

A spectacular inroad into White's position. On 22 PxR, mate follows speedily by QxP+; 23 K-K2, Q-B6+; 24 K-K1, N-Q6 mate.

22 N-B5	B-Q4

The rook remains immune. After 23 PxR, QxP+; 24 K-K1, QxQP; 25 R-N3, QxN White's position is wrecked.

23 K-N3

Seeking asylum behind his imposing phalanx of pawns.

23	N-Q6
24 NxN	

Yet again White cannot pause to pluck off Black's importunate rook. 24 PxR?, QxP+; 25 K-R3, N-B7 mate. After the text, however, there is no way for White to evict Black's powerful constellation of centralised pieces.

24	RxN
25 Q-B2	B-K5
26 Q-B4	N-Q3
27 Q-N8+	K-Q2

28 QR-Q1	Q-R4
29 P-B5	

It was not possible to defend the QP.

29	B-Q4
30 Q-R7	RxQP
31 P-B6	

Equally useless was 31 RxR, QxR; 32 Q-R6, N-K5+; 33 K-R3, Q-KB7; 34 R-N2, Q-B6+; 35 K-R2, N-B3.

31	N-K5+
32 QxN	

Equivalent to resignation, but if 32 K-B4, R-KB7+ or 32 K-R3, N-B7+; 33 K-R2 or N3, Q-B2+ winning either way.

32	BxQ
33 P-B7	Q-K4+
34 K-R3	R-R7 mate

Augustus Mongredien

27

WILLIAMS - STAUNTON
Match game, Bristol, June 1845
Odds of Pawn and Two Moves (remove Black's KBP)

Elijah Williams, President of the Bristol club, was one of Staunton's most ardent admirers at this time, and was so impressed that he uprooted himself and his family from Bristol and moved later in the year to London, where he became editor of the column in the *Field* and published a collection of games played at the Divan under the title *Horae Divanianae*. His strength so improved in the metropolis that he was meeting Staunton on level terms six years later and many of their 1851 contests number amongst the best in the careers of both masters. The present game therefore makes an excellent curtain-raiser, executed as it is by Staunton with supreme confidence and being a game which reveals his thorough assimilation of Philidor's teachings concerning the central pawn mass.

1 P-K4	———
2 P-Q4	N-QB3

Nimzowitsch's Defence!?

3 B-Q3	P-K4

And not NxP; 4 Q-R5+, P-N3; 5 Q-K5 with advantage.

4 N-KB3

Offering a gambit for rapid development after 4 ..., PxP; 5 P-B3. Staunton wisely declines in order to further his own mobilisation.

4	P-Q3
5 B-QB4	B-N5

6 P-KR3	BxN
7 QxB	Q-B3
8 Q-QN3	

With its double attack against Black's QNP and his dormant KN this looks serious, but Staunton has prepared a fine riposte.

8	O-O-O!
9 BxN	NxP
10 Q-B7	

Forcing an ending in which he will be the exchange to the bad, but with outstanding prospects of trapping Black's remaining knight.

10	NxP+
11 K-Q1	NxR
12 QxQ	PxQ
13 B-K6+	K-N1
14 P-QN3	B-N2
15 B-N2	

Black's knight is doomed.

15	KR-K1
16 B-B4	NxP
17 PxN	P-B3
18 N-B3	

It might appear initially as if the position were in White's favour since it is difficult for Black to advance his pawns, but a tactical device comes to Staunton's aid which enables him to set his pawns in motion, and with gain of tempo.

18	P-Q4!

So it's possible after all!

19 PxP	PxP
20 B-N5	

An admission of the failure of his restraining strategy. If 20 BxP, then RxB+!; 21 NxR, R-Q1 and Black comes out a pawn to the good, though this was Staunton's recommendation as best.

20	R-K3
21 K-K2	P-QR3
22 B-Q3	P-K5
23 B-N1	P-B4
24 R-Q1	P-Q5

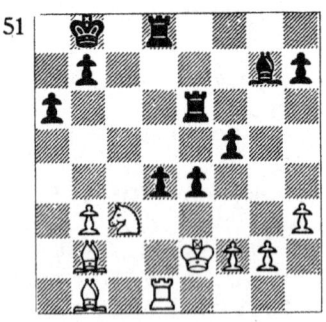

51

This avalanche of central pawns is quite in the style of Philidor. White's minor pieces are no match for Black's rooks since the pawn mass deprives them of any foothold in the centre.

25 N-R4	P-N4
26 N-B5	R-QB3
27 B-R3	P-Q6+
28 K-B1	P-QR4
29 P-QN4	B-B6

Undermining White's QNP. Once this final bastion has caved in the remainder of the game degenerates into a rout.

30 N-N3	PxP
31 B-B1	B-K4
32 B-Q2	R-B6!

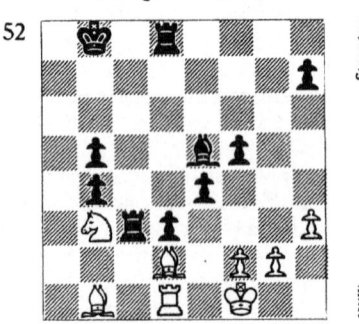

52

A beautifully self-assured move. Of course it would be suicidal for White to capture the rook, thus increasing Black's pawn wedge to titanic proportions, but what he actually plays is also useless.

33 N-R5	K-B2
34 B-R2	R-QR1
35 B-K6	RxN
36 BxP	R-B5
37 BxRP	R-R7
38 P-B4	B-Q5
39 BxKP	

If 39 B-K1, R(5)-B7; 40 BxKP, R-B7+; wins.

39	RxB!

An incisive conclusion.

40 RxR	R-B8+
	Resigns

28

STAUNTON - AMATEUR
Casual game, London, June 1845
Odds of Queen's Knight (remove White's QN)
Bishop's Opening

1 P-K4	P-K4
2 B-B4	B-B4
3 P-QN4	BxP
4 P-B4	

The McDonnell Double Gambit, introduced by that player against Labourdonnais in 1834. On level terms the strongest reply is 4 ..., P-Q4!; 5 KPxP, P-K5; 6 N-K2, N-KB3; 7 P-QB3, B-QB4 with some advantage to Black, as in Mongredien - Morphy, 1st match game, Paris, 1859. Of course with an extra piece, as here, Black can accept such gifts with impunity and, indeed, has the upper hand in this game until the decisive combination on move 14.

4	PxP
5 N-B3	P-Q3
6 P-B3	B-QB4
7 P-Q4	B-N3
8 BxP	N-KB3
9 Q-Q3	O-O
10 P-KR3	NxP

The odds receiver is obviously not without some talent, but three moves later he becomes over-confident and is promptly struck down.

11 QxN	R-K1
12 B-K5	PxB
13 O-O	PxP?

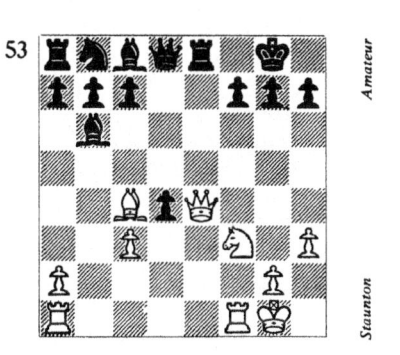

53

A careless mistake which permits Staunton to breach the Black position at its traditionally most susceptible point — KB2. For similar play, from an identical opening, see Game 40.

14 BxP+	KxB

Or K-R1; 15 BxR, P-KR3; 16 N-N5.

15 N-N5+	K-N1
16 QxP mate	

A neat little miniature.

29

KENNEDY - STAUNTON
Match game, London, c. July 1845
Odds of Pawn and Two Moves (remove Black's KBP)

1 P-K4	———
2 P-Q4	P-K3
3 B-Q3	P-B4
4 PxP	Q-R4+

Naturally not BxP?; 5 Q-R5+.

5 N-B3	BxP

This mode of regaining the pawn is an improvement on the method in Game 5.

6 N-K2	N-QB3
7 O-O	N-B3
8 N-N3	O-O
9 P-QR3	

Not a very productive plan. Black's Queen has fulfilled her mission on the Q-side and would welcome a journey home in any event.

9	Q-Q1
10 P-N4	B-N3
11 B-KN5	B-Q5
12 KN-K2	B-N3
13 K-R1	N-K4
14 B-R4?	

Hitherto White's play has been uninspired if not disastrous, but here he begins to reveal a perilous lack of awareness of Black's possibilities. He should have sought control of his KN4 by means of 14 P-R3 or even P-B3, and only then B-R4-B2, hoping to neutralise the effect of Black's powerful KB.

14	N(4)-N5

White's position is already critical since the defence of his KB2 (the traditional target for Black at these odds) has become a virtually insoluble problem. The obvious 15 P-R3 fails against the combination which Staunton brings off in the game itself.

15 N-R4

In the laudable and natural desire to eliminate Black's galling bishop, but now Staunton opens fire with a combinative sequence worthy of McDonnell, Labourdonnais, Morphy or, indeed, any of the paragons of the open, sacrificial style.

15	NxKP!!

Of the several captures available to White at this juncture none offers the slightest shred of salvation.

16 BxQ

If NxB or BxN, there is the reply QxB.

16	N(K)xP+
17 K-N1	N-R6+

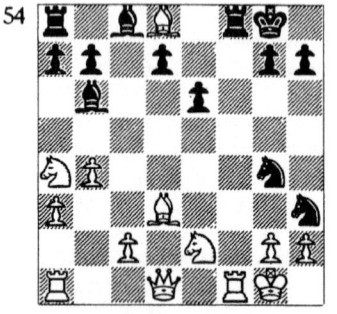

54

18 K-R1	N(5)-B7+
19 RxN	NxR+
20 K-N1	B-K6!!

In the middle of a heavy sacrificial attack with only a rook for Queen and knight this is a superbly cool move, and the only one to win. On the banal NxQ+?; 21 BxB, PxB; 22 NxP, it is White who emerges on top. After the tremendous text move White's whole army is reduced to scattered impotence.

21 Q-N1

Virtual resignation, but the palliative deflecting offer 21 B-KN5 fails against NxQ+; 22 BxB, NxB; with an extra exchange, or even 21 ..., BxB; 22 Q-N1, B-K6! returning to the charge with deadly effect.

21	N-Q8+
22 K-R1	R-B8+
Resigns	

The 'solid plodder' flames again.

30

EVANS - STAUNTON
Casual game, London, c. Aug. 1845
(Staunton gave the odds of Pawn and Two)

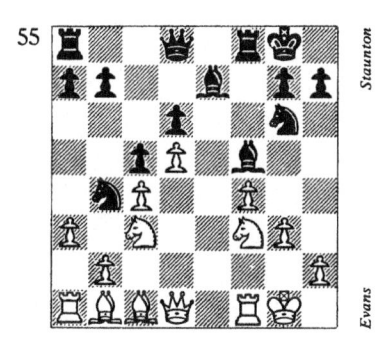

| 13 ...... | BxB |
| 14 PxN? | |

A typical positional mistake for the period. Natural and strong was RxB!, when Black's knight must retreat and White gains time to exploit his extra pawn and control of his K6. The text gives White a passed pawn, but Staunton retains his QB which will enjoy a rich area of activity on the K-side light squares which White has already enfeebled; the sequel of the game will serve to emphasise this very point.

14	B-B4
15 PxP	PxP
16 N-K5	P-QR3
17 P-KN4	

Apparently very forceful, but Black's small crumbs of comfort are gradually beginning to amount to something more tangible — weak light squares and now over-extended pawns as targets for Black's pieces. The temporary initiative White gains by this advance does not compensate him for the permanent structural wounds he inflicts on his own position. It is worth noting that Staunton, in marked contradistinction to many of his contemporaries, had an acute sense of danger where his own King was concerned and very rarely indulged in potentially weakening advances of his pawns. Normally his King was to be seen tucked away securely in a corner and in his liking for safety moves with his King (see move 13 in Game 15, move 15 in Game 54, and move 19 in Game 56) he could be compared to Petrosian, the apostle of prophylaxis in modern Grandmaster chess. An example in Staunton's play can also be seen from the 2nd game of his 1st round match in the London Tournament of 1851, played on 27th May. Brodie - Staunton then went:

1 P-QB4, P-QB4; 2 P-Q3, P-K3; 3 P-K3, P-Q4; 4 PxP, PxP; 5 N-KB3, N-QB3; 6 P-KN3, N-B3; 7 B-N2, B-Q3; 8 N-B3, P-QR3; 9 N-K2, B-N5; 10 P-QR3, O-O; 11 Q-N3, K-R1! (the typical precaution); 12 B-Q2, P-QN4; 13 Q-B2, R-B1; 14 P-N3, R-K1; and Black eventually turned his advantage to account.

17 ......   B-B1
18 N-K4   B-B3
19 P-Q6

This over-optimistic thrust and its corollary (20 NxP) play into Black's hands by exposing all the weaknesses in the White position. At this point consolidation was mandatory and was to be achieved by means of 19 NxN, PxN; 20 R-R3 and, if necessary, N-N3. Black would still have been able to drum up counterplay with moves such as B-Q5+, Q-R5 and P-QN4, but White's pieces would have been well poised for defence. In addition White would have retained a permanent asset in the shape of a protected passed QP. His actual move deprives this important unit of its lifeline.

19 ......   B-K3!

Daring White to capture on his QB5.

20 NxP

Much too dangerous. This simply opens lines for Black's counter-attack.

It might look as if Black, two pawns in arrears and with a White pawn rammed into his position, was being pushed off the board, but appearances can be deceptive.

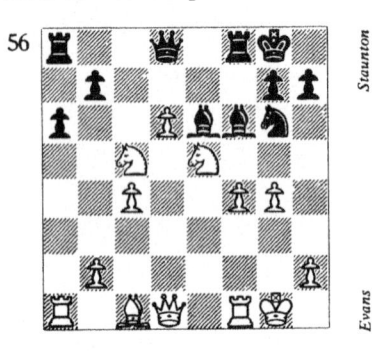

56

20 ......   Q-N3!

The harbinger of a mighty counter-offensive, typical of Staunton's play at odds of Pawn and Two.

21 B-K3

The knight is still virtually immobilised since the QB cannot easily be protected.

21 ......   BxN
22 PxB   RxR+
23 KxR

Hoping to release one part of the pin.

23 ......   R-B1+
24 K-N1

Back again!

24 ......   NxP

The weak squares begin to tell. White cannot defend his KB3 against an incursion by Black pieces, and soon all of the K-side light squares fall prey to the opposition.

25 Q-QB1   N-B6+
26 K-R1   QxQP

White's extra material is swept away and the far-flung K-side pawns fail to offer a shred of defensive cover to White's King. What follows is a severe cautionary tale against the voluntary weakening of one's own K-side.

27 Q-B2   BxNP
28 NxP

Rather irrelevant, but White's position was too far gone for good moves to be of any help.

28 ......   Q-QB3

Those light squares again!

29 N-R5

See Diagram 57

Hoping to drive the Queen away from the fatal diagonal, but Staunton dismisses this gesture with aplomb.

29 ......   N-K8+
30 NxQ

Or K-N1, Q-R8+ with the same finish.

30 ......   R-B8+
31 B-N1   B-B6+
32 Q-N2   BxQ mate

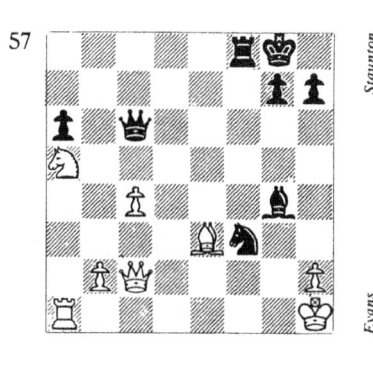

57

The suffocation mate at the close with equal material is delightful. Once offered his chance, Staunton snapped it up with great energy.

31

STAUNTON - AMATEUR
Casual game, London, c. 1845
Muzio Gambit

In the context of the time, opening theory inevitably paid considerable attention to versions of the King's Gambit. William Hartston has expressed the opinion that some of Staunton's analysis was fully equal to, if not better than, various lines analysed in Keres's modern work on this opening. In the following game Staunton shows himself more than a mere analyst of the opening.

1 P-K4   P-K4
2 P-KB4   PxP
3 N-KB3   P-KN4!?

Black has more reputable defences to the King's Gambit, notably 3 ..., P-Q4; but the ambitious Classical Defence has never been refuted.

4 B-B4

Introducing the infamous Muzio Gambit, the most consistent of White's attempts to profit from Black's weakness on the KB-file, albeit at the cost of a piece. Contemporary theory suggests that it should lead to equality. The Kieseritsky Gambit (4 P-KR4, P-N5; 5 N-K5) represents the positional course and in modern play (on those rare occasions when the Classical Defence can be employed at all) this would be White's most likely choice.

4 ......   P-N5

Players who feared the Muzio were content to continue with 4 ..., B-N2.

5 O-O

Clearly White's most sensible course. There are some exotic (and unsound) alternatives: the Ghulam - Kassim

Gambit (5 P-Q4), the Lolli Gambit (5 BxP+) and the McDonnell Gambit (5 N-B3), the last of which is the most respectable of the off-beat deviations at this point. Perhaps the following very attractive game by the great Irishman against Labourdonnais in 1834 influenced Staunton: 5 N-B3!?, PxN; 6 O-O!?, P-QB3; 7 QxP, Q-B3; 8 P-K5, QxP; 9 BxP+, KxB; 10 P-Q4, QxP+; 11 B-K3!, Q-N2; 12 BxBP, N-B3; 13 N-K4, B-K2; 14 B-N5, R-N1; 15 Q-R5+, Q-N3; 16 N-Q6+, K-K3; 17 QR-K1+, KxN; 18 B-B4 mate. 'Furor Hibernicus' was Tartakover's name for the game. Staunton's exploit here might no less be termed 'Furor Britannicus'.

5 ...... PxN
6 QxP Q-B3

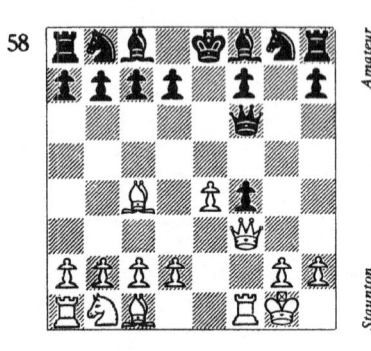

58

The thematic starting position in the Muzio. Black's last move is very definitely best since it not only barricades the KB-file but also impedes the formation of a White pawn centre with P-Q4. The defects of the defence by 6 ..., B-R3? were shown up vividly in a game Keene - Townsend, London 1961, played at the odds of White's Queen's Knight: 6 ..., B-R3; 7 P-Q4, Q-B3 (too late; Staunton here reckoned the only move was N-QB3); 8 P-K5, Q-B4; 9 P-KN3, QxBP; 10 BxP+!, KxB; 11 BxP, BxB; 12 QxB+, K-N2; 13 Q-B7+, K-R3; 14 R-B5, QxR; 15 QxQ, N-QB3; 16 R-KB1, and White won rapidly.

7 P-K5! QxP
8 P-Q3 B-R3
9 N-B3 P-QB3!?

After decades of analysis the main line has finally settled on 9 ..., N-K2; 10 B-Q2, QN-B3 (O-O; 11 QR-K1, Q-B4+; 12 K-R1, N-N3; 13 N-K4, Q-B3; 14 Q-R5, K-N2; 15 B-B3+, P-B3; 16 NxP, RxN; 17 R-K7+, K-B1; 18 QxB+, KxR; 19 Q-N7+, K-K1; 20 BxR, with advantage); 11 QR-K1, Q-KB4; 12 N-Q5, K-Q1; 13 B-B3, R-K1; 14 Q-K2, Q-K3; 15 Q-B3, Q-B4; 16 Q-K2, and the game is equal. A sad comment on such violent openings is that with correct defensive play the premature explosion of energy tends to exhaust rather than enhance the dynamic potential of the position, resulting in an undesirable state of early equilibrium. This fact explains the preference of many modern masters for sophisticated, closed positions with delayed clashes, a preference one can already observe in Staunton's own serious encounters. He only used these premature attacks against weaker opponents, who were unlikely to discover the best defensive resources.

10 BxP

A more enduring attack results from 10 B-Q2, e.g. 10 ..., Q-Q5+; 11 K-R1, P-Q4; 12 QR-K1+, K-Q1; 13 NxP, PxN; 14 B-B3. Staunton in his analyses always recommended B-Q2 as best here, and it was only against opponents much weaker than himself that he ventured on the text move.

10 ...... Q-Q5+?

In a later game against an amateur (c. 1850) Staunton's opponent played the better QxB with the continuation 11 Q-R5, Q-Q5+; 12 K-R1, P-Q4 (this exposes him to further sacrificial attacks. After 12 ..., K-Q1; 13 QxP, K-B2; 14 QR-K1, White may well control the greater part of the board and recover one piece, but Black's position is so impervious that it is doubtful if White has sufficient compensation); 13 QxP+, K-Q1; 14 QR-K1, B-Q2; 15 BxP, PxB; 16 NxP, Q-N2; 17 Q-R5, Q-N3; 18 Q-R4+, K-B1; 19 R-B6!, Q-N2; 20 Q-B4+, N-B3; 21 RxN+, BxR; 22 R-K8+, K-Q2; 23 RxR, Q-K4; 24 Q-N4+, K-Q3; 25 R-Q8+, K-B4; 26 Q-N4 mate.

11 K-R1   BxB
12 QR-K1+ N-K2

Here K-Q1 might provide Black with a more resilient position.

13 R-K4   Q-N2
14 QxB   P-Q4

The point of Black's defence, but ...!

15 BxP!   PxB
16 RxN+!?

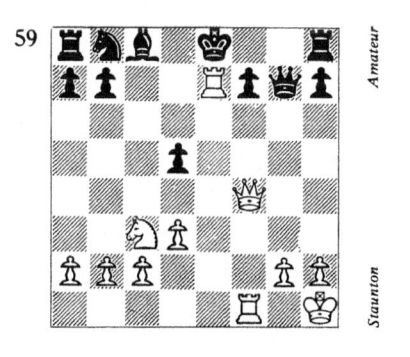

Objectively superior was the more materialistic 16 NxP, N-B3; 17 N-B7+, with a rook and a strong attack for two pieces.

16 ......   KxR
17 NxP+   K-K3

If K-Q2; 18 Q-B7+, K-K3; 19 N-B4+, K-B4; 20 N-R5+, winning.

18 Q-K4+   K-Q2

After K-Q3; 19 P-B4, N-B3; 20 R-B6+, Black could obtain more than sufficient material compensation with QxR, but his King would be horribly exposed. However, Staunton once remarked that the weaker player in an odds game (which is virtually what the Muzio is) is too apt to hang on to material advantage to his ultimate cost, and he undoubtedly felt confident that Black would play anything rather than 20 ..., QxR. If 20 ..., K-B4; 21 Q-K3+, N-Q5; 22 P-N4 mate. If 20 ..., K-Q2; 21 Q-B4!, K-K1 (against both Q-B7+ and RxP); 22 Q-Q6, threatening N-B7 mate. If 20 ..., B-K3; 21 Q-B4+, K-B4 (K-Q2; 22 Q-B7+, K-K1; 23 RxB+, winning); 22 Q-B7 (threatening P-N4+), BxN; 23 Q-Q6+, K-Q5; 24 QxB+, K-K6; 25 Q-K4+, K-Q7; 26 R-B2+.

19 Q-K7+   K-B3
20 Q-B7+   KxN
21 P-B4+   K-Q5?

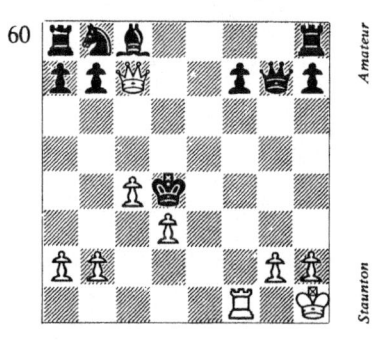

The final error. He had to play K-K3, when White's only line is 22 P-Q4! (planning P-Q5 mate), QxP; 23 QxP+, K-Q3; 24 R-B6+, QxR! (not K-B4; 25 Q-K7+, KxP; 26 P-N3+, K-N4; 27 P-R4+, K-R4; 28 Q-K1+, Q-N5; 29 Q-K5+, P-N4; 30 Q-B7 mate); 25 QxQ+, K-B2; 26 QxR, N-B3; 27 QxP+, B-Q2 and White's passed pawns represent an element of great strength in this position.

22 Q-Q6+	K-K6
23 Q-B4+	KxP
24 R-Q1+	K-B7
25 Q-Q2 mate	

See Diagram

Final position

A King hunt (illustrated clearly by the diagram) which the relevant anthologies have previously overlooked.

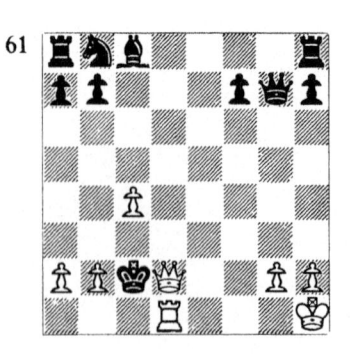

61 *Amateur* / *Staunton*

32

HORWITZ - STAUNTON
2nd match game, London, Feb. 1846
Sicilian Defence

1 P-K4	P-QB4
2 P-KB4	P-K3
3 N-KB3	N-QB3
4 B-K2	P-Q3
5 O-O	KN-K2
6 P-B4	N-N3
7 P-Q3	B-K2
8 N-B3	B-B3

Although Staunton had some years since appreciated the strength of the fianchettoed Queen's Bishop, it was only much later that he came round to the equivalent idea on the K-side, and then only after the intermediate variation B-K2-B3 which he plays here. He probably feared the weakness, after P-K3 and P-KN3, of his KB3 and KR3 squares, which he avoids in the present game. A similar weakness on the Q-side is hardly serious, but it could be worrying in the King's field. The 24th game of the match began 1 P-K4, P-QB4; 2 B-B4, P-K3; 3 N-QB3, N-QB3; 4 P-B4, P-QR3; 5 P-QR4, P-KN3; 6 N-B3, B-N2; and it is greatly to Staunton's credit that he first appreciated the possibility of the weakness and then realised that the KB fianchetto really was on. Today we fianchetto on the K-side without thinking, but Staunton had to work it all out for himself from scratch by a process of pure thought. A very striking example of something similar will be found in *Dynamic Chess* by Coles, but it occurred over sixty years later, long after the thinking had already been done. In the adjoined position

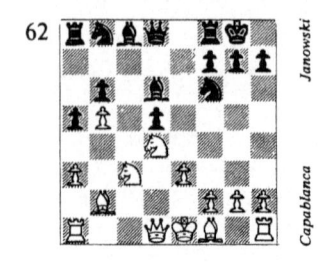

62 *Janowski* / *Capablanca*

Capablanca, against Janowski at San Sebastian in 1911, had a feeling that P-N3 was required for White, but feared the weakness and chose B-K2-B3, giving himself

Great Chess Match between Mr. Staunton and Mr. Horwitz. (No wonder the Staunton pattern sets became popular!)

endless trouble later.
9 Q-K1   O-O

In the 4th game of the match he preferred 9 ..., P-QR3; 10 K-R1, O-O; 11 B-K3, R-N1; 12 P-QR4, N-Q5; 13 B-Q1, B-Q2; 14 BxN!, with slight advantage to White which was later squandered by errors.

10 B-K3   B-Q5

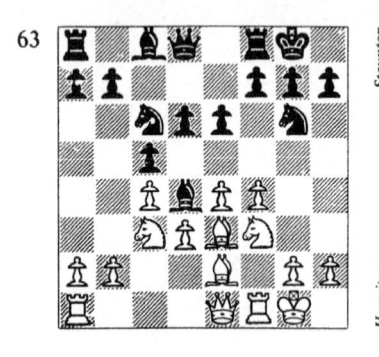

63

Staunton
Horwitz

11 Q-Q2   NxP

Staunton considered that this threw away such advantage as he had, and afterwards recommended Q-B3 first.

12 BxB	NxB+
13 NxN	PxB
14 N(2)xP	Q-N3
15 Q-KB2	N-QN5

NxN with equality was better (Staunton).

16 N-K1	B-Q2
17 P-QR3	N-B3
18 N-N5!	

A splendid move by Horwitz, winning a pawn by force. Staunton's attempt to hold it merely gets him into worse trouble.

18	Q-B4
19 P-QN4	Q-K4
20 N-KB3	Q-B5
21 P-N3	Q-R3
22 NxQP	P-QN3
23 P-N5	N-Q1
24 N-K5	B-B1

B-K1 would be even more disastrous after 25 NxB, RxN; 26 NxP, Q-N3; 27 N-Q6, but the game is long past saving.

25 N(5)xP	NxN
26 NxN	Q-B3
27 N-R6+!	PxN
28 QxQ	RxQ
29 RxR	K-N2
30 QR-KB1	P-R3
31 R-B7+	K-N3
32 P-K5	PxP

White announced mate in 4. A good incisive game by Horwitz. Up to the position in Diagram 63, after which he began to go wrong, Staunton was in fact pursuing a line he had first used as White in the 16th match game against Saint-Amant, which began 1 P-QB4, P-QB4; 2 N-QB3, P-K4; 3 P-K3, N-QB3; 4 P-QR3, P-B4; 5 P-Q3, N-B3; 6 KN-K2, P-Q3; 7 N-N3, B-K2; 8 B-K2, O-O; 9 O-O, P-KR3; 10 B-B3, K-R2; 11 B-Q5,

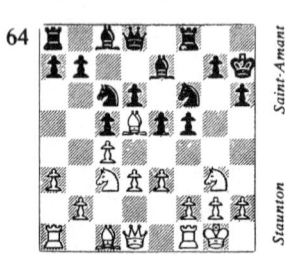

64

Saint-Amant
Staunton

Q-K1; 12 R-N1, P-QR4; 13 N-N5, Q-Q1; 14 P-N3. That the whole conception was still relevant in the next century can be seen from the opening of the game Nimzowitsch - Romih at San Remo 1930, which went 1 P-QB4, P-K4; 2 N-QB3, P-QB4; 3 P-KN3, P-Q3; 4 B-N2, N-QB3; 5 P-Q3, P-B4; 6 P-QR3, B-Q2; 7 P-QN4, R-N1; 8 P-N5, N-R4; 9 B-Q5,

See Diagram 65 opposite

9 ..., N-KB3; 10 B-N5, B-K2; 11 BxN, BxN; 12 R-B1, Q-K2; 13 P-K4, and White won on

65 *Nimzowitsch–Romih*

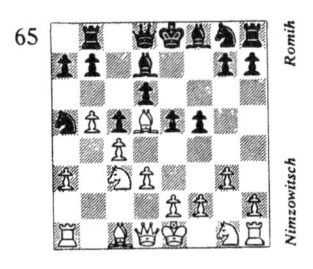

the 32nd move. Nimzowitsch had the advantage, of course, of playing his game after Staunton had discovered that a K-side fianchetto was feasible instead of the roundabout method used here by the old master. A similar early arrival of the bishop on Q5 can be seen in the Quinteros - Andersson game quoted after Game 42.

33
HORWITZ - STAUNTON
20th match game, London, 17th Apr. 1846
Sicilian Defence

Steinitz in his *Modern Chess Instructor* declared: 'It is specially as regards the power of the King that the modern school deviates from the teachings and practice of old theorists and chess masters, and we consider it established that the King must be treated as a strong piece both for attack and defence.' Steinitz may have regarded himself as the leader of the 'modern school', but in this game the 'old theorist' anticipates the Steinitzian dictum by several decades, just as he anticipated so many positional themes allegedly introduced years after his time by the established pedagogues of chess history.

1 P-K4	P-QB4
2 P-KB4	

Staunton's games with Black probably did a lot to banish this antiquated continuation from serious play. In recent years it has been re-introduced but only with the substitution of 5 B-N5+ for Horwitz's B-K2.

2	P-K3
3 N-KB3	P-Q4
4 PxP	PxP
5 B-K2?	

Much too passive, as indicated above.

5	B-Q3
6 P-B3	N-QB3
7 P-Q3	Q-B2
8 P-KN3	

After this weakening move Black already stands better, but the alternative defence by Q-Q2 would severely congest White's pieces.

| 8 ...... | N-B3 |
| 9 N-R3 | P-QR3 |

It is quite right to prevent N-QN5 exchanging one of Black's excellent bishops.

10 N-B2	O-O
11 P-Q4	R-K1
12 O-O	B-Q2
13 K-N2	R-K2

Staunton's plan of doubling rooks on the K-file is methodical but does not meet the needs of the position which require something sharper. Much more to the point was B-B4! now that White has foolishly put his King on KN2, with the plan of transferring this piece to the dominating square K5. In that case Black would probably have been able to decide the game by a direct attack against White's King. The course Staunton adopts is much slower.

14 R-K1	QR-K1
15 B-B1	Q-N3
16 RxR	RxR
17 P-N3	

Necessary to develop his QB.

17 ......   PxP

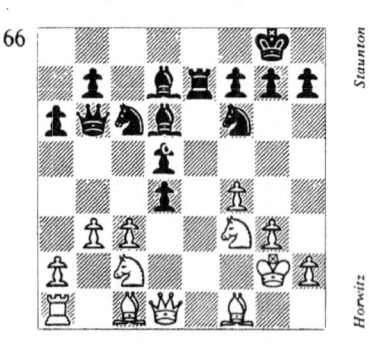

66

Even now B-B4! would have been very strong.

18 N(2)xP   B-KN5

Black retains a definite initiative but White has defensive prospects.

19 B-Q3   N-K5

The win of a pawn by NxN; 20 PxN, BxN+ is not possible, since White then replies 21 KxB! (21 ..., QxQP?; 22 BxP+), when White's King is in no immediate danger and Black has suddenly surrendered a bishop.

20 B-N2	B-QB4
21 Q-B2	BxN(Q5)
22 NxB	NxN
23 PxN	R-B2

Black's grip on the light squares and the lack of scope for White's bishops promise Black a permanent advantage. The exposed situation of White's King also hampers the defence.

24 Q-N1

Incredibly the only square!

24 ......   B-B6+!

At last this bishop hits the recommended diagonal.

25 K-N1

KxB is out of the question.

25 ......   P-B4

Staunton points out that N-B6 achieves nothing after 26 BxP+, K-R1; 27 Q-Q3.

| 26 Q-K1 | R-K2 |
| 27 R-B1 | |

Black's pieces have attained their optimum positions and now he is faced with the problem of how to make any progress. The solution is ingenious; Staunton enlists the aid of his King in order to concentrate sufficient force for a decisive assault.

| 27 ...... | K-B2! |
| 28 B-B1 | P-N4 |

Made possible by his previous move.

29 PxP

Giving in too easily. Q-K3 offers a tougher resistance. Now the light squares cave in.

| 29 ...... | NxP(4) |
| 30 Q-Q2 | K-N3! |

The way in which Staunton succeeds in maintaining his pieces on their key squares by protecting them with his King is truly remarkable. White could kick the knight with 31 P-KR4, but that would be awfully loosening. What he actually plays is not much better.

31 R-B8   Q-K3

Massing for the final infiltration.

32 R-Q8

It would have been a slight improvement to keep the rook at home to defend the back rank. Horwitz's resistance is not very impressive.

| 32 ...... | B-N5 |
| 33 Q-B4 | N-B6+ |

Staunton demonstrates in his own

notes that White can even win if Black goes astray with N-B2? e.g. 34 R-N8+, K-R4; 35 B-B1! Presumably such variations provided the bait for Horwitz to launch his rook into Black's hinterland. But the accurate, and rather obvious, text move decides the game in Black's favour.

  34 K-N2 Q-K8
  35 R-N8+ K-R4!
    Resigns

The final position with all of Black's pieces co-operating to give mate is most unusual. There is no defence to R-K7+. Even 36 RxB fails: 36 ..., R-K7+; 37 KxN, Q-B7 mate or 37 BxR, QxB+; and mates next move.

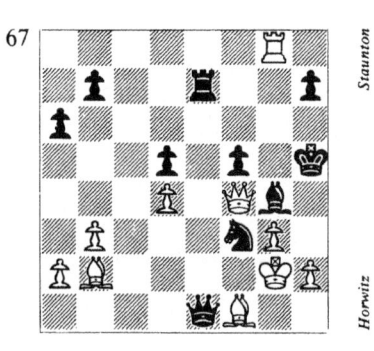

34

HORWITZ - STAUNTON
24th match game, London, 30th Apr. 1846
Sicilian Defence

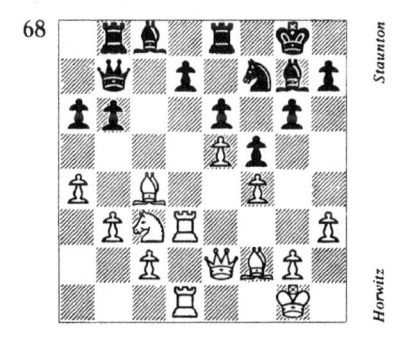

Horwitz has obtained considerable pressure on Black's position but has weakened the dark squares on his Q-side. Staunton's defence appears to have been hard put to it to hold the position, but he has skilfully reserved options of counter-attack as soon as opportunity permits. Now he feels the time has come and, like the great master he is, he appreciates the strength of his long diagonal QR1-KR8 so that, though he has his eye on White's Q-side weakness, he views it not merely as a target in itself but as part only of a double attack, the other part being against White's King's position, and under this alternating leverage one or the other will give. This breadth of vision anticipates the style of Lasker by more than half a century.

22 ...... B-R3!

A delightfully unobtrusive preparatory move by which he hopes to weaken the long diagonal even further.

23 P-N3

Falling in too readily with Black's plan, though he cannot prevent the basic strategy from maturing anyway. If 23 B-N3 or B-K3, Black could still play 23 ..., B-B1 and continue more or less as in the game. Alternatively, he could even start up a third threat with K-R1, R-N1 and P-KN4, undermining the White KP.

23 ...... B-B1

With its mission accomplished this bishop now eyes the Q-side weakness.

24 K-R2   Q-B3

The twin threats of P-QN4 (trapping White's KB) and B-QN2 (more powerful now with White's QB still on KB2 because of the mating threat) suddenly reveal the dynamism of Black's defence. Even if the White QB were standing on K3 or N3, Black is still prepared at a suitable moment to play B-QN2, making a 'positional sacrifice' of the Q-file to gain compensating flank flexibility.

25 R(3)-Q2

A vain attempt to stave off P-QN4.

25 ......   B-N5
26 B-Q4   BxN
27 BxB   P-QN4
28 R-Q6

He realises his game has gone and sets a last despairing trap.

28 ......   NxR
29 PxN   B-N2

Not falling for PxB; 30 Q-K5. White could now resign, but struggled on for

Bernhard Horwitz

nearly twenty more moves before throwing in his hand. The remaining moves were:

30 PxP	PxP
31 BxP	QxQB
32 BxP	B-B6
33 R-Q3	BxQ
34 RxQ	KR-Q1
35 BxP+	K-B1
36 P-Q7	B-N4
37 P-R4	BxP
38 B-B4	B-N4
39 BxB	RxB
40 K-R3	P-R4
41 R-B6	K-N2
42 R-B7+	K-R3
43 R-B4	R-Q8
44 P-QN4	R(4)-Q4
45 K-N2	R(4)-Q7+
46 K-B3	R-Q5
47 R-B8	RxP
48 K-K3	R(8)-Q5
Resigns	

35

HARRWITZ - STAUNTON
16th match game, London, Sept. 1846
Odds of Pawn and Two Moves (remove Black's KBP)

This game assumes the form of a pseudo-Benoni and, taken in conjunction with Games 36 and 39, each on the same opening plan, it provides us with an opportunity of expanding our appreciation of Staunton's deep sense of positional understanding and his remarkable facility for conducting play at these odds. The three games together form a valuable thematic unity.

1 P-K4	———
2 P-Q4	P-K3
3 P-QB4	

Possibly too ponderous a move at these odds. With Black's KBP missing, it looks more natural to keep the square QB4 available for the bishop. The solid developing move N-KB3, though hardly ever played at this point with these odds, must be the right one. An example of the odds receiver taking the other extreme and going berserk with a premature attack occurs in one of the match games Brown - Staunton, London, 1841, which continued 3 B-Q3, P-B4; 4 P-K5, P-KN3; 5 P-KR4, PxP; 6 P-R5, Q-R4+; 7 K-B1, QxKP; 8 PxP, P-KR3; 9 P-N7?, QxP; 10 Q-R5+, K-Q1; 11 B-N5+, K-B2; 12 N-KB3, N-QB3; 13 N-R3, BxN; 14 PxB, N-B3; 15 B-B4+, P-Q3; 16 Q-QN5, N-Q4; 17 Q-N3, R-B1. Black has now consolidated effectively and went on to win.

| 3 ...... | P-B4 |
| 4 P-Q5 | P-Q3 |

This pseudo-Benoni gives the game a very modern look.

5 P-B4

Given that the odds receiver at Pawn and Move or Pawn and Two succeeds in avoiding obvious tactical mistakes, the master player is obliged to rely for his winning chances on his ability to spot *potential* weaknesses. Though P-KB4 is decidedly not a mistake, it gives Black hope for the future in that it creates a basis for White's K-side to become porous later on.

5	N-KR3
6 N-KB3	N-R3
7 N-B3	B-K2
8 P-QR3	O-O
9 B-Q3	B-R5+
10 P-N3	B-K2
11 P-R3	N-KB2
12 B-K3	N-B2
13 Q-B2	P-K4
14 O-O-O	B-B3
15 QR-N1	P-QR3
16 P-KN4	

Up to this point White's play cannot be seriously faulted, but this impetuous advance allows Staunton to establish hegemony over the central dark squares, especially his own K4, which grants him full compensation for his pawn.

| 16 ...... | PxP |
| 17 BxKBP | N-K4! |

A neat tactical trick comes to Black's aid, enabling him to occupy K4 with a piece rather than a pawn, when his position would be deprived of all its dynamism.

18 BxN?

Submitting too readily to Black's plan.

| 18 ...... | BxB |
| 19 NxB | Q-N4+ |

The point.

20 K-N1   QxN

The Queen can be shifted from this dominating post only by 21 Q-R2!, which should have been White's response. But as his next move shows, he holds unjustified dreams of a direct K-side attack, so is naturally reluctant to offer an exchange of Queens.

21 P-KR4?	B-Q2
22 P-N5	P-N4
23 P-R5	R-B6
24 R-N2	R-N1

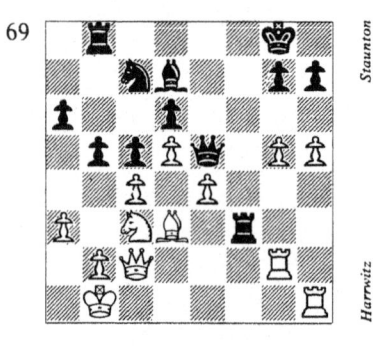

69

Staunton

Harrwitz

Staunton handles his attack in strikingly modern fashion, operating simultaneously on two fronts. In fact, this position bears a marked resemblance to an Old (or Czech) Benoni (1 P-Q4, N-KB3; 2 P-QB4, P-B4; 3 P-Q5, P-K4) which has been mishandled by White. Indeed, many contemporary players as White, when faced with this defence, failed to appreciate that under no circumstances must the blockading square K5 be ceded to a Black piece. Yet Staunton grasped this as long ago as 1846! The threat now of course is 25 ..., PxP; 26 BxP, RxN.

25 N-K2	PxP
26 BxP	B-R5
27 Q-B1	RxP

The Black pieces converge for a decisive onslaught. What ensues is pure desperation on White's part.

28 N-N3	RxN
29 RxR	QxR
30 P-N6	P-R3
31 R-B1	Q-K4
32 B-Q3	N-N4
33 R-B5	Q-Q5
34 R-B3	N-B6+
35 K-R1	N-Q8
Resigns	

36

HARRWITZ - STAUNTON
19th match game, London, Sept. 1846
Odds of Pawn and Two Moves

1 P-K4	———
2 P-Q4	P-K3
3 P-QB4	P-B4
4 P-Q5	P-Q3
5 P-B4	N-KR3
6 N-QB3	N-B2
7 N-B3	B-K2
8 B-Q3	N-QR3
9 O-O	O-O
10 P-QR3	B-B3
11 P-K5	

Harrwitz this time avoids letting Black control a strong K4 square, which so many of Staunton's other opponents failed to provide against in this opening.

11 ...... B-K2

If PxKP; 12 BPxP, BxP; 13 NxB, NxN; 14 BxP+, KxB; 15 Q-R5+ (Staunton).

12 Q-K2?

P-B5 would have enabled him to maintain and even increase the first player's advantage at these odds, for then 12 ..., PxBP; 13 P-K6, N-R1 puts a fearful cramp on Black's game.

12	N-R3
13 Q-QB2	N-QB2
14 BxP+	K-R1
15 B-K4	R-QN1
16 P-R3	P-QN4
17 PxNP	PxQP
18 NxP	NxN
19 BxN	

At this point White is clearly on top.

19 ...... RxNP
20 P-KN4?

The same brand of mistake as committed by Evans in Game 30. White loosens his own position in a quest for an attack which proves to be ephemeral. When giving odds, Staunton had to rely on occasional lapses of this kind for his compensation.

20 ...... R-N3

To defend his K-side against White's plan of transferring his KB to the diagonal QN1-KR7. Obviously the positionally correct reply was 21 P-K6! setting up a crippling blockade, but the reply chosen, though consistent, reveals the subtle difference in quality between the World Champion and some of his main opponents. The striking thing about this game is Staunton's phoenix-like resurrection from the ashes of his position.

21 B-R2	PxP
22 B-N1	P-N3
23 PxP	

The capture with the Knight looks better, but White wanted to get his QB into play.

23	N-N1
24 B-Q2	B-N2
25 B-B3	BxN
26 P-K6+	B-B3
27 RxB	

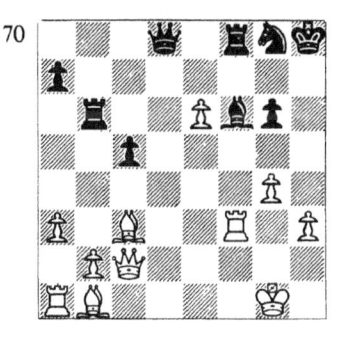

From this precarious situation, Staunton suddenly launches a victorious counter-attack, very much like a conjuror producing a 10-ton elephant from a small top-hat.

27	B-Q5+
28 K-N2	RxR
29 KxR	

If 29 QxP, Q-R5; 30 KxR, Q-B7+; 31 K-K4, Q-K7+; 32 K-B4, Q-K6+; 33 K-B5, N-K2+.

29	RxKP
30 B-R2	Q-R1+
31 K-N3	R-K6+
32 K-R4	P-N4+
33 KxP	Q-Q1+
Resigns	

For mate follows quickly.

Daniel Harrwitz

37
STAUNTON - HARRWITZ
21st match game, London, Oct. 1846
Ponziani Opening

1 P-K4	P-K4
2 N-KB3	N-QB3
3 P-B3	

An historic moment! This ancient opening, which Staunton did so much to revive that it was for some years known as 'Staunton's Opening', often leads to obscure and unusual positions. The basic idea is to form a broad pawn centre.

3 ...... P-B4!?

Harrwitz follows the recommendation of the 18th century Italian law professor, Domenico Ponziani. It is in effect a reversed Vienna Opening. The chief alternatives are: (i) P-Q4, most commonly played in the era of Steinitz and Tchigorin, with the continuation 4 B-N5!? (Q-R4 is better, but was not held to be good until after Staunton's death), PxP; 5 NxP, Q-Q4!; 6 Q-R4, N-K2; 7 P-KB4 (Staunton's patent), with a complicated game in which both players have problems. (ii) N-B3, the modern continuation, when White retains a nominal advantage after 4 P-Q4.

4 P-Q4   BPxP

Black can also consider (i) P-Q3 first suggested by Morphy's uncle in *Le Palamede* in 1846, though after 5 KPxP, PxP; 6 NxP, N-B3 White's advantage is not clear. (ii) KPxP? with several promising replies for White, e.g. 5 P-K5, PxP?!; 6 NxP, B-N5; 7 B-KN5 as in a game Evans - Harrwitz.

5 NxP   N-B3

Q-B3, analogous to the Latvian Gambit, is less dangerous for White after 6 N-N4 or 6 NxN.

6 B-QN5

This move, originating with Staunton, has been ignored by writers on the Ponziani from Steinitz onwards, though it may well be the best move! Normally White plays 6 B-KN5 when 6 ..., Q-K2!, by analogy with the Vienna, improves upon 6 ..., B-K2 as in the much-quoted game Rosenthal-Anderssen, Baden-Baden 1870.

6 ...... P-QR3?

As in the Vienna, Black should play Q-K2; 7 BxN, NPxB; 8 O-O, Q-K3 (intending B-Q3); although after 9 P-B3, White has chances to obtain an initiative. Harrwitz's move simply loses a tempo by comparison.

7 BxN   NPxB

If QPxB; 8 B-N5, B-Q3; 9 QN-Q2, B-KB4 (slightly better is Q-K2; 10 N-N4); 10 Q-N3, with an excellent position for White, according to Staunton's *Handbook*.

8 B-N5   R-QN1

Staunton claimed that Black has no good move. If 8 ..., B-K2; 9 BxN, and 10 Q-R5+, or 8 ..., B-N2; 9 Q-N3, or again 8 ..., B-Q3; 9 QN-Q2.

9 P-QN4!?

Rather extravagant to the modern eye, although it may be good. Q-K2 is also promising. Staunton's choice has the virtue of clamping down a firm blockade on Black's doubled QBP. A very advanced theme for 1846!

9 ......   B-N2

The bishop becomes very bad. P-QR4 could be tried, offering a pawn to shift the blockade. Staunton would almost certainly have parried this

break-out attempt with the reinforcing 10 P-QR3.
10 Q-R4
Staunton later came to regard O-O as better. E.g. 10 ..., P-Q4? (a terrible move which no modern master would consider); 11·P-B3, P-KR3 (or B-K2; 12 PxKP, O-O; 13 N-Q2 with advantage); 12 BxN, PxB (QxB; 13 PxP); 13 PxKP, PxN; 14 Q-R5+ mating in five. Also possible is 10 Q-N3! (to induce P-Q4) and if 10 ..., Q-K2; 11 O-O, P-Q3 then 12 N-N4 is advantageous to White.
10 ......   P-Q4?
B-K2 was much better. Harrwitz played like a child in this game; in other words, he was out of his class.
11 O-O
Staunton rightly ignores the trap 11 NxP?, Q-Q2; 12 P-N5, R-R1 and without this Black's last move is just a positional error. Black's doubled QBPs are now transformed into an irreparable weakness, obstructing his own pieces and particularly imprisoning his QB.

11	P-R3
12 B-R4	Q-Q3
13 B-N3	

White has a clear advantage, and in the sequel his opponent can find no way to disentangle his pieces.

13	R-N1
14 N-Q2	R-B1
15 N-N3	N-Q2
16 N-R5	N-N3
17 Q-B2	B-R1

18 P-B3!

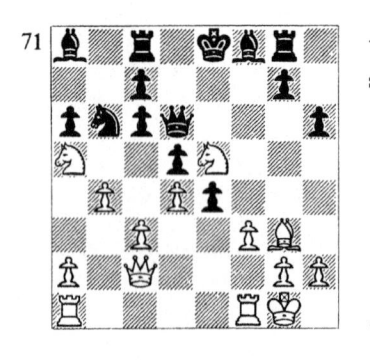

71

Opening up the position. The beginning of the end.

18	PxP
19 RxP	Q-K3
20 R-K1	B-K2
21 N(K)xP	

The final demolition.

21	QxR+
22 BxQ	BxN
23 Q-N6+	K-Q1
24 NxB+	**Resigns**

The gulf in chess understanding between the two players is obvious, and though Harrwitz's play was unimpressive one cannot help admiring Staunton's appreciation of blockade technique — years ahead of his time. His taming of Black's QB and the knight play round the complex of weak squares arising from the doubled QBPs foreshadows similar achievements by Nimzowitsch and Petrosian in the following century.

38

STAUNTON - AMATEUR
Casual game, London, 1847
Evans Gambit

1 P-K4	P-K4	18 QxQB	N-B3
2 N-KB3	N-QB3	19 QR-Q1	B-Q7
3 B-B4	B-B4	20 KR-K1	
4 P-QN4	BxP		
5 P-B3	B-R4		
6 O-O	P-Q3		
7 Q-N3	Q-K2		

N-R3! is a good move here, not fearing 8 P-Q4, O-O; 9 BxN, PxB when the absence of a dark-squared bishop for White is of more significance than the wreckage of Black's K-side pawns.

8 P-Q4	PxP
9 P-K5	PxKP
10 B-R3	Q-B3
11 PxP	P-K5
12 N-N5	N-R3
13 NxKP	QxP

It is hard to take Black's moves very seriously. He simply takes everything he can lay his hands on with no thought of consolidation or defence. One is scarcely surprised when Staunton bowls him over without difficulty.

14 QN-B3	BxN

Of course!

15 N-N5!	N-R4
16 BxP+	K-Q1
17 N-K6+	BxN

Or K-Q2; 18 Q-N5+, P-B3; 19 Q-N5, Q-B3; 20 QR-Q1+ (Staunton).

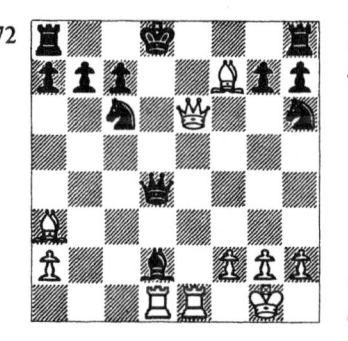

72

20	NxB
21 QxKN	Resigns

Black is in an awful mess and can hardly move at all. In particular White threatens 22 R-K2 so the best defence is 21 ..., K-B1; but White could then decide matters with the coup 22 B-B8! tying up Black even more. If then 22 ..., Q-Q2; 23 QxQ+, KxQ; 24 RxB+ and Black must surrender a piece. An edifying gamelet, but Black's play did not merit exhaustive analysis. Still, it is refreshing to observe the ease with which Staunton's combinative skill beat inferior opposition.

39

LOWE - STAUNTON
Match game, London, Dec. 1847
Odds of Pawn and Two Moves (remove Black's KBP)

1 P-K4	——
2 P-Q4	P-K3
3 P-QB4	P-B4
4 P-Q5	P-Q3
5 N-QB3	B-K2
6 B-Q3	B-B3
7 KN-K2	N-K2
8 N-B4	P-K4
9 N-R5	N-N3
10 O-O	O-O
11 P-B4?	

Yet another example of an opponent mistakenly granting Staunton the freedom of the key central dark squares, namely Black's K4 and Q5.

11	PxP
12 NxP	B-Q5+
13 K-R1	N-K4
14 B-K2	P-QR3
15 B-Q2	P-QN3
16 Q-K1	R-R2!
17 Q-N3	QR-KB2!

A highly advanced device to double rooks on the open KB-file. The belief that this rook manoeuvre was a Russian invention in the 'Modern Benoni' (1 P-Q4, N-KB3; 2 P-QB4, P-B4; 3 P-Q5, P-K3) and dates from the 1950s is quite a misconception. It was mentioned by Nimzowitsch in 1927, and here we can see that it actually dates back to Staunton and 1847!

18 P-KR4	R-B3
19 P-R5	Q-K1
20 QR-K1	B-Q2
21 N-Q1	P-QN4
22 P-N3	P-N5
23 N-B2	Q-B2
24 N(2)-R3	P-R3
25 Q-R4	BxN
26 QxB	QN-Q2

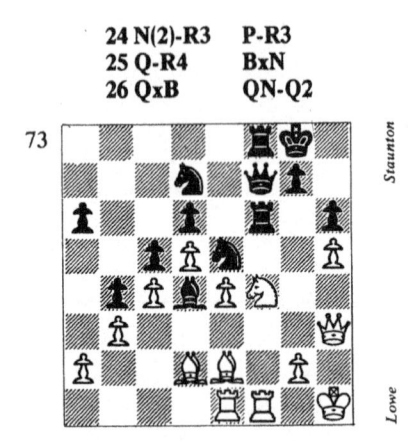

73

An imposing position for Black, but it was not necessary for White to go downhill as rapidly as he does.

27 N-K6?	RxR+
28 RxR	QxR+!

A typical Staunton sacrifice, i.e. one in which he could analyse out a forced win. He was less happy giving up material for nebulous compensation.

29 BxQ	RxB+
30 K-R2	B-N8+
31 K-N3	B-B7+
32 K-R2	

Or 32 K-B4, B-N8+; 33 K-N3, N-KB3 with the threat of continuations similar to the actual game.

32	N-KB3
33 P-N3	N(3)-N5+
34 QxN	

Otherwise mate is round the corner.

34	NxQ+
35 K-R3	N-K6
36 BxN	BxB

37 N-B7	B-Q5
38 NxP	R-QR8
39 K-N4	RxP
40 N-B7	R-QN7

41 N-N5	B-K4
Resigns	

White has carried on somewhat too long.

40

STAUNTON - AMATEUR
Casual game, London, Dec. 1850
Odds of Queen's Rook (remove White's QR)
Bishop's Opening

1 P-K4	P-K4
2 B-B4	B-B4
3 P-QN4	BxP
4 P-B4	

For another example of McDonnell's Double Gambit at different odds see Game 28.

4	PxP
5 N-KB3	B-K2
6 P-Q4	B-R5+
7 P-N3	PxP
8 O-O	PxP+
9 K-R1	B-K2?

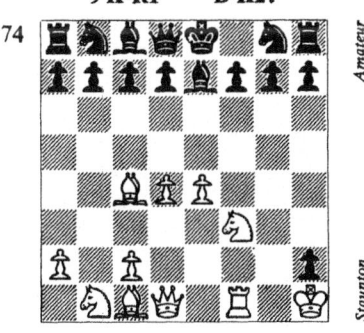

74

Amateur / Staunton

Since Black has a whole rook's start, there is little point in attempting an objective discussion of this gamelet.

White's energetic gambit play has created undoubted chances, but against any sort of correct defence the White attack would certainly founder. Black's last move is the kind of blunder one has to hope for from a Rook odds player and it lets Staunton in with a decisive, if not too difficult, combination.

10 BxP+	KxB

If K-B1, Staunton gave 11 B-N3, N-KB3; 12 N-N5, P-Q3; 13 Q-R5, Q-K1; 14 NxP+, RxN; 15 QxR.

11 N-K5+	K-K1
12 Q-R5+	P-N3
13 NxNP	N-KB3
14 RxN	P-Q3
15 N-B8 mate	

This game, and such games as Nos. 28 and 31, demonstrate that Staunton was equally at home in the sharp and violent openings current in the first half of the 19th century as in the more sophisticated positional openings, such as the Sicilian Defence, the English Opening and the Queen's Gambit Declined, with which we normally associate him.

41

HORWITZ - STAUNTON
Casual game, London, May 1851

From a friendly game at the Giuoco Piano Opening, played just before the opening of the 1851 Tournament.

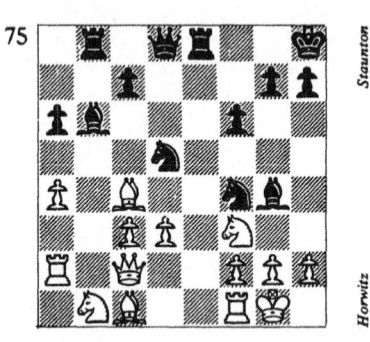

Staunton's position is loaded with dynamic energy, which was released after:

20 KBxN	N-K7+
21 K-R1	QxB
22 P-B4?	

An awful move. Now Staunton unleashes a holocaust. Horwitz had obviously overlooked the threat.

22	QxN!
23 P-R3	

A pitiful move, but PxQ allows BxP mate, with White's King boxed away in the corner.

23	BxBP
24 N-Q2	

Or 24 PxQ, BxP+; 25 K-R2, B-N6 mate.

24	N-N6+
25 K-R2	Q-B5
26 N-B3	NxR+
27 K-R1	

Can you see the point?

27	Q-R7+!
28 NxQ	N-N6 mate

A more advanced version of the mate in Game 11. Poor Horwitz was never given a chance.

THE STAUNTON SYSTEM IN DEFENCE

In many of his games from the 1851 International Tournament in London Staunton employed that group of moves which, as described in the Biography, can be identified as his 'system'. So before proceeding to an examination of the tournament and subsequent games it seems appropriate to pause and examine more closely the operation of the Staunton System, which was first noted by Coles in the *B.C.M.* of October 1947 and elaborated by him in an article in January 1969, later reprinted in Keene's *Flank Openings*.

As a Black defence it combined the virtues of flexibility and solidity. The prototype can be found in the 4th game of Staunton's 1846 match with Horwitz. **Horwitz - Staunton**, Sicilian Defence — 1 **P-K4, P-QB4; 2 P-KB4, P-K3; 3 N-KB3, N-QB3; 4 P-B4, P-Q3; 5 B-K2, KN-K2; 6 O-O, N-N3; 7 P-Q3, B-K2; 8 N-B3, B-B3** (a roundabout fianchetto); **9 Q-K1, P-QR3; 10 K-R1, O-O; 11 B-K3, R-N1; 12 P-QR4, N-Q5; 13 B-Q1, B-Q2; 14 BxN, PxB; 15 N-K2, P-N4;** with a sharp struggle from which Black eventually emerged victorious. In the 24th game Staunton streamlined the defensive idea and so arrived at his System for the first time. **Horwitz - Staunton**, Sicilian Defence — 1 **P-K4, P-QB4; 2 B-B4, P-K3; 3 N-QB3, N-QB3; 4 P-B4, P-QR3; 5 P-QR4, P-KN3!; 6 N-B3, B-N2; 7 O-O,**

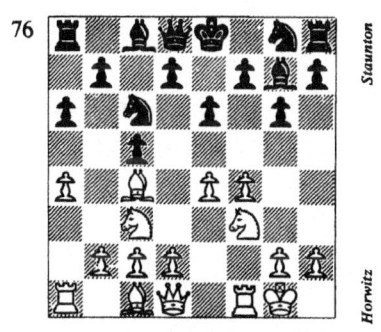

76

7 ..., **N-R3** (Staunton was not bound by fetishes concerning the eccentric development of his cavalry); **8 P-Q3, P-B4; 9 Q-K1, O-O; 10 B-K3, P-N3; 11 P-R3, N-K2; 12 P-K5, B-N2; 13 P-Q4, PxP; 14 NxP, Q-B2;** reaching a difficult position which turned in Black's favour after a complex middle-game battle.

The very novelty and subtlety of the ideas underlying Staunton's System often seemed to confuse the adepts of more open games against whom he was so frequently pitted, causing them to collapse almost without a struggle. Examine the 4th game of his 2nd round match with Horwitz in the 1851 tournament. **Horwitz - Staunton**, Sicilian Defence, 12th June 1851 — 1 **P-K4, P-QB4; 2 B-B4, N-QB3; 3 P-QR3, P-K3; 4 N-QB3, P-KN3; 5 KN-K2, B-N2; 6 O-O, P-QR3; 7 P-QR4, KN-K2; 8 N-B4, P-N3; 9 P-Q3, B-N2; 10 B-K3, R-QB1; 11 B-R2, O-O; 12 R-N1, Q-B2;**

77

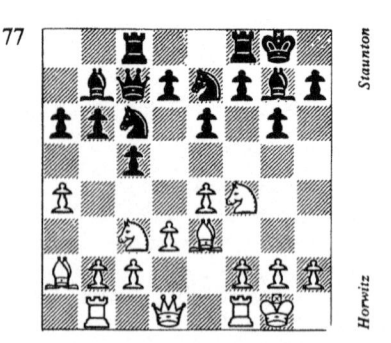

13 N-R3, N-N5 (in contrast with Black's smooth deployment of his forces White's pieces seem disjointed and incapable of co-operation); **14 B-N3, P-Q4; 15 PxP, PxP; 16 P-Q4, Q-B3!; 17 N-K2, P-B5; 18 P-QB3, PxB; 19 PxN, QxP** (the harvest); **20 R-R1, QxP; 21 R-R3, R-B7; 22 B-B1, KR-B1; 23 N(3)-B4, P-QR4; 24 N-Q3, Q-B5; 25 B-K3, B-QR3; 26 N(2)-B1, P-R5; 27 R-K1, N-B4; 28 Q-N4, BxP; 29 BxB, NxB; 30 Q-N5, RxN; 31 NxR, N-B7** (QxN!; 32 RxQ, RxR+; 33 QxR, N-K7+); **32 R-Q1, NxR; 33 PxN, P-N7; Resigns.**

Even Elijah Williams, who by this time must be regarded with the greatest respect and who was himself a disciple of Staunton's treatment of the closed game, was not immune to similar rough treatment at the hands of Staunton's System, as seen in the 1st game of their match after the tournament.

Williams - Staunton, Bird's Opening, July 1851 — **1 P-KB4, P-QB4; 2 P-K3, P-K3; 3 N-KB3, P-KN3; 4 B-K2, B-N2; 5 O-O, N-K2; 6 N-B3, P-Q4; 7 B-N5+, N-Q2; 8 N-K2, O-O; 9 P-B4,**

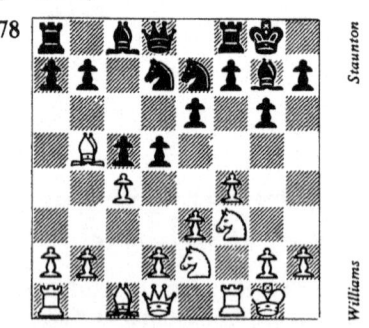

78

9 ..., N-KB3; 10 N-K5?, P-QR3; 11 B-R4, PxP; 12 N-N3, P-QN4; 13 B-B2, B-N2; 14 Q-K2, N(3)-Q4; 15 N-B3, P-B4; 16 P-QR3, N-QB3; 17 R-N1, Q-Q3; 18 P-KR4, QR-K1; 19 P-R5, P-K4; 20 RPxP, RPxP; 21 PxP, N(3)xP; 22 P-N3, N-B5; 23 Q-Q1, NxN+; 24 NPxN, N-Q6; 25 P-B4, Q-Q4; 26 Q-K2, NxB; 27 KRxN, P-B6; 28 R-Q1, PxP; 29 RxP, B-Q5; 30 K-B1, Q-B3; 31 R-Q3, R-B2; 32 Q-B2, B-N2; 33 R(N)-Q1, B-KB1; 34 K-K2, P-B5; 35 PxP, PxP; 36 R-B3, B-N2; 37 K-Q2, R-Q2+; Resigns.

That Williams could acquit himself more honourably against Staunton — and even against his dreaded system — we shall soon see! Meanwhile, to our muttons and the 1851 Tournament.

42

HORWITZ - STAUNTON
London Tournament, 31st May 1851
2nd round, 2nd match game.
Sicilian Defence

It has become customary to think of Staunton in 1851 as a much reduced player. Admittedly his health was fragile and he was weighed down by the organisational problems of the tournament. But what his play had lost in robustness and precision it had gained in depth, complexity and richness. Critics point to his defeat by Anderssen as indicative of his decline, but there is little doubt that Anderssen was indeed the best player in the 1851 tournament, and there is no disgrace in losing to a superior.

1 P-K4 P-QB4
2 P-KB4 N-QB3
3 N-KB3 P-K3
4 P-B4

Although Nimzowitsch might have condoned this move, it looks wrong in view of the hole on Q4. B-N5 is best here.

4 ...... P-KN3
5 N-B3

Against 5 P-Q4, a possible counter would be 5 ..., B-N2 followed by 6 PxP, Q-R4+; or by 6 P-Q5, N-Q5. But Staunton would probably have played 5 ..., PxP; 6 NxP, NxN (or P-QR3); 7 QxN, P-B3 followed by N-K2-B3. If this suggestion for Staunton seems extravagant, one should examine a closely analogous position, with Staunton playing White, which occurred only some five or six weeks later. The game in question is given in full since it reveals Staunton's truly staggering mastery of a strategy so 'modern' that it is, even now, virtually unacceptable to many master players — the strategy of acceptance of weakness in the pawn structure (those holes which were such anathema to Steinitz and Capablanca), not to obtain dynamic counterplay but for the more abstruse reward of flexibility! This strategy is so new and strange to most players that eyebrows are raised even when it has been adopted by such pioneers as Ulf Andersson, Taimanov, Ljubojevic and Petrosian. Staunton-Williams, 6th match game, 1851: 1 P-QB4, P-K4; 2 P-K3, N-KB3; 3 P-KN3, P-Q4; 4 PxP, QxP; 5 P-B3!, B-QB4; 6 N-B3, Q-Q3; 7 Q-B2, P-QR3; 8 P-QR3. By rights his QN3, Q3 and KB3 should be horribly weak, but Staunton makes such a success of covering this light square complex that he even turns his K4 into an 'overprotection' springboard for his own attack (see his 17th move). 8 ..., N-B3; 9 N-R3, O-O; 10 N-B2. A development reminiscent of his play following diagram 76. 10 ..., B-N3; 11 B-K2! Further evidence of Staunton's freedom of mind. No slavish fianchetto here! 11 ..., N-K2; 12 O-O, Q-B3; 13 B-Q3, R-QN1; 14 P-QN4, R-Q1; 15 B-N2. The Black Queen dare not accept the offer of the KBP in view of the knight discovery. 15 ..., P-KR4; 16 QR-Q1, P-R5; 17 N(3)-K4!,

See Diagram 79 overleaf

17 ..., NxN; 18 QxQ, NxQ; 19 BxN,

79 Williams / Staunton

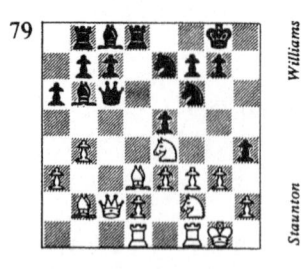

PxP; 20 PxP, B-Q2; 21 K-N2, P-B3. The pressure on Black's centre pawn from the wings becomes too much, so that his King's security has to be reduced. 22 B-Q5+. Complete conquest of the light squares!! 22 ..., K-B1; 23 B-N3, K-K2; 24 KR-K1? Time trouble of the days before clocks. Black was playing so slowly that White over-hastily tries to speed up the game. With 24 P-Q4! he could have secured his advantage since 24 ..., B-K3 is then answered by 25 P-Q5. Now Black equalises. 24 ..., B-K3!; 25 B-R4, K-B2; 26 BxN, PxB; 27 P-Q4, PxP; 28 PxP, P-R4; 29 N-K4, PxP; 30 PxP. Agreed Drawn — a bitter disappointment no doubt to Staunton after his superbly original strategic build-up.

5	B-N2
6 B-K2	P-Q3
7 O-O	KN-K2
8 P-QR3	

White's opening play creates a somewhat disjointed impression.

8 ...... P-QR3

There is more point to this move when played by Black since a subsequent P-QN4 would certainly enhance the scope of his KB in fianchetto.

9 R-N1 O-O
See Diagram

The full Staunton System emerges. Horwitz once again fails to come up with any satisfactory retort and by

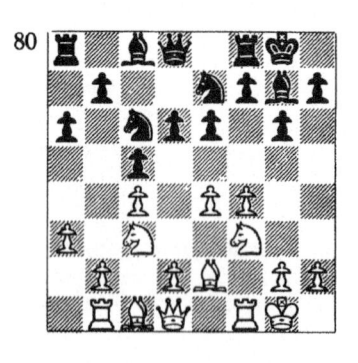

80 Staunton / Horwitz

move 20 his game lies in ruins.

10 Q-B2

He was obviously afraid to play the consistent P-QN4 in view of 10 ..., PxP; 11 PxP, Q-N3+; 12 K-R1, NxP. However, he could then make an interesting gambit of it with 13 B-R3, P-QR4; 14 P-Q4.

10 ...... P-B4

Establishing a blockade that spans the entire central zone. The mobility of White's pawns is severely restricted and Horwitz's attempt to undertake central activity (based on the vulnerability of Black's QBP) results only in the disintegration of his own centre.

11 P-Q3	B-Q2
12 B-K3	R-B1

A 'semi-mysterious' rook move. Actually Black's intention is fairly transparent: N-Q5 followed by P-Q4 or P-QN4 with play against White's QBP. White's remedy is not particularly efficacious, but his position is to be distrusted in view of the weakness of his Q4 and the cluttered arrangement of his pieces behind his none too secure pawn front.

13 P-K5 N-Q5!?

Ingenious but possibly not best. There is nothing wrong with the simple PxP; 14 BxP, PxP!; when White has insufficient compensation for his pawn.

14 NxN?

Falling in with Black's plans. Correct was 14 BxN!, PxB; 15 PxP, PxN; 16 PxN, QxP; 17 PxP, QxP; 18 RxP, B-QB3; 19 R-N3, Q-Q3; 20 Q-Q2! when it is Black who has been forced to give up a pawn for unclear compensation.

14	PxN
15 BxP	N-B3!

The point of Black's play. This blow eliminates White's centre and galvanises the Black pieces into action.

16 B-K3	PxP
17 PxP	BxP
18 Q-Q2	Q-B2
19 P-KN3	

Hoping to get in P-Q4, but now disaster looms up from a fresh angle. White had to play 19 B-B4!, giving up the square Q4 for good (19 ..., BxB; 20 QxB, QxQ; 21 RxQ, P-K4; 22 R-B2, N-Q5 with great advantage) but preventing the combination which is now possible.

19	BxP!

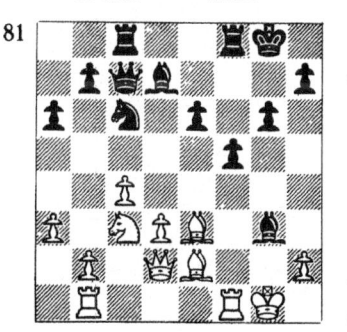

81

With the justification: 20 PxB, QxP+; 21 K-R1, N-Q5!; 22 BxN, B-B3+; 23 N-Q5, PxN; 24 B-KB3, Q-R5+; picking up the strong bishop on the ill-fated square. The weakness of his Q4 in this game is the bane of White's existence.

20 B-B3

A sensible decision. As so often after a material gain the inferior party obtains a temporary initiative as a sort of natural right. Naturally it takes time for Black to extricate his KB and this gives White the opportunity to set in motion, at last, his centre and Q-side pawns. There follows a period of consolidation on Staunton's part.

20	B-Q3
21 P-Q4	P-N3
22 P-N4	B-K2
23 P-B5	

P-Q5? cedes his beautiful K5 square to Black's knight, in which case the absence of any pawn shelter for White's King would soon begin to tell.

23	PxP
24 QPxP	B-B3
25 B-K2	

Or 25 B-B4, BxN; 26 QxB, QxB; 27 BxN, Q-N4+; 28 B-N2, B-B3.

25	N-N1
26 B-KB4	Q-N2

Typically Staunton occupies the significant diagonal bearing down towards White's King.

27 B-Q6	KR-Q1
28 B-QB4	N-B3

The consolidation nears completion. Black now has the twin threats of N-Q5 and B-Q5+. Horwitz's next move is a trifle desperate.

29 N-K4	B-Q5+
30 N-B2	N-K4
31 B-K2	N-B6+?

Unnecessary complications. With 31 ..., Q-Q4!, threatening BxN+ and B-B3, the game would have come to a speedy end.

32 BxN	QxB
33 QxB	B-B3
34 N-K4	Q-N5+
35 K-B2	BxN

With an extra pawn and some attack Black should still win easily enough, but Staunton's play from this point lacks conviction, evidence that at times now he had difficulty in standing up to a long and hard game played without any break.

36 R-N2	Q-B6+
37 K-K1	QxP
38 R(1)-B2	B-Q4
39 P-R4	Q-R8+
40 K-Q2	K-B2?

Missing another win. In his notes Staunton gave RxB!; 41 PxR, R-B5; 42 Q-B6, Q-B8+; 43 K-K2, R-K5+ with a definite pull.

41 P-R5	Q-R8
42 PxP+	KxP
43 R-KR2	Q-K5
44 QxQ	BxQ
45 K-K3	R-Q2
46 R-R2	R-B3
47 R-QR1	R(2)xB

A necessity perhaps if he is to win.

48 PxR	RxP
49 R-N1+	K-B3
50 RxP	K-K4

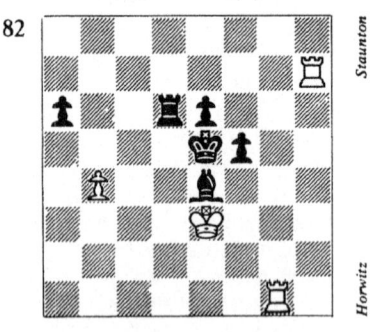

82

Obviously Black stands better and White will experience difficulty in holding on to his QNP, but his next blunder cuts short all hopes of resistance and robs us of an interesting endgame. The following sequence is an indication of the sort of play which might have ensued: 51 R-R7, P-B5+; 52 K-K2, P-B6+; 53 K-K1 (K-K3, R-Q6+), K-B5; 54 R-B7+, K-K6; 55 R-N3, R-B3; 56 K-Q1, B-B7+; 57 K-K1, B-B4; 58 K-Q1, K-B7; 59 R-N5, R-Q3+; 60 K-B1, K-K7.

51 R-QB1??

Ending with a whimper!

51	P-B5+
52 K-B2	BxR
Resigns	

An interesting game, typical of Staunton's play in many respects, but too unevenly played to be numbered amongst his very best achievements. His lack of accuracy at critical moments reveals his increasing ill health and the strain of tournament organisation worries.

A game in which one might think the Black forces were handled by Staunton, did we not know that it was an absolutely modern example, was Quinteros - Andersson, Nice Olympiad 1974, which went: 1 N-KB3, N-KB3; 2 P-B4, P-B4; 3 P-KN3, P-QN3 (the Q-side fianchetto, which originated with Staunton and which he often used in versions of the Sicilian, which is what this game soon resembles); 4 B-N2, B-N2; 5 P-Q3, P-K3; 6 P-K4, P-Q3; 7 N-B3, B-K2; 8 O-O, P-QR3 (prophylaxis to prevent N-N5 after his Q-B2); 9 P-QR3, Q-B2; 10 N-K1, N-B3 (now the White pawn formation bears a striking resemblance to Horwitz's in the preceding game); 11 N-B2, N-Q2; 12 P-QN4, B-B3 (the roundabout K-side fianchetto, as in Game 32, which Staunton played before elaborating his own System); 13 B-Q2, N-Q5; 14 NxN, BxN; 15 R-N1, B-QB3; 16 N-K2, B-B3; 17 Q-N3, O-O; 18 P-N5, B-N2; 19 P-QR4, PxP; 20 BPxP, KR-B1; 21 KR-B1, Q-N1; 22 R-B2, R-R2; 23 R(1)-QB1, Q-R1 (typical of Staunton's build-up of diagonal pressure, though his favourite square for his Queen was usually QB3, as in Game 34); 24 R-R2, R-Q1 (under pressure from all these strategic devices White soon cracks); 25 P-B4, R-QB1; 26 B-K3, P-Q4; 27 P-K5, B-K2; 28 P-Q4, PxP; 29 RxR+, BxR; 30 NxP, N-B4; 31 Q-N1, RxP; 32 RxR, QxR; 33 P-B5, B-Q2; 34 Q-KB1, Q-R6; 35 Q-KB4, N-Q6; 36 Q-B1, NxP; 37 B-B4, B-B4; 38 Resigns.

43

STAUNTON - HORWITZ
London Tournament, 17th June 1851
2nd round, 7th match game.
English Opening

Were one asked to select the very best game played by Staunton, one might narrow the short list down to four — the 5th and 21st match games against Saint-Amant (Games 17 and 23), the 8th match game against Williams (Game 48) and the following beautiful blockading game against Horwitz.

1 P-QB4
Tartakower wrote of this move in his *500 Master Games* : 'A remarkable feature of Staunton's play is the number of ultra-modern ideas with which he was familiar, e.g. the restricted centre, the fianchetto development, bilateral work, the theory of the local engagement, etc., and, last but not least, the English Opening (sometimes called the Staunton Opening).'
1 ...... P-K3
2 N-QB3 P-KB4
An early move of the KBP seemed to be a great favourite with Horwitz, but he rarely followed up this ambitious move with any noteworthy energy or aggression.
3 P-KN3 N-KB3
4 B-N2 P-B3
Horwitz plans to strongpoint the central light squares, his QB3 and Q4, as further evidenced by the subsequent manoeuvre with his QN, with a view to restricting the scope of White's KB. This is not a bad plan, but he ruins it through overcaution on moves 10 and 11.
5 P-Q3
Already preparing a counterstroke directed at the very light squares upon which Horwitz has built his faith. P-Q4 would also be quite good, transposing into a Dutch Defence.
5 ...... N-R3
6 P-QR3 B-K2
7 P-K3 O-O
8 KN-K2 N-B2
9 O-O P-Q4
10 P-N3
The Staunton System is here used with the White pieces. The double fianchetto and the restricted centre reveal a striking affinity with the Reti System of 70 years later.
10 ...... Q-K1?!
Dubious. Why not P-K4!, establishing a foothold in the centre and creating a pleasant square for the QN on K3?
11 B-N2 Q-B2?!

P-K4 was still the move. Staunton now takes prophylactic measures against this and soon seizes the initiative himself.

12 R-B1

The 'semi-mysterious' rook move was seen in Game 42, when Staunton played his System as Black.

12 ...... B-Q2

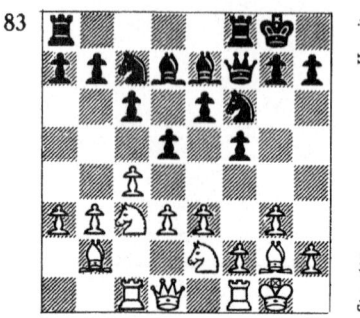

'Black's plan is to complete his mobilisation behind a curtain of pawns. White, however, does not wait and himself starts an affray in the centre' (Tartakover).

13 P-K4!

Reti in his system similarly reserved the right to advance the KP in preference to the QP.

13 ...... BPxP
14 QPxP QR-Q1
15 P-K5

Black is driven back all along the line.

15 ...... KN-K1
16 P-B4 PxP
17 PxP

The splitting of White's Q-side pawns is of no consequence and is outweighed by his far-ranging bishops and his potential grip on the square Q6.

17 ...... B-B4+

Embarking on a harmless adventure — harmless for White, that is. It is, however, difficult to suggest any constructive alternative.

18 K-R1 B-K6
19 QR-N1 P-KN3

This move is worse than useless and only serves to create a twin weakness on his KB3 to balance the existing weakness of his Q3 but, as the old adage goes, in a bad position the bad moves come of themselves.

20 Q-N3 B-B1
21 N-K4

Menacing both of the weak points in Black's game.

21 ...... B-N3
22 QR-Q1 N-R3

Evidently Horwitz wanted to prevent P-QB5 followed by N-Q6. In fact, on the previous move Staunton could have chosen 22 P-QB5, B-R4; 23 N-Q6, but he probably did not want to release his Q5 square for occupation by a Black knight.

23 Q-B3 RxR

If Q-B2 then 24 N-Q6! would emphasise the point of White's 23rd move.

24 RxR N-B4
25 N-Q6 Q-B2

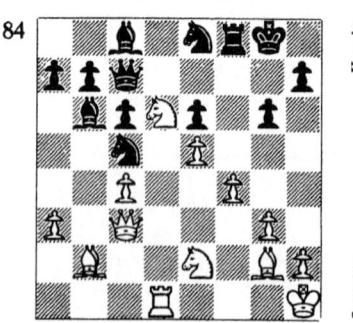

White establishes his powerful outpost in any case. It is obviously out of the question for Black to capture the knight since the massed White battalions on the long dark diagonal would soon deliver mate.

26 Q-B2

Parrying N-R5.

26 ..... N-N2

Hoping to emerge via KB4 or KR4, but Staunton squashes this possibility while simultaneously setting in motion an ominous 'steam-roller' of pawns on the K-side.

27 P-N4! Q-K2
28 B-Q4

Planning to dislodge the Black knight from QB5 and then to proceed with P-QB5, entirely suffocating the opposition. White's advantage has reached such immense proportions that the surrender of his Q5 to a Black knight is no longer of any significance.

28 ..... Q-QB2

Black can only move to and fro. Any positive action on his part would result in a deterioration, rather than amelioration, of his prospects. Reduction to such negative tactics is definite proof that Horwitz has been outgeneralled on a vast scale.

29 P-QR4

Faced with the threat of P-R5, Black gives in and allows P-QB5. If he tries the more stubborn 29 ..., P-QR4 then 30 R-N1!, exploiting the relative looseness of Black's KB, would soon oblige further concessions.

29 ..... N-R3
30 P-QB5 B-R4
31 Q-N3 P-N3
32 N-K4

The logical consequence of Black's error on move 19.

32 ..... PxP

N-K1 makes no substantial difference. It does look better here to play NxP, to eliminate one of White's minor pieces, but then there ensues the beautiful variation: 33 BxN!, PxB; 34 N-B6+, K-R1; 35 Q-KR3, N-K1; 36 R-Q7!!, and Black loses his Queen.

33 N-B6+ K-R1

If RxN; 34 PxR, and Black's knight hangs.

34 Q-KR3 N-K1
35 B-R1

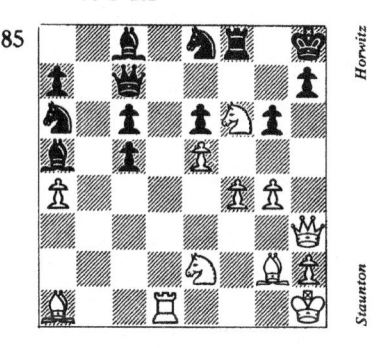

85

Horwitz

Staunton

Staunton's deployment of his pieces creates a wonderfully aesthetic impression, highlighted by this sweeping retreat of his bishop. Black's men, trapped on useless squares, can hardly enter play at all, and in view of the threat 36 R-Q7! (as in previous note) Black must exchange on his KB3, after which his execution cannot long be delayed.

35 ..... NxN

'Now the long black diagonal definitely comes to life' (Tartakover).

36 PxN K-N1
37 B-K5 Q-QN2
38 B-K4

Preparing for the demolition sacrifice BxNP.

38 ..... Q-KB2

Can White's passed pawn be blockaded where it stands?

39 N-N1!!

A brilliant reply. The knight is now free to manoeuvre to K5 or KN5, providing a cruelly negative answer to the previous question.

39 ..... B-Q1
40 P-N5 B-N2
41 N-B3 R-K1
42 B-Q6

86

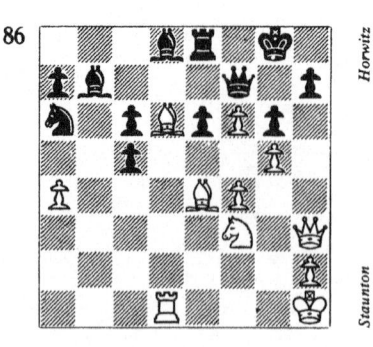

Horwitz / Staunton

Putting the finishing touches to his encirclement of the Black army. The threat (with curiously Nimzowitschian overtones) is to deliver mate to Black's Queen by N-K5.

42 ...... BxP

As hopeless as anything else.

43 PxB QxP
44 N-N5 Q-N2
45 B-K5 Q-K2
46 BxNP **Resigns**

'I must admit that this admirable game, which I first played over in my early teens, was a major contributory factor towards the adoption of Flank Openings in my own games' (Keene). That Staunton's moves and methods retain as much validity today as they had some 125 years ago can be seen from the following game played in a recent County match.

Keene (Cambridge) Penrose (Essex)
English Opening
March 1974

1 P-QB4, P-QB4; 2 P-QN3, N-QB3; 3 B-N2, P-K4; 4 N-QB3, P-KN3; 5 P-N3, B-N2; 6 B-N2, KN-K2; 7 P-Q3, O-O; 8 P-K3, P-Q3; 9 KN-K2, B-B4; 10 O-O, Q-Q2; 11 N-Q5, NxN; 12 PxN, N-K2; 13 P-K4, B-R6; 14 Q-Q2, QR-K1; 15 QR-K1, P-KR4; 16 P-B4, P-N3; 17 B-QB3, K-R2; 18 Q-N2,

87

Penrose / Keene

18 ..., N-N1; 19 P-B5, BxB; 20 KxB, B-R3; 21 N-N1, N-B3; 22 B-Q2, Q-Q1; 23 N-B3, N-Q2; 24 PxP+, PxP; 25 BxB, KxB; 26 Q-Q2+, K-N2; 27 N-N5, RxR; 28 RxR, N-B3; 29 Q-KB2! (stronger than the capture of the exchange), Q-K2; 30 N-K6+, K-B2; 31 P-KR3, R-KN1; 32 P-KN4, PxP; 33 PxP, P-KN4; 34 Q-B5, R-N3; 35 R-R1, Q-K1; 36 R-R7+, K-N1; 37 RxP, K-R1 and Black resigned, for 38 N-N7!, RxN; 39 QxN, Q-N3; 40 QxQ, RxQ; 41 R-QN7 is decisive.

44

ANDERSSEN - STAUNTON
London Tournament, 20th June 1851
Semifinal, 3rd match game.
Scotch Gambit

This match ended 4 - 1 in Anderssen's favour, and afterwards Bird wrote: 'Whether Staunton in his best form could have made even games against Anderssen is a question upon which opinions differ. Certainly his play in these games lacked the precision and taste which characterized it a few years previously, when he succeeded in vanquishing all comers.' In each of the two following games the loser played better and then slipped up, tragedies for the players involved.

1 P-K4	P-K4
2 N-KB3	N-QB3
3 P-Q4	PxP

Inferior is NxP, as Staunton discovered in one of his many games against Cochrane in 1842. Cochrane then continued 4 NxP, N-K3; 5 B-QB4, P-QB3; 6 NxKBP!? (not strictly necessary, but quite in Cochrane's ebullient style), KxN; 7 BxN+, KxB; 8 O-O, K-B2; 9 B-K3, N-K2; 10 P-KB4, P-Q4; 11 P-B5, K-N1; 12 P-B4, P-QN4; 13 PxNP, PxNP; 14 N-B3, B-N2; 15 P-K5, P-N5; 16 P-B6, PxP; 17 PxP, N-N3 (PxN; 18 P-B7+, K-N2; 19 B-Q4+); 18 P-B7+, K-N2; 19 Q-Q4+, Resigns.

4 B-QB4

Nowadays 4 P-B3 (The Goring Gambit) is the popular gambit continuation, which is still capable of claiming its victims, as in the game Ljubojevic - Olafsson, Las Palmas 1974, which continued 4 ..., P-Q6; 5 BxP, P-Q3; 6 P-KR3, N-B3; 7 B-KB4, B-K2; 8 QN-Q2, N-Q2; 9 N-B4, B-B3; 10 B-B2, O-O; 11 O-O, N(2)-K4; 12 N-K3, B-K3.

4 ......   B-B4

Natural and best — unless, that is, Black prefers the Two Knights Defence with N-B3.

5 O-O	P-Q3

Here N-B3; 6 P-K5, P-Q4 transposes into the Max Lange Attack. However, there is nothing at all wrong with the text.

6 P-B3	N-B3?!

B-KN5 is best here. Now the game becomes a version of the Giuoco Piano somewhat inferior for Black.

7 PxP	B-N3
8 N-B3	B-N5
9 B-K3	O-O
10 P-QR3	Q-K2
11 Q-Q3	BxN
12 PxB	Q-Q2

Immediately eyeing the weakened White's King's position.

13 K-N2	N-KR4
14 N-K2	N-K2
15 N-N3	NxN

It looks better to retreat with N-KB3, but Staunton, with a typical touch of master imagination, has conceived a secondary plan of attack against White's QP and does not want to waste time before carrying it out.

16 RPxN	P-Q4
17 B-R2	QR-Q1
18 QR-Q1	P-QB3
19 R-KR1	N-N3
20 R-R5	PxP

21 PxP	Q-N5!
22 QR-KR1	RxP!!

A nasty shock for White, who had quite failed to spot that Staunton had this second objective as well as the White King. If now BxR, N-B5+; 24 K-B1, NxR; or even 24 ..., NxQ; 25 RxP, Q-Q8+; 26 K-N2, QxR+; 27 RxQ, BxB; 28 R-Q1, BxNP; 29 RxN and Black has the advantage either way.

23 Q-B3	RxP

Also playable is 23 ..., QxKP+; 24 P-B3, Q-Q6; 25 BxR, QxB; 26 QxQ, BxQ with definite compensation for the exchange.

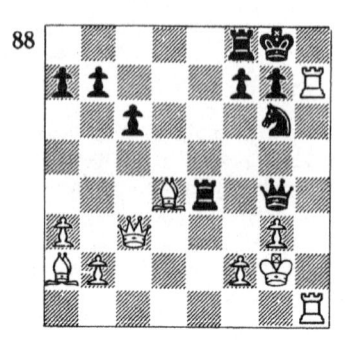

24 RxP	B-Q5
25 BxB	

Adolf Anderssen

25 ...... RxB?
Completely overlooking White's cunning riposte. Staunton should have played N-B5+, and then 26 K-N1, Q-Q8+; 27 K-R2, QxB; 28 QxQ, RxQ; 29 R-R4, N-K3! (N-K7; 30 K-N2, RxR; 31 RxR, leaves the Black knight slightly stranded); after which Black has a solid extra pawn in the ending. If White tries 26 K-R2 then KxR; 27 PxN, R-KR1; 28 BxBP, RxP and his position is critical.

26 R(1)-R4!

Winning for White now.

26	NxR+
27 RxN	QxR
28 PxQ	RxP
29 Q-KN3	R-R4
30 P-B4	R-QN4
31 P-N4	R-Q1
32 B-B4	R-Q7+
33 K-N1	R-Q8+
34 K-B2	R-KB4
35 Q-N4	R(8)-Q4
36 BxR	RxB
37 Q-B8+	Resigns

45

STAUNTON - ANDERSSEN
London Tournament, 21st June, 1851
Semifinal, 4th match game.
Giuoco Piano

1 P-K4	P-K4
2 N-KB3	N-QB3
3 B-B4	B-B4
4 P-B3	N-B3
5 P-Q4	PxP
6 P-K5?!	P-Q4
7 B-QN5	N-K5
8 PxP	B-N5+
9 QN-Q2	

Staunton suggested that B-Q2 was better here.

| 9 ...... | O-O |
| 10 O-O | B-N5 |

Black has emerged from the opening with an easy game, thanks largely to Staunton's insipid 6th move.

11 BxN	PxB
12 Q-B2	QBxN
13 NxB	R-N1

A typical Anderssen pawn offer to swing his rook into aggressive action on the other wing. It would probably have been advisable for Staunton to resist the temptation to capture the QBP.

14 QxP	R-N3
15 Q-B2	P-KB4
16 P-QR3	B-K2
17 P-QN4	P-B5
18 N-K1	R-KR3

White is condemned to passive defence.

19 P-B3	N-N4
20 N-Q3	N-K3
21 B-N2	Q-K1
22 QR-B1	Q-R4
23 P-R3	R-N3
24 N-B2	R-N6
25 K-R2	R-B4
26 Q-B6!?	Q-N3
27 R-KN1	R(4)-N4
28 N-N4	P-KR4
29 N-B6+	

See Diagram overleaf

A last fling.

| 29 ...... | K-B2?? |

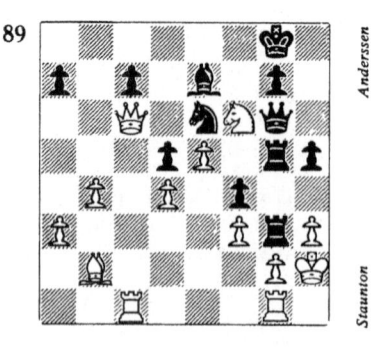

Of this move Anderssen wrote: 'Just as I was about to deliver the death blow Staunton suddenly said to me — after I had moved, but without actually making his reply — 'It's checkmate.' That was a real thunderbolt for me!'

30 Q-K8 mate

Of course 29 ..., BxN won out of hand. After 30 QxN+, K-R2; 31 PxB, RxNP+; 32 RxR, RxR+; 33 K-R1, Q-N6! White cannot even protect his KN2 with 31 R-B2, since the Black Queen denies the square to White's pieces. For that reason Staunton later queried the accuracy of his own 22nd move.

46

WILLIAMS - STAUNTON
London Tournament, 7th July, 1851
Play-off, 1st match game.
Sicilian Defence

Even more than to his defeat by Anderssen, the critics pointed to Staunton's relative lack of success against Williams as an indication of his diminishing stature. What has not been realised is the true strength of Williams, no longer the mere provincial amateur of six years earlier but an accomplished master reaching the peak of his powers. The two series of games between the men in 1851, first in the play-off for prizes in the tournament and then in a challenge match, include some of the finest games to have been played amongst Englishmen. Out of the nineteen played in the two contests four now follow - with honours even.

```
1 P-K4     P-QB4
2 P-KB4    N-QB3
```
Better is P-K3, to meet 3 N-KB3 with P-Q4, as adopted by Staunton in Game 33. The early development of Black's QN gives White's KB a useful pinning square on QN5.
```
3 N-KB3    P-K3
4 B-N5!    P-KN3
5 BxN      NPxB
```
Larsen - Perez, Amsterdam 1964, saw the alternative recapture QPxB. After 6 P-Q3, B-N2; 7 O-O, N-K2; 8 N-B3, O-O; 9 Q-K1, P-N3; 10 P-QR4, B-QR3 White could have confirmed his advantage with 11 P-QN3. Staunton's choice looks like the better recapture but Black's pawn structure remains unwieldy and his dark squares are weak. In view of this

4 ..., KN-K2 should have been played.

    6 P-B4   B-KN2
    7 Q-K2   Q-N3

This leads to unpleasantness for Black, but P-Q3; 8 P-K5, P-Q4; 9 N-B3 planning N-QR4 is scarcely any improvement. It will be noticed that in this game Staunton succumbs to a White strategy which is broadly similar to the one he himself adopted in Game 25, where it is highly probable that Williams was part of the opposition.

    8 P-K5!   N-R3
    9 N-B3   N-B4
  10 N-K4   O-O
  11 P-Q3   R-N1
  12 O-O   P-Q4
  13 N-B3

White could not hold his pawn after 13 PxP e.p. With the text White prepares P-QN3, B-R3 and N-QR4, winning Black's front QBP, against which there is no antidote.

  13 ......   B-QR3
  14 P-QN3   Q-B2
  15 B-R3   KR-Q1

An admission of defeat.

  16 BxP   B-KB1
  17 B-B2   Q-R4
  18 QR-B1   R-Q2
  19 P-KN4   N-N2
  20 N-Q1   P-R4
  21 P-KR3   B-K2
  22 N-K3

It is quite clear that White is going to decide matters by direct attack against Black's King.

  22 ......   P-Q5
  23 N-N2   P-QB4
  24 N-N5   BxN

Doubtless an unwilling decision, but White was planning to proceed with N-K4 and B-R4.

  25 PxB   B-N2
  26 N-B4   PxP
  27 PxP   Q-N3
  28 B-N3   Q-B3

A characteristic Staunton diagonal attack, but in the present situation it is of no avail.

  29 Q-R2   N-K1
  30 R-QB2   P-B4

Sheer desperation in the face of Q-R6 and R-R2.

  31 NPxP e.p.   R-R2
  32 NxNP!

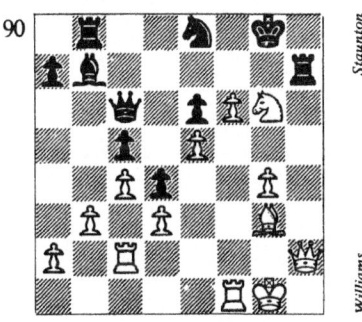

A neat Queen sacrifice, but not difficult to calculate. Obviously RxQ fails against 33 P-B7+ and Staunton's *zwischenzug* fails to help.

  32 ......   NxP
  33 PxN   RxQ
  34 RxR

There is no defence to R-R8+. Staunton's next move is as good, or bad, as anything else.

  34 ......   R-K1
  35 R-R8+   K-B2
  36 N-K5 **mate**

47

WILLIAMS - STAUNTON
London Tournament, 16th July 1851
Play-off, 5th match game.
Bird's Opening

1 P-KB4

Known as the Dutch Opening at the time, this move acquired its new nomenclature some 30 years later, when Bird began to adopt it in international tournament play.

1 ...... P-Q4
2 P-K3 P-QB4
3 N-KB3 P-K3

There cannot be anything objectively wrong with this, but N-KB3 looks more flexible.

4 B-N5+

Williams seemed quite familiar with the Nimzowitschian development of his KB.

4 ...... B-Q2
5 BxB+ NxB

Today one would recapture with the Queen, followed by the emergence of the knight on B3.

6 O-O

P-QN3 deserved attention. Staunton now forestalls this promising development of White's QB.

6 ...... P-KN3
7 P-B4 P-Q5!

Unfavourable was PxP; 8 N-R3, N-N3; 9 NxP, NxN; 10 Q-R4+, Q-Q2; 11 QxN where White's mobilisation is superior and he exerts nagging pressure against Black's QBP.

8 Q-K2

Not 8 PxP, PxP; 9 NxP?, Q-N3!

8 ...... B-N2
9 P-K4 N-R3
10 P-Q3 O-O
11 P-KR3

The upshot of the opening phase is that White has built up a solid position with long-term chances of a K-side attack, but Black is not without counterplay.

11 ...... P-B4

A useful prophylactic measure.

12 QN-Q2 P-R3

Preparing an offensive on the other wing.

13 N-N5 R-K1
14 P-K5 P-N4
15 P-QN3 R-N1
16 N(2)-B3 B-B1
17 Q-KB2 R-N2!

Staunton's subtle defence of his K-side from the extreme Q-wing must command our respect. The point of this move is to secure the KRP against possible White irruption.

18 Q-R4 N-N1!

The corollary to his previous move.

19 B-R3

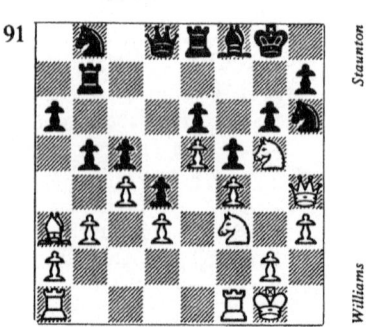

Thus far Staunton has defended excellently and now, by continuing with 19 ..., P-N5; 20 B-B1, N-B3 followed by Q-Q2 and R-QR1, he would have maintained level chances. The move he — unwisely — plays looks natural enough, but he falls victim to a remarkably elaborate combination.

19 ......　　Q-B2?
20 NxQP!!

One doubts if Staunton had given this move a second glance. Clearly PxN in reply loses to 21 BxB and QxN.

20 ......　　P-N5

Apparently a complete and satisfactory answer. 20 ..., Q-Q2 would be elegantly refuted by 21 N(4)xKP, RxN; 22 NxR, QxN; 23 P-Q4!, P-N5 (PxP; 24 BxB); 24 P-Q5! with advantage. But, as will be seen, the text move meets a similar fate.

21 N(4)xKP　　RxN

Or Q-K2; 22 NxB, QxN; 23 B-N2 with advantage.

22 NxR　　Q-K2

Staunton's defence is ingenious but insufficient.

23 QxQ　　RxQ
24 NxB　　PxB

So White has won the exchange and two pawns, but his knight is trapped. However, White's tremendous combination is not yet at an end.

25 NxNP　　PxN
26 P-QN4!

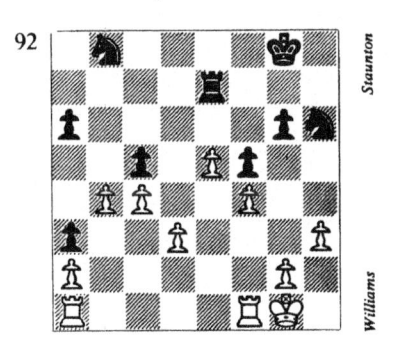

92

The final point of White's grandiose conception inaugurated on move 20.

This move guarantees him three connected central passed pawns.

26 ......　　PxP

Or R-Q2; 27 PxP, RxP; 28 KR-Q1, wins.

27 P-Q4　　R-QB2
28 QR-B1　　K-B2
29 P-Q5　　R-B4
30 K-B2

This central pawn avalanche is strangely reminiscent of Staunton's odds game victory over Williams six years earlier (Game 27).

30 ......　　P-R4
31 K-K3　　P-R5
32 K-Q4　　N-R3
33 R-QN1

Threatening RxP.

33 ......　　R-R4
34 KR-B1　　P-N6

Black's only chance is to push his pawns.

35 P-B5　　N-QN5

93

Not that it matters much, but 35 ..., N-KN1, rushing the reserves to the scene of battle, would have been better.

36 K-B4　　N-R3

Too late Staunton realises that his intended NxRP fails against 37 R-K1, P-N7; 38 P-K6+, and Black's passed pawns stand idly by whilst White's march on to their coronation.

37 P-B6　　N-KN1
38 P-Q6　　K-K3

39 P-B7	NxP
40 PxN	N-K2
41 K-N4	R-R1
42 KxP	K-Q2
43 PxP	PxP+
44 KxP	N-B3
45 RxN	KxR
46 R-B1+	**Resigns**

An outstanding game by Williams, the merit of which is heightened by the high calibre of Staunton's resistance.

48

STAUNTON - WILLIAMS
8th match game, London, July 1851
Bird's Opening

If one attempts to pick out Staunton's most impressive game, the choice can be narrowed down to four, as suggested in the introductory note to Game 43. Probably the palm should go to this present game. During the 1974 Capablanca Memorial tournament the game was demonstrated to a number of grandmasters, including Andersson and Ribli, without the names of the contestants being revealed, and the most popular guesses as to the identity of the leader of the White forces were Gideon Barcza or Bent Larsen! We have the advantage over the grandmasters; we *know* that the player of White was Staunton and that the game was played over a century ago.

1 P-KB4   P-K3

Almost any reply is playable against White's first move.

2 P-K3   P-KB4

This copycat method might appear strange to modern eyes, but was fairly well accepted theory at the time. The 9th match game, Kolisch-Anderssen, London 1861, began 1 P-KB4, P-KB4 2 N-KB3, N-KB3; 3 P-K3, P-K3; 4 B-K2, B-K2; 5 O-O, O-O; 6 P-QN3, P-Q3. The 10th game in the present match began similarly.

3 P-KN3	N-KB3
4 B-N2	P-Q4
5 N-KB3	P-B4
6 P-N3	

These opening moves can be compared with those in the 7th game of the match just finished between Buckle and Lowenthal, in which the former was White: 1 P-KB4, P-KB4; 2 P-QN3, N-KB3; 3 P-N3, P-K3; 4 B-QN2, B-K2; 5 B-N2, P-B3; 6 N-QB3, N-R3; 7 N-R3, P-Q3; 8 O-O, O-O; 9 P-K3, B-Q2; 10 Q-K2, P-R3; 11 KR-K1, Q-B2; 12 N-B2, P-K4; 13 PxP, PxP; 14 N-Q3, B-Q3; 15 P-K4!, and White stands better. Not great play, of course, but the *ideas* are interesting and demonstrate concepts which were being explored by English players at the time — double fianchetto, delayed central thrust, etc., concepts which derive in the first place from Staunton. In *Flank Openings* Keene points to an interesting parallel. Buckle in the above game put his knights on QB3 and Q3 and attacked the centre with a delayed P-K4. In the game Reti-Yates New York 1924, no less than 73 years later, White, a leading Hypermodern, placed his knights on KB3 and K3 and attacked the centre with a delayed P-Q4!, viz.: 1 N-KB3, P-Q4; 2 P-B4, P-K3; 3 P-KN3, N-KB3; 4 B-N2, B-Q3; 5 P-N3, O-O; 6 O-O, R-K1; 7 B-N2, QN-Q2; 8 P-Q3, P-B3; 9 QN-Q2, P-K4; 10 PxP, PxP; 11 R-B1, N-B1; 12 R-B2, B-Q2; 13 Q-R1, N-N3; 14 KR-B1, B-B3; 15 N-B1, Q-Q2; 16 N-K3, P-KR3; 17 P-Q4!,

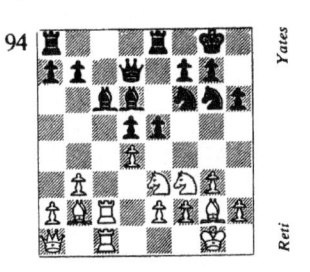

94 *Yates / Reti*

17 ..., P-K5; 18 N-K5, and White stands very well.

6	N-B3
7 O-O	B-Q3
8 B-N2	O-O
9 Q-K2	B-B2

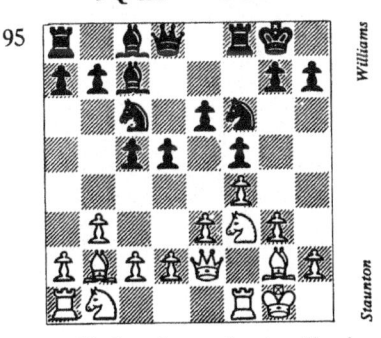

95 *Williams / Staunton*

It would be dogmatic to dismiss Williams's treatment of the opening as 'rustic' or 'provincial' out of a personal dislike of such a Stonewall set-up which weakens the dark squares, especially Black's K4. For examine the following, the opening of a game in a 1973 Interzonal tournament in which the winner (Black) is a strong grandmaster who qualified from this event for the 1974 Candidates' series, the final eliminating stage in the quest for the World Championship.

Torre - R.Byrne, Leningrad 1973
1 P-KN3, P-KB4; 2 B-N2, N-KB3; 3 P-QB4, P-K3; 4 P-N3, B-K2; 5 B-N2, O-O; 6 P-B4, P-Q4 (Byrne gives this a !); 7 N-KB3, P-B4 (and this too); 8 O-O,

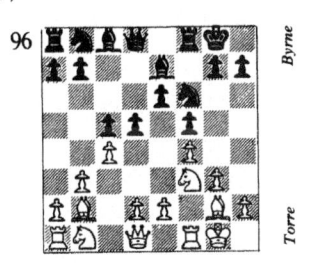

96 *Byrne / Torre*

8 ..., P-QN3; 9 P-K3, B-N2; 10 Q-K2, N-B3; 11 N-B3, Q-Q2; 12 N-Q1, QR-Q1; 13 N-B2, N-K5?!; 14 P-Q3, NxN; 15 KxN, B-B3; 16 BxB, RxB; 17 PxP, QxP; 18 N-K5, Q-Q3; 19 BxN, BxB; 20 R-KN1, B-N2; 21 P-KN4, Q-B2; 22 R-N3, R-Q4; and now 23 Q-N2!, cementing his grip on the dark squares, would have given White at least equality. Instead he played the careless 23 QR-KN1? and succumbed to the exchange sacrifice 23 ..., RxN!; 24 PxR, QxP which swept away all of his strongpoints. The resemblance between the openings of this modern game and the game under review is quite astonishing.

10 N-R3

This 'eccentric' development, avoiding obstruction of the QB's diagonal, seems more effective than Torre's rather confused deployment of his knight.

10 ......   P-QR3

P-QN3 and B-N2 came strongly into consideration at this point.

11 QR-Q1

A very subtle and deep move which creates *potential* pressure against Black's pawn centre. Seventy years later Reti wrote (a propos 'new' hypermodern opening systems): 'as the opening is in general a struggle for domination in the centre, the characteristic feature of every such new system will be a desire to *direct pressure against the centre without fixing the middle pawns too soon.*' By the 1920s everyone had forgotten about Staunton. Reti starts his *Masters of the Chessboard* with Anderssen, Morphy and Steinitz. It cannot be claimed that Staunton had the slightest influence on the Hypermoderns — but to suggest that in some respects he was ahead of his time would be an under-statement!

11 ...... P-QN4
12 P-B4

A thrust which affords a convenient moment to examine Staunton's 'hypermodernity' more fully. In his admirable collection of Reti's Best Games Harry Golombek wrote: 'Reti's own writings ... explained how it was observation rather than immediate control of the centre at which his opening efforts were aimed. The Black central pawns were to be teased on to commit themselves into advanced positions. Then White would use them as objects of attack, whilst one or other of his fianchettoed bishops would become powerful along a diagonal which had been inevitably opened for it by the advance of the Black pawns. This explanation revealed that, far from being 'stupid', this opening was the subtlest on the board.' This description of Reti's endeavours in the 1920s is an equally accurate description of Staunton's opening strategy in the present game. That Staunton's undermining of the Black centre in this and other games was not fortuitous, but undertaken in an entirely deliberate and conscious manner, can be seen from one of his own notes to the 12th game of his Paris match with Saint-Amant, in which he was White: 1 P-QB4, P-QB4; 2 N-QB3, P-B4; 3 P-K4,

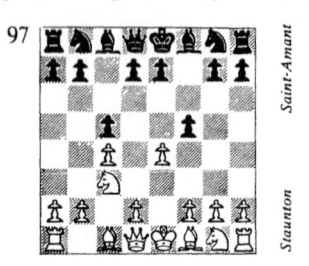

97 *Saint-Amant / Staunton*

'A forcible reply', wrote Staunton, 'to Black's last move, since if he now takes the King's Pawn, the White Knight comes into excellent play on his King's side, and, if he does not take the Pawn, his own centre pawns are sure to be broken up and displaced.' It is, in fact, the introductory move of a well-conceived plan to break up his opponent's pawn position. The game continued: 3 ..., P-Q3; 4 B-Q3, P-K3; 5 N-R3, N-KB3; 6 PxP, PxP; 7 O-O, B-K2; 8 P-QN3, N-B3; 9 B-N2, O-O; 10 N-B4, N-KN5 (all very similar to the 6th game, quoted in the notes to Game 18); 11 N(4)-Q5, B-B3; 12 NxB+, NxN; 13 N-K2, N-KN5; 14 P-B4, P-QN3; 15 P-KR3, N-R3; 16 R-B3, Q-R5; 17 R-N3, P-N3.

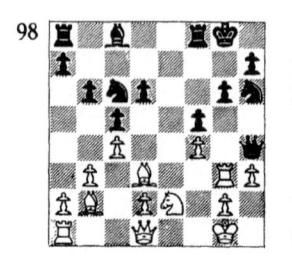

98 *Saint-Amant / Staunton*

Here Staunton played the weak 18 Q-K1, but still won after many vicissitudes. Konig pointed out that White could have launched a decisive attack with 18 Q-B2!, B-N2; 19 Q-B3! (a Queen manoeuvre absolutely typical of Staunton's play in the later 1840s and early 1850s), N-Q5; 20 NxN, QxR; 21 N-B6, with advantage. Staunton's double fianchetto systems and his undermining strategy were enthusiastically adopted by the English participants in the tournament of 1851 and Imre Konig saw this as proof that 'one eminent player can create a school.' Marmaduke Wyvill, who came second only to Anderssen, was called by Staunton 'one of the finest players in England', possibly because he belonged to the Staunton school, as the following extract shows. Wyvill's 15th move is in the same class as Staunton's 12th in the game under review.

Wyvill - Lowe, London 1851
1 P-QB4, P-K4; 2 P-K3, P-QB4; 3 N-QB3, N-QB3; 4 P-KN3, B-K2; 5 B-N2, P-Q3; 6 P-Q3, N-B3; 7 P-QR3, B-K3; 8 KN-K2, P-Q4; 9 PxP, NxP; 10 O-O, O-O; 11 Q-B2, NxN?; 12 PxN, B-Q4; 13 P-K4, B-K3; 14 B-K3, Q-Q2; 15 P-KB4!

99 *[diagram, Lowe/Wyvill]*

(The flanking blow to undermine Black's centre). 15 ..., P-B4; 16 PxKP, NxP; 17 N-B4, N-N5; 18 B-Q2, P-B5?; 19 P-Q4, B-B2; 20 P-K5, QR-N1; 21 P-R3, N-R3; 22 P-Q5, B-B4+; 23 K-R1, Q-K2; 24 QR-K1, and White won crushingly.

This game received Staunton's full approval, doubtless because he recognised a strategy at work of which he was the legitimate and acknowledged sire.

12 ...... NPxP

A plausible idea. P-N5; 13 N-B2 does nothing to hinder White's projected P-Q4, while QPxP allows the unpleasant 13 N-K5!

13 PxP R-N1
14 BxN!!

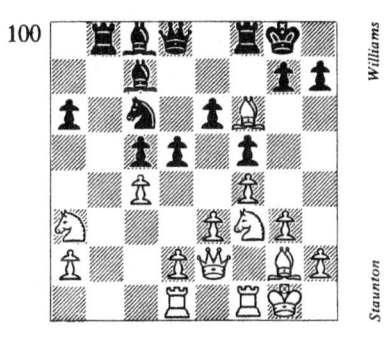

100 *[diagram, Williams/Staunton]*

A startling exchange of what appears to be his most illustrious piece, but Staunton wishes to subject his opponent's central pawns to intense bombardment (in true 'hypermodern' style) and this move is the essential prelude thereto. What enhances the merit of the text move is the existence of an attractive, but stereotyped, alternative in 14 B-QR1, which would probably have been the nearly automatic choice of most other players in this position.

14 ...... QxB

As it turns out, RxB would have been a slight improvement, but Williams obviously wished to terminate the vis-a-vis of his Queen with White's rook.

15 PxP PxP
16 P-Q4

The delayed fixing of the middle pawns. Black's QP is transformed

into a grave weakness.
16 ...... P-B5
What could be more natural? Black relieves the pressure and simultaneously creates a protected passed pawn. At this point Williams must have felt quite content with his position. It was extremely hard to appreciate at precisely this moment that Black **had** to make the courageous decision to abandon his QP with 16 ..., PxP. After 17 NxP, the QP is untenable but Black retains drawing chances in view of his bishop pair and the vulnerability of White's KP. After the text events develop virtually by force until the end of the game. Black has several possibilities to diverge but he seems to be lost whatever he does.
17 N-K5 N-N5
What else? If N-K2; 18 N(3)xP, PxN; 19 QxP+ and QxB. Or if Q-Q3; 18 N(3)xP, PxN; 19 QxP+, and QxN. Such neat tactics operating within the framework of a grand strategy are one of the hallmarks of a great player.
18 N(3)xP!
Ostensibly intending the meagre transaction 18 ..., PxN; 19 QxP+, R-B2; 20 NxR, QxN; which is by no means convincingly in White's favour.
18 ...... PxN
19 P-QR3!

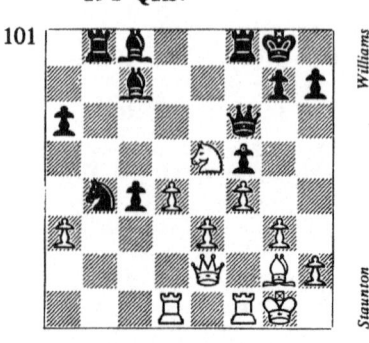

101

Here we have it! If 19 ..., N-Q6; 20 NxP & Black's N expires in mid-board — a piquant variation indeed, though 19 QxP+, R-B2; 20 P-QR3 (not NxR, QxN), B-K3; 21 P-Q5, was even stronger. Staunton's profound positional energy and acute tactical perception give the lie to Morphy's slightly negative appraisal of his talents.
19 ...... BxN
Unable to succour his knight, Black still hopes to preserve his QBP.
20 QPxB Q-B2
Maintaining the lifeline to his QB5.
21 PxN RxP

102

Staunton's achievement in this game is a matter for constant wonder. It took depth of vision beyond common experience to appreciate at move 14 that Black, in this position, stands to lose, even with equal material and in possession of his two passed pawns.
22 R-Q6
Threatening B-Q5. If now 22 ..., K-R1; 23 B-Q5, Q-B2; 24 R-QB6, Q-N2; 25 RxBP, QxB; 26 RxR, B-N2; 27 RxB, QxR; 28 R-R1, R-R1; 29 Q-Q2, with an extra pawn and well centralised pieces. Black's QRP will find it hard to achieve lift-off. Another possibility after 22 ..., K-R1; 23 B-Q5 is Q-R2; 24 BxP, RxB; 25 QxR, QxP+; but after 26 K-N2, B-N2+; 27 K-R3, White's King seems perfectly safe and Black has little to show for the exchange. If

instead of 22 ..., K-R1; Black tries 22 ..., B-K3; White plays 23 Q-Q2, with threats of QxR and of RxB and B-Q5.

| 22 ...... | B-N2 |

23 P-K6!

Only by relentless tactical blows can the positional advantage be maintained. Staunton rightly said this was 'the only move'.

| 23 ...... | Q-B2 |
| 24 R-Q7 | Q-B1 |

25 Q-Q1!

25 BxB, RxB; 26 RxR, QxR; 27 QxP, gives White the advantage, but Staunton justifiably plays for more. The threat of Q-Q4, consummating the diagonal attack, forces Black to his knees.

| 25 ...... | B-B3 |

Or P-B6 (preventing Q-Q4); 26 P-K7, R-K1; 27 BxB, RxB; 28 Q-Q5+.

| 26 BxB | QxB |
| 27 Q-Q4 | R-B3 |

See Diagram 103

| 28 R-Q6 | |

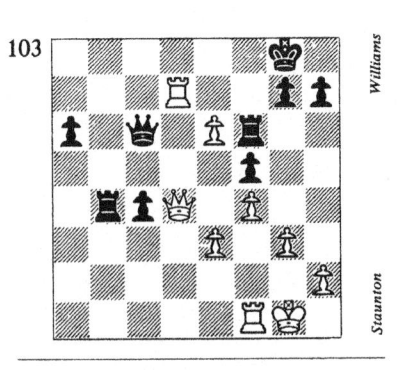

Accurate to the last. On P-K7 the resistance flickers on with 28 ..., K-B2. Or 28 R-Q8+, R-B1; 29 P-K7, R-K1.

| 28 ...... | Q-N4 |

If Q-N2; 29 R-Q8+, R-B1; 30 RxR+ and mates.

29 R-Q8+	R-B1
30 RxR+	KxR
31 Q-Q6+	K-K1
32 R-Q1	**Resigns**

A most elegant and incisive masterpiece.

49

WILLIAMS - STAUNTON
9th match game, London, August 1851
Sicilian Defence

1 P-K4	P-QB4
2 N-KB3	P-K3
3 P-Q4	PxP
4 NxP	N-QB3
5 B-K3	N-B3
6 B-Q3	B-K2
7 O-O	O-O
8 N-QB3	P-Q4

See Diagram

If this rather unusual opening sequence, with its early P-Q4 for

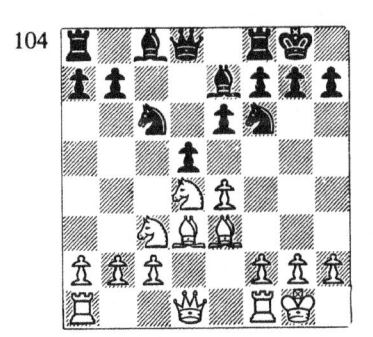

Black, strikes a chord in the reader's mind, let him look at the 21st game from the celebrated 1972 match Spassky - Fischer, Reykjavik:
1 P-K4, P-QB4; 2 N-KB3, P-K3; 3 P-Q4, PxP; 4 NxP, P-QR3; 5 N-QB3, N-QB3; 6 B-K3, N-B3; 7 B-Q3, P-Q4; 8 PxP, PxP; 9 O-O, B-Q3; 10 NxN, PxN; 11 B-Q4, O-O; 12 Q-B3, B-K3;= . Alexander's comment on this opening was: 'In this game Black develops in a straightforward, almost old-fashioned way, keeping his Queen on Q1, playing P-Q4, accepting the drawback of an isolated QP and getting free play for his pieces. Fischer is reported as saying that he got the idea from playing through some of Anderssen's games, and I can believe it — it has an Anderssenian flavour. It will probably become an important addition to the Sicilian player's repertoire and, unless refuted, is one of the more important theoretical innovations of the match.' Possibly Fischer had in mind some games from Anderssen's match against Kolisch, played in London in July 1861. The opening game, with Anderssen Black, went: 1 P-K4, P-QB4; 2 N-KB3, P-K3; 3 P-Q4, PxP; 4 NxP, N-KB3; 5 B-Q3, N-B3; 6 B-K3, P-Q4; 7 PxP, PxP; 8 O-O, B-Q3; 9 P-KR3, P-KR3; 10 Q-B3, O-O; 11 N-B3, N-K4. The 3rd and 7th games of the match followed similar lines. But, as will shortly appear, this variation has an even more extensive prehistory!

**9 NxN   PxN
10 P-K5**

The course adopted by White here is not promising. He strengthens — and expands — Black's centre, while the cramping effect of White's pawn on K5 is quite minimal. In pursuing this line Williams was simply proceeding along the main line of the theory of the day, however positionally erroneous it may have been! PxP, as chosen by Spassky against Fischer and by Kolisch against Anderssen, is a strategically more correct method.

**10 ......   N-K1
11 N-K2   P-KB4**

Damping down White's K-side ambitions. 12 PxP e.p., BxP would be a very negative reply, but as White plays he rapidly exhausts his possibilities for activity.

**12 P-QB3   P-QR4
13 P-KB4   P-B4
14 P-QN3   B-N2**

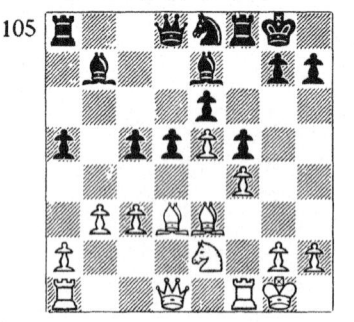

105 *Staunton / Williams*

The disadvantages of 10 P-K5 are already becoming apparent, so this may be a convenient point to pause for a review of mid-19th century thought on this variation, which will show how Williams was only playing in line with current opinion. One of the earliest games to set the pattern was Szen - Anderssen in the 6th game of their 2nd Round match in the 1851 London tournament:
1 P-K4, P-QB4; 2 P-Q4, PxP; 3 N-KB3, N-QB3; 4 NxP, P-K3; 5 B-K3, N-B3; 6 B-Q3, B-K2; 7 O-O, O-O; 8 P-QB3, P-Q4; 9 NxN, PxN; 10 P-K5, N-K1; 11 P-KB4, P-KB4; 12 N-Q2, P-B4; 13 P-KN4, P-N3; 14 P-N5, N-B2; 15 P-KR4, B-N2; 16 N-B3, Q-Q2; 17 K-B2, Q-B3 (a Stauntonian manoeuvre); 18 B-K2, QR-Q1; 19 Q-B2, P-Q5; 20 PxP,

PxP; 21 NxP, Q-N7+; 22 K-K1, B-N5+; 23 B-Q2, RxN; 24 BxB, RxB; 25 QxN, RxNP; 26 R-B2, Q-N8+; 27 R-B1, Q-N6+; 28 K-Q1, RxB; 29 KxR, B-R3+; 30 K-Q2, Q-Q6+; Resigns. Yet in the following game from the final of the same tournament Anderssen falls a victim to the selfsame strategical blunder previously committed against him. Anderssen - Wyvill: as above for 7 moves and then 8 N-Q2, P-Q4; 9 NxN, PxN; 10 P-K5,

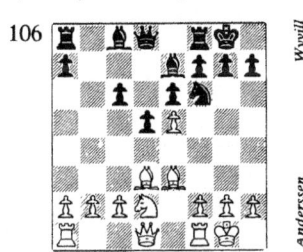

106

10 ..., N-Q2; 11 P-KB4, P-KB4; 12 R-B3, P-B4; 13 R-R3, R-B2; 14 P-QN3, P-N3; 15 N-B3, N-N3; 16 B-B2, P-Q5; 17 B-R4, N-Q4; 18 Q-Q2, P-QR4; 19 BxB, RxB; 20 N-N5, N-K6; 21 Q-B2, B-N2; with an excellent game for Black who went on to win decisively. Before condemning Williams, Szen and even Anderssen for their lack of strategic foresight in running themselves into dead-end situations by P-K5, we should look at something of a curiosity — three of Anderssen's games, in all of which he had White, from his Paris match with Morphy in 1858. The 6th game went: 1 P-QR3!?, P-K4; 2 P-QB4, N-KB3; 3 N-QB3, P-Q4; 4 PxP, NxP; 5 P-K3, B-K3; 6 N-B3, B-Q3; 7 B-K2, O-O; 8 P-Q4, NxN; 9 PxN, P-K5;

See Diagram 107

10 N-Q2, P-KB4; 11 P-KB4, P-KN4; 12 B-B4, BxB; 13 NxB, PxP; 14 PxP, Q-K1; 15 O-O, Q-B3; 16 Q-N3, Q-Q4; 17 R-N1, P-N3; 18

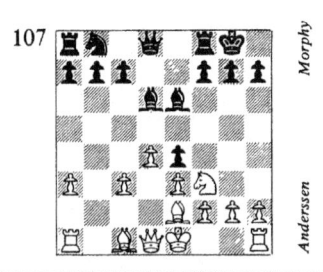

107

Q-R2, P-B3; 19 Q-K2, N-Q2; 20 N-K3, Q-K3; 21 P-B4, N-B3; 22 R-N3, K-B2; 23 B-N2, QR-B1; 24 K-R1, R-KN1; 25 P-Q5! and White stands better. The 8th game varied with 11 ..., Q-R5+; 12 P-N3, Q-R6; 13 B-B1, Q-R3; 14 P-B4, P-B3; 15 P-B5, B-QB2; 16 B-B4, with some initiative for White. The 10th game of the match varied from the 6th a little earlier with 8 O-O, NxN; 9 NPxN, P-KB4; 10 P-Q4, P-K5; 11 N-Q2, R-B3; 12 P-KB4, R-R3 (just as in Anderssen - Wyvill with the colours reversed!); 13 P-N3, N-Q2; 14 N-B4, BxN; 15 BxB+, K-R1; 16 R-R2, Q-K2; 17 P-QR4, N-B3; 18 Q-N3, P-QN3 and White's positional superiority was incontestable; he went on to win in 77 moves. That Morphy himself should have repeatedly subscribed to the dubious treatment adopted by Williams in the present game shows without doubt that many 19th century masters overestimated the value of the K-side attack (either by R-KB3-KR3 or by P-KR3, K-R2, R-KN1 and P-KN4) in comparison with the long-term advantages of flexibility and central control. Morphy's persistent adoption of this rigid attacking formation must surely exonerate Williams from censure for his handling of the opening.

15 P-KR3   Q-Q2
16 K-R2   Q-B3

Staunton's patent alignment of the Queen and bishop.

17 R-KN1   R-Q1

Staunton later thought this premature, and suggested P-N3 followed by N-N2, a further indication of his advanced prophylactic outlook.

18 P-KN4

One of the stock methods of attack referred to earlier, but it stands little chance, given Black's fluid central preponderance.

18 ......   P-N3
19 PxP   PxP

Opening the KN-file but also ceding to Black a beautiful 'Nimzowitschian' blockade square on his K3. (Interested readers may care to compare Game 12 in Nimzowitsch's *My System).*

20 Q-B2   N-N2
21 N-N3   K-R1
22 Q-K2   N-K3

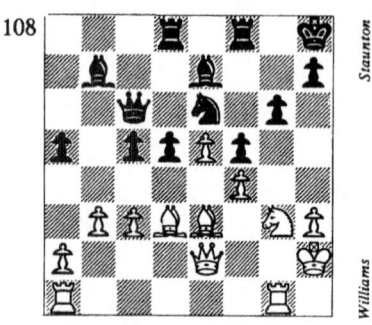

As Nimzowitsch was to write 80 years later: 'Strategical law is law, and law shall be kept! And the law says — a passed pawn shall be blockaded!'

23 QR-QB1   P-Q5

A logical incursion into White's territory.

24 PxP   NxQP

Less convincing is RxP; 25 B-B4, NxP; 26 Q-B1 (Staunton).

25 BxN   RxB
26 R-B4   R(1)-Q1
27 RxR   RxR

White's situation is critical; his KBP is sickly and his King is exposed to rolling fire along the long diagonal.

28 B-N5   Q-B6
29 R-KB1

29 QxQ, BxQ; 30 R-KB1, R-Q7+ is murder.

29 ......   Q-Q4
30 B-B4   Q-Q1
31 Q-K3   Q-Q2
32 N-K2   R-Q7
33 P-QR4

Or 33 P-K6, Q-Q5; 34 QxQ+, PxQ; with decisive advantage, the more so since Black's King can rush to KB3 intending to annex the KP.

33 ......   Q-B3

Reverting to his favourite theme, even more effective now that his Rook is in a dominating position.

34 R-KN1   Q-B6

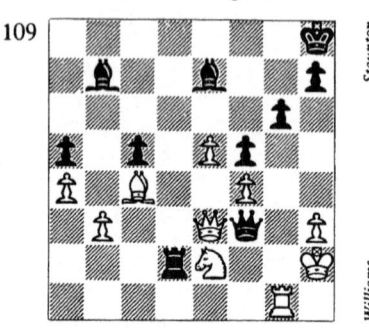

The exchange of Queens is forced, since 35 QxR, Q-B7+; 36 R-N2, QxR mate.

35 QxQ   BxQ
36 R-N2

Or 36 K-N3, BxN; 37 R-N2, BxB; 38 RxR, BxP; 39 R-Q7, B-B1; with advantage to Black.

36 ......   B-R5
37 K-N1   BxR
38 KxB   K-N2
39 K-B3   R-Q1
40 N-B3   R-Q7
41 N-K2   R-Q8
42 K-N2   P-R3

Heralding the decisive manoeuvre — P-N4, undermining White's centre in the endgame, which will extinguish any hopes White may have been cherishing of erecting a light-squared fortress position.

43 N-N3	BxN
44 KxB	P-N4
45 K-B3	R-QB8
46 PxP	PxP
47 P-K6	R-B6+
48 K-N2	K-B3
49 B-Q5	K-K2
50 B-B4	P-B5
51 B-Q5	K-Q3
52 B-B4	R-K6
53 K-R2	R-N6
Resigns	

Zugzwang. Any move sheds at least one pawn.

50

JAENISCH - STAUNTON
8th match game, London, 25th August 1851
Vienna Gambit

1 P-K4	P-K4
2 N-QB3	N-KB3
3 P-B4	

The Philidor continuation 3 B-B4, gives more chances of a lasting initiative than this Vienna interpretation. For many years the 'rook sacrifice line' was considered to be Black's answer to 3 B-B4, but this feeling has been challenged recently by some precise analysis emanating from T.D.Harding: 3 B-B4, NxP; 4 Q-R5, N-Q3; 5 B-N3, N-B3; 6 N-N5, P-KN3; 7 Q-B3, P-B4; 8 Q-Q5, Q-K2; 9 NxP+, K-Q1; 10 NxR, P-N3; 11 P-Q3, B-QN2; 12 P-KR4!, P-B5; 13 Q-B3, N-Q5; 14 Q-N4, B-KR3; 15 N-R3, N(3)-B4; 16 N-N5, P-Q4; 17 P-QB3, N-N4; 18 B-Q2, QBxN; 19 O-O-O, and Black has insufficient compensation for the exchange.

3 ......   P-Q4

The only move to deserve serious consideration.

4 PxQP

Normal is 4 BPxP, NxP; and then either 5 Q-B3, 5 P-Q3 or 5 N-B3. Now the game has transposed into a Falkbeer Counter Gambit.

| 4 ...... | P-K5 |
| 5 P-Q4?! | |

This is no better than the line adopted by Jaenisch in the 2nd game of the match: 5 P-Q3, B-QN5; 6 PxP, NxKP; 7 Q-Q4, BxN+; 8 PxB, O-O; 9 N-B3, R-K1; 10 B-K2, N-Q3; 11 B-N2, R-K5; 12 Q-B2, N-B5; 13 O-O-O, NxB; 14 KxN, Q-Q3; 15 R-Q4, RxP; 16 RxR, QxR; and having regained his pawn Staunton went on to win. Since the text leaves Black with a powerful and inviolate KP, White should go in for an unclear variation subsequently advocated by Keres: 5 Q-K2!, B-KB4; 6 NxP, NxN; 7 P-Q3, Q-R5+; 8 K-Q1, Q-K2; 9 PxN, BxP.

5	B-QN5
6 B-B4	NxP
7 BxN	QxB
8 N-K2	B-N5

This is superior to O-O; 9 O-O, Q-K3; 10 P-B5!, followed by P-B6

with a dangerous K-side attack.
9 O-O   KBxN
10 NxB!
The only move to keep White afloat. 10 PxB, Q-B5 is quite horrible for him.
10 ......   Q-Q2
11 Q-K1   P-KB4
Necessary to maintain the long-term advantage of the passed KP, although Black's QB gets slightly cut off in the process. 11 ..., QxP+ would be a serious mistake, allowing White to rid himself of his chains at the temporary cost of a mere pawn, e.g. 11 ..., QxP+; 12 B-K3, Q-B5; 13 P-KR3, B-Q2; 14 R-Q1, N-B3; 15 B-Q4 (Staunton), or 13 Q-N3, P-KB4; 14 P-KR3, followed by QxP (Tartakover)
12 B-K3
12 NxP, PxN; 13 QxP+, Q-K3; 14 QxP, Q-QB3! would be a dubious escapade, since White's three pawns' compensation do not form any sort of coherent majority. Another attempt at a radical solution would be 12 P-KR3, B-R4; 13 P-KN4, B-N3; 14 PxP, BxP; 15 NxP, but after the simple 15 ..., O-O! it would be apparent from White's weak QP and KRP, together with his smashed King's position, that his violence had recoiled on his own head.
12 ......   O-O
13 Q-R4
Hoping to get Black's bishop stranded, but Staunton thwarts all of his opponent's efforts with quietly impressive and solid positional play.
13 ......   R-B3
The fight for the offside bishop intensifies.
14 P-KR3   R-KR3
15 Q-B2   B-R4
See Diagram
White's adventure with his Queen has not been entirely wasted since Black's

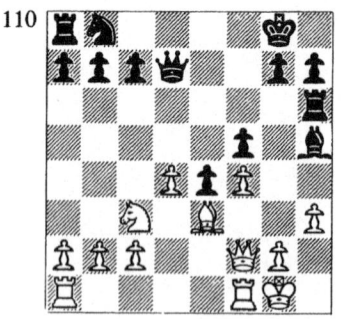

110

Staunton

Jaenisch

KR and QB have been driven into a corner. White should now have sought to enliven his QB by 16 P-Q5! Instead he undermines Black's KP, but only by a course of head-on collision.
16 P-KN4?! B-B2
Stronger, according to Staunton, was the blunt 16 ..., R-KN3! E.g. 17 NxP,BxP; 18 PxB, PxN; 19 P-N5, Q-B4; or 18 N-B5, BxP+; 19 K-R2, Q-B2; 20 KxB, R-N5; but not 16 ..., R-KN3; 17 NxP, PxP?; 18 P-B5, R-QB3; 19 N-N3, B-B2; 20 PxP, and White consolidates his position in readiness for a K-side advance.
17 P-KR4   B-B5
18 KR-K1   PxP
19 NxP   B-Q4
20 P-B5   R-QN3
21 B-N5   N-R3
22 P-B4
An unjustified pawn sacrifice. However, 22 P-B6, fails against R-KB1, so White had to resort to the defensive 22 P-N3, R-KB1; 23 N-N3, hoping to push Black back with a rush of his Q-side pawns. But even in that case the shattered White K-side is always likely to be his ruin.
22 ......   BxP
From now on White's every ingenious attempt founders on Staunton's rock-like defence.
23 N-B5   P-N6!

'A good reply, as White cannot defend three pawns at the same time (the KBP, the QP and the QNP)' (Tartakover).
24 QxP
Or 24 NxQ, PxQ+; 25 KxP, RxP+.

24	QxP
25 R-K5	Q-N3
26 P-N3	B-B2
27 N-Q7	

Fishing in the proverbial troubled waters. Indeed, after 27 NxN, RxN; White would have little compensation for his pawn minus and the porous K-side.

27	R-Q3

Threatening RxN and RxQP, annihilating the lynch-pin of White's position. In view of these dire circumstances White has little choice but to 'win' the opposing Queen.

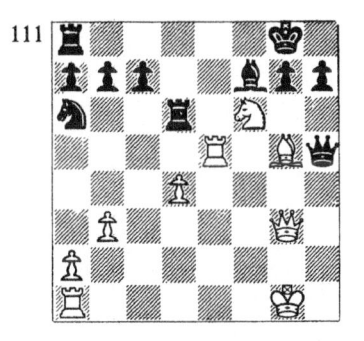

28 P-R5	QxP
29 N-B6+	

111

Staunton
Jaenisch

The climax of White's attack, but Black's resources are sufficient. However, if 29 B-K7, then R-KN3 is an adequate response.

29	PxN
30 BxP+	Q-N3
31 R-KN5	RxB
32 K-R2	R-K1
33 R-KN1	QxR
34 QxQ+	R-N3
35 Q-Q2	P-B3
36 RxR+	BxR

'The contest of ideas has come to an end; now technique has its say. In point of material values, the rook, bishop, knight and pawn are superior to the Queen, but her mobility retains to the end practical chances of obtaining perpetual check' (Tartakover).

37 Q-N5	N-B2
38 Q-QR5	N-N4
39 P-Q5	P-N3
40 Q-Q2	R-Q1

Winning a second pawn.

41 P-R4	RxP
42 Q-B4	N-Q3
43 Q-B6	R-Q7+
44 K-N1	R-Q8+
45 K-R2	R-Q7+
46 K-N1	R-Q8+
47 K-R2	R-Q4
48 Q-Q8+	N-K1
49 Q-K7	R-Q7+
50 K-N1	R-Q6
51 P-N4	R-Q5
52 P-N5	PxP
53 PxP	R-Q4
54 Q-K6+	B-B2
55 Q-N4+	K-B1
56 Q-N4+	N-Q3

In modern master chess such a position would probably be resigned by White, but in 1851 the achievement of victory from such a situation was regarded as a minor technical triumph!

57 Q-R3	K-K1
58 QxP	RxP
59 Q-B7	R-N8+
60 K-R2	R-N7+
61 K-N1	N-B5
62 Q-B6+	K-K2
63 Q-K4+	B-K3
64 QxP+	K-Q3

See Diagram 112 overleaf

There was no point in conserving both of his extra pawns. Black can win comfortably with the QNP.

112

Staunton

Jaenisch

65 Q-KN7	P-N4
66 Q-B8+	K-Q4
67 Q-Q8+	K-B3
68 Q-K8+	B-Q2
69 Q-K4+	K-B2
70 Q-Q4	

He retained more chance of his perpetual check with 70 Q-B4+, K-N2; 71 Q-K4+, B-B3; 72 Q-K7+, K-R3; 73 Q-B6, K-N3; 74 Q-Q8+, etc.

70	B-B3
71 Q-B5	K-N2
72 K-B1	

And here Q-K7+ looks more promising.

72	R-Q7
73 K-K1	R-Q2
74 K-K2	R-Q7+
75 K-K1	R-Q4
76 Q-B8	N-K4
77 Q-N7+	K-R3

| 78 Q-QB7 | P-N5 |

Hooray! Start hanging out the flags!

79 Q-B8+	K-N4
80 Q-N8+	K-B5
81 Q-N6	P-N6
82 K-K2	B-N4
83 Q-B7+	K-N5+
84 K-K3	R-B4
85 Q-Q8	N-Q6
86 Q-Q4+	B-B5
87 K-Q2	P-N7
88 Q-B3+	K-R5
89 K-B2	

If 89 Q-B2+, B-N6!; 90 QxN, R-Q4 wins.

| 89 ...... | B-N6+ |
| 90 K-N1 | B-R7+ |

Not falling for the stalemate.

| 91 KxB | RxQ |
| **Resigns** | |

It is quite refreshing to see a mid-19th century game in which accurate defence triumphs against stormy aggression. The techniques of prophylaxis and consolidation were foreign to most masters in the pre-Steinitz era. After this gruelling contest it is little wonder that Jaenisch collapsed to lose the next game in just over 20 moves, though in view of Staunton's health one might have expected it to be the other way round.

51

STAUNTON - JAENISCH
9th match game, London, 26th August 1851
Scotch Gambit

1 P-K4	P-K4
2 N-KB3	N-QB3
3 P-Q4	PxP
4 B-QB4	B-B4
5 O-O	P-Q3

For comments on this opening see Game 44.

6 P-B3   PxP

Too perilous. Correct is B-KN5! fighting for the initiative, even at the cost of his extra pawn. E.g. 7 Q-N3, BxN; 8 BxP+, K-B1; 9 PxB, N-K4! and Black has a good position according to an analysis by Keres.

7 NxP   B-K3

'Black's position is already unsatisfactory, and neither the text move nor other continuations ... could prevent White from taking advantage of his opponent's twisted central position' (Tartakover). If 7 ..., N-B3; 8 B-KN5, and it is not easy for Black to break the pin.

8 BxB	PxB
9 Q-N3	Q-B1
10 B-K3!	

Staunton's improvement over some previous games of the match in which he selected 10 N-KN5, N-Q5; 11 Q-R4+, P-B3; 12 B-K3, and now the 1st match game continued 12 ..., P-N4; 13 Q-Q1, P-K4; 14 P-QN4!, BxP; 15 BxN, PxB; 16 QxP, BxN; 17 QxB, N-B3; 18 P-K5, N-Q4; 19 Q-B3, Q-Q2; 20 P-K6, Q-K2; 21 N-B7, R-KB1; 22 KR-K1, Q-B3; 23 NxP+, K-K2; 24 Q-KN3, QxP+!! (a brilliant defence); 25 QxQ, RxQ; 26 KxR, KxN; 27 QR-B1, R-K1; 28 R-B2, P-B4; 29 R-K4, P-B5; when Black's compensation for the exchange should have been sufficient to draw, although in fact Staunton won after a Jaenisch blunder on move 39. The 5th game diverged with 12 ..., P-K4; 13 BxN, BxB; 14 Q-N3, Q-Q2; 15 N-K2, B-N3; 16 QR-Q1, N-R3; 17 N-KB3, Q-K2; 18 P-QR4, O-O-O. Staunton's 10th move in the present game wrecks his pawn structure but opens sufficient attacking lines in compensation. In addition it prepares a double central battering ram since P-K4-K5 is now available twice.

10	BxB
11 PxB	N-B3
12 N-KN5	N-Q1

Another aspect of Staunton's 10th move — N-Q5 to defend the KP is no longer an option for Black.

13 QR-B1

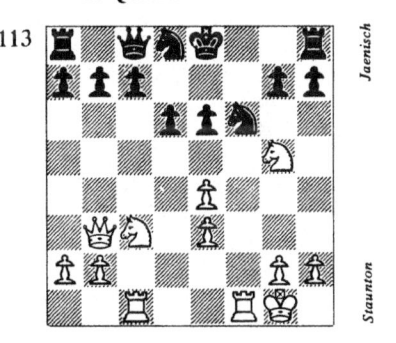

113

Threatening N-QN5.

13	P-QR3
14 N-R4	Q-Q2

Or R-QN1?; 15 N-N6!, netting Black's Queen.

15 P-K5!

The first ram.

15 ......   P-R3

If PxP; 16 N-B5, or if P-N4; 16 PxN, PxN; 17 Q-B2.

16 N-KB3   P-QN4

Black has overlooked White's 20th move and continues to remain oblivious to the possibility until Staunton confronts him with it over the board. If 16 ..., N-Q4; then 17 PxP, QxP; 18 QR-Q1, gives White a powerful game. E.g. 18 ..., Q-K2 (to parry P-K4); 19 N-K5!, or 18 ..., Q-N5; 19 RxN, QxQ; 20 RxN+!

17 PxN   PxN
18 Q-B2   PxP
19 Q-N6+   K-K2?

Allowing an instant debacle. He had to try Q-B2; 20 QxQ+, NxQ; 21 RxP, O-O; when White retains a vast plus with 22 N-Q4, but Black could still fight.

20 N-K5!   QPxN
21 QxP+   Resigns

K-K1; 22 QxR+, K-K2; 23 Q-B8 mate, or K-Q3; 22 KR-Q1 mate. ' 'Simple means, convincing results' might be the motto of this game, which is typical of Staunton at his best' (Tartakover).

52

ALLIES - STAUNTON
Exhibition game, Edinburgh, 5th July 1852
Odds of Pawn and Two Moves (remove Black's KBP)

Staunton gives the names of the White team as Gordon, Meikle and Robertson. Brien in the *Chess Player's Chronicle* wrongly substitutes Donaldson for Robertson. Many clergymen of the day were reluctant to be known by their parishioners to be indulging in so frivolous a pastime as chess, especially since cash stakes were often involved even in the most casual of games, so they often played under pseudonyms. The Rev. Gordon was more often 'Gamma', the Rev. Donaldson 'Delta', and against Morphy six years later the Rev. Owen took the name 'Alter'.

1 P-K4   ——
2 P-Q4   N-QB3
3 P-Q5   N-K4
4 P-KB4

White's opening plan cannot really be recommended. They loosen their position and chase Black's knight round to a square where it bolsters up the shaky K-side. Even in the similar, but solider, Alekhine Defence some seventy years later, Tartakover said of this sort of position that White had his initiative to defend.

4 ......   N-B2

5 N-KB3   P-Q3
6 B-Q3   P-B3
7 P-B4   B-N5
8 O-O   P-KN3

The only good way of introducing his KB into play.

9 N-B3   B-N2
10 B-K3   N-B3
11 Q-B2

A positional error which gives Staunton the chance to weaken White's dark squares. White should have safeguarded his KN4 with P-KR3.

11 ......   BxN!

Very alert of Staunton. White must either weaken his pawn structure with 12 PxB, which is unpleasant in view of the open KB-file, or else part with his valuable QB.

**12 RxB   N-N5
13 N-K2**

Careless. K-R1, a move Staunton would never have missed, was the most sensible here against the threat of NxB; 14 RxN, B-Q5.

**13 ......   NxB
14 RxN   Q-N3**

Now the White players suffer from a series of embarrassing pins, which they never quite succeed in shaking off.

**15 Q-Q2   N-K4!
16 P-KR3**

16 PxN?, B-R3 would emphasise Black's dark square influence, while if 16 K-R1, N-N5; 17 R-B3, N-B7+

**16 ......   O-O
17 K-R2   B-R3
18 R-KB1   R-B2**

How is White to untangle in the face of Black's threat to double rooks on the KB-file? 19 P-KN3 looks plausible, but then P-KN4!, exploiting the pin which has arisen on the KB-file, creates new problems. The method chosen by White may even be best, but it gives Staunton an opportunity to display his profound understanding of the principles of blockade and his remarkably advanced sensitivity to weak square complexes of a certain colour. At the moment White's K-side dark squares do not appear to be so weak and his pawns look as if they retain a measure of flexibility. But compare this position with the situation five moves later!

**19 P-KN4   QR-KB1
20 R-N3   B-N4!!**

A tremendous move. The bishop is heading for the superb blockading square KR5.

**21 P-N3   B-R5
22 R-K3**

They would do much better to get off the weak dark square complex with R-N2.

22 ......   P-N4!

White's reply is forced.

23 P-KB5   P-KR4!

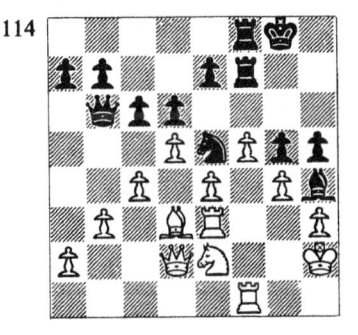

114

Taking advantage of the omission on White's 22nd move. The once healthy White K-side pawns have been reduced to a helpless petrifact, obstructing their own pieces and providing a ready target for Black's forces. White cannot defend his KNP, while the opening of the KR-file also spells disaster for him. Nimzowitsch would have been delighted with Staunton's achievement in this game. He once wrote that 20th century masters no longer sacrificed for brutal attacks, as did their 19th century counterparts, but for subtle positional reasons or in order to induce a blockade of the opposing army. He was probably totally unaware that Staunton had been thinking along similar lines over half a century before his time.

**24 PxRP   R-R2
25 R-KN1**

A blunder or a sacrifice? White may

have been relying on the ultimate capture of Black's KNP to obtain compensation for the loss of the exchange, but this never comes to fruition under favourable circumstances. However, Black's threats on the KR-file would in any case have decided the game in his favour.

25 ......   B-B7

From now on Staunton's technique makes light work of the problem of winning.

26 R(1)-N3   RxRP
27 K-N2

Or 27 N-B4, BxR; 28 RxB (QxB, N-N5+), PxN.

27 ......   BxR(K6)
28 RxB   K-B2
29 R-N3   R(B)-KR1
30 N-N1   P-N5
31 B-B1   R-KN1

Refusing to get bogged down by PxP+; 32 K-R2.

32 K-R2   R(4)-R1
33 Q-B4   PxRP
34 RxR   RxR
35 NxP   R-N5
36 Q-B2   QxQ+
37 NxQ   R-N1
38 B-K2   PxP
39 KPxP   K-B3
Resigns

53

STAUNTON - AMATEUR
Casual game, Scotland, August 1852
Sicilian Defence

An interesting game from the point of view of the opening and an attractive blockading performance by Staunton, though the opposition was not really worthy of his steel.

1 P-K4   P-QB4
2 P-Q4   PxP
3 N-KB3

The order of Staunton's moves creates an odd impression. Perhaps he was angling for a gambit line with 3 ..., P-K4; 4 P-B3, PxP; 5 QNxP, when White seems to have excellent compensation for his pawn.

3 ......   P-K3
4 NxP   P-QR3

In 1852 they already knew about this! Perhaps the Black player was influenced by one of Staunton's games as Black against Anderssen in the tournament of 1851 (See notes to Game 56).

5 P-KN3

Staunton counters with another idea which the moderns probably regard as their own prerogative. Compare the opening of the 4th game in the quarter-final Candidates' match between Fischer and Taimanov, Vancouver, 25th May 1971: 1 P-K4, P-QB4; 2 N-KB3, N-QB3; 3 P-Q4, PxP; 4 NxP, Q-B2; 5 N-QB3, P-K3; 6 P-KN3, P-QR3; 7 B-N2, N-B3; 8 O-O, NxN; 9 QxN, B-B4; 10 B-B4!, P-Q3; 11 Q-Q2, P-R3 (N-Q2!); 12

QR-Q1, P-K4; 13 B-K3, B-KN5; 14 BxB, PxB; 15 P-B3, B-K3; 16 P-B4, R-Q1; 17 N-Q5, and White went on to win a beautiful game. Such lines as this represent some of the main highways of modern opening theory.

| 5 ...... | B-B4 |

Out of place here. Either N-QB3 or Q-B2 would be more suited to the needs of the position. After the text Staunton exploits the weakness of the dark square complex (his QB5, Q6 and K5), which he normally masked so deftly in his own games as Black in similar lines.

6 N-N3	B-R2
7 B-N2	N-K2
8 B-B4?	

N-B3 is more accurate, for after the text Black could have rid himself of the hole on his Q3 by the straightforward 8 ..., P-Q4 with a fine position.

8	QN-B3?
9 B-Q6	O-O
10 N-B3	P-QN4

Staunton has already started to strangle Black on the dark squares, and now he is able to draw the noose tighter. Black's best chance lay in 10 ..., P-B4 when 11 P-K5, P-B5! would give him counterplay on the K-side. More probably White would have met 10 ..., P-B4 with 11 O-O!, PxP; 12 NxP, R-B4; 13 P-QB4, with a considerable pull.

| 11 P-K5 | B-N2 |
| 12 N-K4 | R-K1 |

| 13 N(4)-B5 | |

The whole complex is now occupied.

13	B-B1
14 O-O	N-B4
15 P-QB3	NxB
16 PxN	BxN
17 NxB	Q-N3
18 P-QN4	

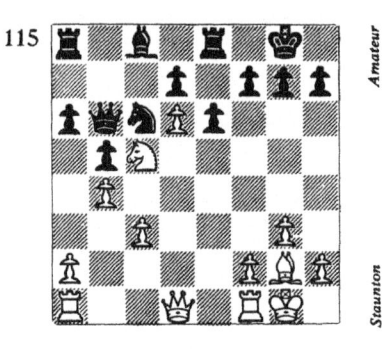

115

White's game plays itself. His position is so good that the victorious 'petite combinaison' soon arises of itself.

18	P-QR4
19 R-K1	PxP
20 PxP	R-R2
21 P-QR3	N-N1
22 Q-Q4	N-R3
23 NxKP!	

A welcome end to Black's torment.

23	QxQ
24 NxQ	RxR+
25 RxR	**Resigns**

None too soon anyway, but now if K-B1; 26 NxP.

54

STAUNTON - LOWENTHAL
Casual game, London, Jan. 1853
Giuoco Piano

A peculiar game. After an undistinguished opening noteworthy points arise — Staunton's prophylactic move with his King, his seizure of a dominating central position after a Black error, the way in which this entrenched position enables him to fend off Black's apparently dangerous attack and the spectacular final blockade with his knights.

1 P-K4	P-K4
2 N-KB3	N-QB3
3 B-B4	B-B4
4 P-Q3	N-B3
5 N-B3	

This rather uninspired Four Knights variation was a favourite of Buckle's.

5	P-Q3
6 P-KR3	O-O
7 O-O	N-K2
8 B-KN5	P-B3
9 BxN	PxB
10 P-Q4	B-N3
11 B-N3	N-N3
12 N-K2	Q-K2
13 Q-Q3	K-R1
14 QR-Q1	R-KN1
15 K-R1	

The prophylactic move.

15	B-K3?
16 P-Q5!	

And now the centre.

16	PxP
17 BxP	QR-Q1
18 P-B4	Q-Q2

Now the Black attack threatens.

19 N-R2!	N-R5
20 P-KN3!	BxP
21 R-KN1	N-N3
22 P-KN4	

Isolating a portion of Black's army.

22	BxBP
23 QxB	BxR
24 RxB	

With all the light squares under

Johann Jacob Lowenthal

White's control Black's rook and two pawns are no match for the enemy minor pieces.

24	N-B1
25 N-KB3	N-K3
26 N-R4	N-N4
27 Q-B1	K-N2
28 N-N3	K-B1
29 N-R5	NxP

Now he has a third pawn, but it makes no difference. No doubt he hoped for 30 BxN, RxP but it was a thin hope.

| 30 N-B5 | N-Q7 |
| 31 Q-K2 | |

See Diagram

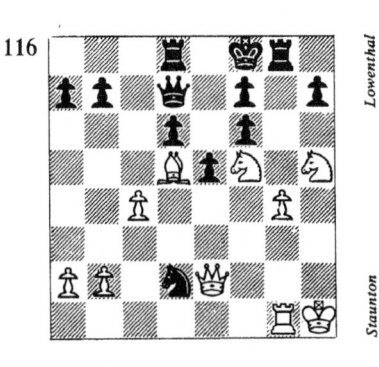

31	Q-B1
32 QxN	R-N4
33 NxBP	RxN
34 PxR	QxKBP
35 Q-R6+	K-K2
36 N-N4	K-Q2
37 Q-R3	K-B2
38 R-KB1	Resigns

55

STAUNTON - VON DER LASA
5th match game, Brussels, August 1853
Ruy Lopez

Can one legitimately discuss chess and music in the same terms? At times it is difficult to suppress a suspicion that there are 'correspondances', as Baudelaire put it, between such games as the following and, say, a Bruckner symphony, where a turgid expanse is suddenly illuminated by successive flashes of brilliant light.

1 P-K4	P-K4
2 N-KB3	N-QB3
3 B-N5	N-B3
4 Q-K2!?	

See Diagram 117

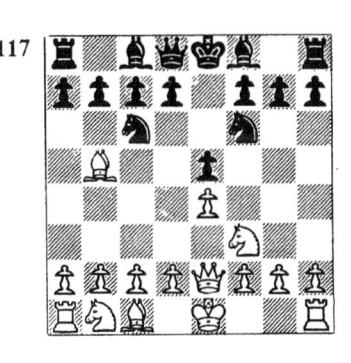

The main line of the Berlin Defence (4 O-O, NxP) still enjoys untroubled health and was successfully employed by Smyslov as Black in several games from the Alekhine Memorial tournament at Moscow 1971. Very little attention has been devoted to this alternative 4th move for White, reputedly a suggestion of the Spanish chessplaying 'bishop' (if bishop he was), Ruy Lopez in person. This neglect may be because Keres's authoritative work on the opening, dated 1969, condemns it, but only on the basis of a game played in 1897!! Janowski - Winawer then went 4 Q-K2, B-K2; 5 O-O, P-Q3; 6 P-Q4 (P-B3!?), PxP; 7 NxP, B-Q2; 8 NxN, PxN; 9 B-Q3, O-O; 10 N-B3, R-K1= Bronstein, however, feels that the potential of 4 Q-K2 has not yet been exhausted and played the move against Panno in a 1973 Interzonal, with the continuation 4 Q-K2, B-K2; 5 P-B3, P-Q3; 6 P-Q4, B-Q2; 7 P-Q5, N-QN1; 8 B-Q3, P-B3; 9 P-B4, N-R3; 10 N-B3, O-O; 11 P-KR3, N-B4; 12 B-B2, PxP; 13 BPxP, Q-B2; 14 B-Q2! and White stands better.

4 ...... P-QR3

Keene - Milner-Barry, Cambridge, 1971, varied at this point with 4 ..., B-B4; 5 P-B3, O-O; 6 O-O (BxN!?), P-Q3; 7 P-Q3, B-Q2; 8 B-R4!, N-K2; 9 BxB, NxB; 10 P-Q4, B-N3; 11 P-QR4, P-QB3; 12 PxP, PxP; 13 N-R3, N-N3; 14 N-B4, Q-K2; 15 P-KN3, P-KB4; 16 P-R5, B-B2; 17 P-N3, PxP; 18 KN-Q2, N-B3; 19 B-R3, P-B4; 20 N(2)xKP, P-QN3; 21 N(B)-Q2, NxN; 22 NxN, Q-K3; 23 P-QN4, BPxP; 24 BPxP, KR-Q1; 25 N-N5, Q-N6; 26 KR-N1, Q-Q6; 27 Q-R5, P-KR3; 28 N-K6, R-Q3; 29 NxB, QR-Q1; 30 R-Q1, QxR+; 31 RxQ, RxR+; 32 K-N2, Resigns. A good example of the legendary Spanish bishop's very own 4th move. After 25 N-N5 Black is in great trouble from the twin threats of Q-R2+ and Q-KR5. 'A game I cannot resist quoting since I so rarely play 1 P-K4' (Keene).

5 B-R4!

Far superior to BxN? which R.Byrne chose against Smyslov at Moscow 1971. After 5 ..., QPxB; 6 N-B3, B-Q3; 7 P-Q4!?, PxP; 8 NxP, O-O; 9 B-Q2, B-QN5; 10 N-B3, Q-K2 Black already stood slightly better.

5 ...... P-QN4
6 B-N3 B-B4
7 P-B3

The *Handbuch* line at the time ran 7 P-QR4, R-QN1; 8 PxP, PxP; 9 N-B3, P-N5; 10 N-Q5, O-O; 11 O-O, P-Q3; 12 P-R3, B-K3. Staunton's move looks like an improvement.

7 ...... O-O
8 P-Q3 P-Q3
9 B-N5

This pin is annoying for Black since his KB is on the wrong side of the central pawn chain, which renders it difficult for him to raise the siege of his KN.

9 ...... B-K3
10 QN-Q2 Q-K2
11 B-Q5 B-Q2
12 N-R4 QR-N1
13 N-B5 Q-Q1
14 P-QN4 B-N3
15 Q-B3

Threatening N-R6+!

15 ...... BxN

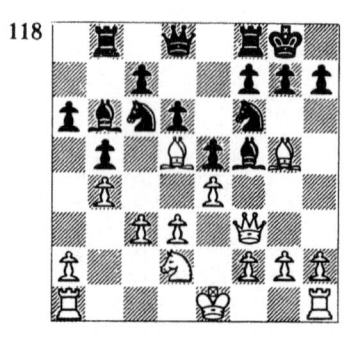

118

16 PxB?

A very weak move which lets slip his advantage. White had two very good alternatives here: (i) 16 BxQN!, when

Black's QB must retreat and the unpleasant pin on Black's KN has been intensified. (BxQN would also have been the correct reply to 13 ..., BxN). Or **(ii)** the more direct 16 QxB, when N-K2 fails against the simple 17 BxN!, NxQ; 18 BxQ. After the move chosen by Staunton the game drifts into an arid waste where the contest is characterised by turgid manoeuvres rather than by brilliant ideas.

16	N-K2
17 B-N3	P-Q4
18 BxN	PxB

It is probably best to inflict this weakness on Black's K-side, but his position is so solid that it causes him no trouble as yet.

19 O-O	Q-Q2
20 P-N4	K-R1
21 K-R1	P-B3
22 R-KN1	R-N1
23 N-B1	P-QR4
24 P-QR3	Q-Q3
25 N-N3	B-B2
26 R-N2	R-R1
27 N-R5	

von der Lasa has co-ordinated his defences well and he holds a slight advantage on the Q-side and in the centre, but the debility of his front KBP makes it unlikely that he should entertain thoughts of victory.

27	PxP
28 BPxP	P-R3
29 Q-K3	K-R2
30 Q-B5	KR-Q1

Obviously not QxQ; 31 NxP+, K-N2; 32 N-R5+, etc.

31 Q-B1	B-N3
32 R-R2	R-R3
33 R-N3	B-Q5
34 R-R3	N-N1
35 N-N3	K-N2
36 N-R5+	K-B1

White could hardly have made progress against 36 ..., K-R2.

37 P-B4

The sole method of inconveniencing the opposition.

37 ...... R-K1?!

Black did not wish to permit the return of White's knight to the centre after 37 ..., PxP; 38 NxP, but in that case 38 ..., R-K1! would have maintained the balance of forces. The move chosen is good enough but it demands an inspired defence in subsequent play.

38 P-N5!

Staunton begins to wake up and lightning flashes across the barren land.

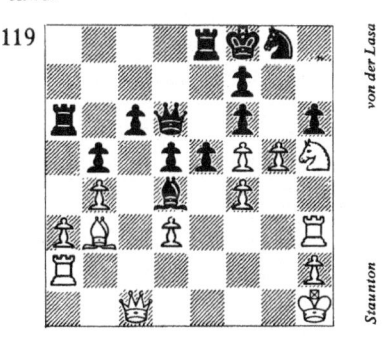

119

38 ...... KPxP

There was an intriguing defensive idea available at this point in 38 ..., RPxP; 39 PxNP, PxP; allowing the apparently decisive 40 QxNP. But then comes 40 ..., Q-R3!!; 41 QxQ+, NxQ; 42 N-B6 (What else does White have apart from this attempt to win a piece? If his Queen steps aside from the exchange on move 41, then Q-B8+ is always a nasty possibility), R(1)-R1!; 43 RxN, K-N2; 44 N-N4, RxP; 45 P-B6+, K-N1 and there seems to be no way for White to retain his extra piece (46 RxR, RxR; 47 B-Q1, R-R8) or to exploit the caged Black King (46 N-K3, RxR; or 46 R-KN2, R-R8+). White's most sensible course is to steer for equality with 46 R-R5, RxR; 47 BxR, RxB; 48 NxP, — a droll variation this, with

White's dreaded 'Spanish bishop' a prisoner in his own camp.

39 PxRP   NxP
40 NxP(4) NxP

After N-N1 either 41 R-KN2 or 41 R-R7 would be inconvenient for Black, and not quite sufficient was the sacrificial line 40 ..., QxN; 41 QxQ, R-K8+; 42 K-N2, R-N8+; 43 K-B3, R-B8+; 44 K-N3, RxQ; 45 KxR, B-K4+; 46 K-B3, NxP.

41 R-R8+   K-K2
42 R-K2+   B-K4
43 NxP+!

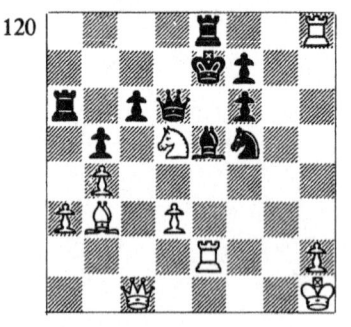

120
von der Lasa / Staunton

43 ......   QxN+?

Actually, with White's bishop hanging on Q5 and Black's threat of N-N6+, this Queen sacrifice looks rather promising for Black and he doubtless expected to get three pieces for the Queen; but he has overlooked Staunton's excellent 45th move. He should either play 43 ..., PxN; 44 RxR+, KxR; 45 Q-B8+, K-K2; 46 QxN, and Black's best line is probably 46 ..., RxP; 47 P-Q4, RxB; 48 PxB, PxP; 49 RxP+, K-B1; with a likely draw, or else he should play 43 ..., K-Q1; when there is nothing clear for White, who could even lose by falling into the trap 44 RxR+, KxR; 45 NxP+, QxN; 46 Q-B5, N-K6!; with a Queen check on KB8 to follow or 46 Q-KB4, N-K2!; and White comes out minus a piece. The game at this point is remarkably rich in complex variations.

44 BxQ   RxR
45 Q-KB4!

Shattering Black's illusions. He now at last demolishes the opposition.

45 ......   PxB
46 RxB+   PxR
47 QxP+   K-Q2
48 QxR   RxP
49 Q-K5   N-Q3

If N-K2; 50 Q-N8! wins.

50 QxP   R-R5

The smoke has cleared and Staunton has reached an advantageous technical ending, the sort of exercise he could handle to perfection.

51 Q-Q4   K-K3
52 P-R4   R-R3
53 K-R2

Inexperienced players often try to win such positions without the aid of the King, thus jeopardising their chances of victory. As seen in Game 33, Staunton was well aware of the power of the King, even in the middle-game, so in this simplified position he makes the utmost use of this most important piece.

53 ......   N-B4
54 Q-B5   N-Q3
55 K-R3   R-R6
56 Q-K3+   K-B4
57 Q-B2+   K-K3
58 Q-K2+   K-B4
59 P-R5   N-B5
60 Q-B2+   K-N4
61 QxP   RxP+
62 K-N2   R-Q7+
63 K-B1   R-Q3
64 Q-K8   R-B3+
65 K-K2   R-QN3
66 K-Q3   R-Q3+
67 K-B3

Creeping round the corner.

67 ......   R-QN3
68 K-Q4   R-Q3+
69 K-B5   R-B3

70 QxP **Resigns**
R-B4+; 71 KxN, RxQ; 72 KxR is an obviously hopeless King and pawn ending, while 70 ..., N-K6; 71 Q-K8!, leaves Black horribly tied up and bound to lose a piece for the QNP. After an unpromising start this game gave rise to some acute and fascinating tactical variations.

To be fair to von der Lasa — and in a way to Staunton, since it shows just how strong an opponent he was up against in this match — we append another game from the contest with the same opening.

Staunton - von der Lasa
9th match game
1 P-K4, P-K4; 2 N-KB3, N-QB3; 3 B-N5, N-B3; 4 Q-K2, B-Q3!? (this was something of a fetish with the Berlin school. In the 1st game of his 1846 match with Staunton, Horwitz as Black played 1 P-K4, P-K4; 2 N-KB3, N-QB3; 3 B-N5, Q-B3; 4 N-B3, B-Q3); 5 P-B3, O-O; 6 O-O, R-K1; 7 P-Q3, P-KR3; 8 N-R4? (QN-Q2! and P-Q4), N-K2; 9 B-QB4, P-B3; 10 Q-B3, B-B2; 11 BxRP?!, P-Q4!; 12 B-N3, B-N5; 13 Q-N3, PxB; 14 P-KR3, K-R2; 15 PxB, R-KN1; 16 Q-B3 (if P-B3, B-N3+ followed by N-R4-B5 with a strong attack for the pawn), NxNP; 17 QxP+, R-N2; 18 Q-B3, Q-Q2; 19 Q-K2, QR-KB1; 20 QN-Q2, N-N3; 21 NxN, RxN; 22 N-B3, R(3)-B3; 23 B-Q1, RxN!; 24 PxR, N-R7!!; 25 KxN, R-B5; 26 R-KN1, R-R5+; 27 K-N2, Q-R6 mate. It was a sure sign of lack of form with Staunton when he set off in pursuit of material advantage at the cost of position. Some masters — Steinitz, Korchnoi, even Fischer — enjoy a reputation for 'heroic materialism', to quote a phrase from Sir Kenneth Clark's *Civilisation,* but Staunton's best games occur when he plays for positional advantage without too much regard for material considerations.

56

VON DER LASA - STAUNTON
12th match game, Brussels, August 1853
Sicilian Defence

1 P-K4	P-QB4
2 P-Q4	PxP
3 N-KB3	N-QB3
4 B-QB4	

This makes an odd impression to modern eyes, not that the move is unusual in combating the Sicilian, but a more clear-cut course would be to recapture the pawn.

4	P-K3
5 NxP	B-B4

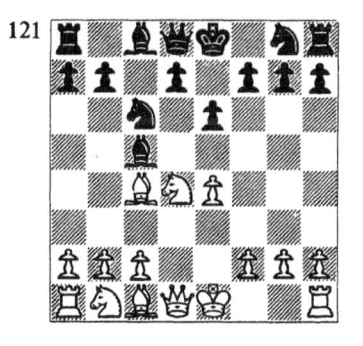

A 19th century development of the bishop which went right out of fashion because it was considered to result in a weakness on Black's Q3. However, it has been much revived in recent years, chiefly in the form 1 P-K4, P-QB4; 2 N-KB3, P-K3; 3 P-Q4, PxP; 4 NxP, P-QR3; 5 B-Q3, B-B4; 6 N-N3, B-R2 as in Karpov - Hubner, Graz 1972, and in Calvo - Korchnoi, Havana 1966. A game Poutrus - Keene, London 1964, continued 7 O-O, Q-R5; 8 N(1)-Q2, N-KB3; 9 N-B3, Q-R4; 10 Q-K2, N-B3; 11 B-K3, B-N1! and Black won. Other modern examples of Black developing his KB on QB4 are Botterill - Basman, Eastbourne 1973, which went: 1 P-K4, P-QB4; 2 N-KB3, P-K3; 3 P-Q4, PxP; 4 NxP, B-B4; 5 N-N3, B-N3; 6 N-B3, N-K2; 7 B-KN5, O-O; 8 B-K2, P-B4; 9 PxP?, BxP+! with advantage. Timman - Basman, Hastings 1973-74, varied with the better 7 B-KB4, O-O; 8 B-Q6, P-B4; 9 P-K5,

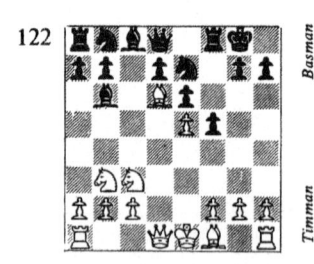

QN-B3; 11 O-O, R-B2; 12 K-R1, P-B5; 13 N-K4, N-B4; 14 B-R5, P-N3; 15 B-N4, N-N2; 16 Q-B3, P-KR4; 17 B-R3, Q-R5; 18 N-B6+, with advantage to White. To review further the 19th century practice at this opening, still earlier versions are to be found, e.g. von der Lasa - Anderssen, Breslau 1846: 1 P-K4, P-QB4; 2 P-Q4, PxP; 3 N-KB3, N-QB3; 4 B-QB4, P-K3; 5 NxP, B-B4; 6 N-KB3 (in the present game against Staunton he improves on this with N-N3), KN-K2; 7 N-B3, O-O; 8 P-QR3, N-N3; 9 O-O, P-B4; 10 PxP, RxP; 11 B-Q3, R-R4; 12 P-KN4?, R-R6; 13 K-N2, RxN; 14 KxR, Q-R5; 15 K-N2, N(B)-K4; 16 P-R3, P-N3; 17 BxN, PxB; 18 B-B4, B-N2+; 19 P-B3, NxBP; 20 RxN, Q-B7+; Resigns. Or again Anderssen - Staunton, First game in semifinal match in the 1851 London tournament: 1 P-K4, P-QB4; 2 P-Q4, PxP; 3 N-KB3, P-K3; 4 NxP, B-B4; 5 N-QB3, P-QR3; 6 B-K3, B-R2; 7 B-Q3, N-K2; 8 O-O, O-O;

122

9 ..., QN-B3; 10 Q-Q2, P-B5; 11 O-O-O, R-B2; 12 B-Q3, N-B4; 13 KR-K1, Q-R5; 14 N-K4, B-Q1; 15 P-N3 and White stands better. This last example is proof that 19th century theory still survives, is valid and should not be neglected, since it follows the 1st game in the final match in the 1857 New York tournament between Morphy and Paulsen right up to 9 P-K5, when Paulsen continued 9 ..., P-QR3; 10 B-K2,

123

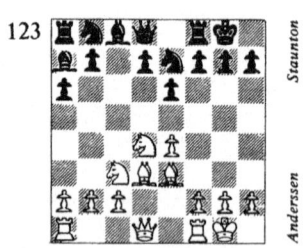

9 Q-R5 (reminiscent of the play in Game 19), N-N3; 10 P-K5, Q-B2; 11 QR-K1, P-N4; 12 P-B4, B-N2; 13 N-K4, and White stood better. Besides the Morphy - Paulsen example quoted above, there were three more specimens of the variation in their games from the New York tournament. In the 4th game play went:
1 P-K4, P-QB4; 2 N-KB3, P-K3; 3 P-Q4, PxP; 4 NxP, B-B4; 5 N-N3,

B-N3; 6 N-B3, N-QB3; 7 B-KB4,
P-K4; 8 B-N3, KN-K2; 9 B-QB4,
O-O; 10 N-N5, P-QR3; 11 N-Q6,
B-B2; 12 P-QR4, N-N3; 13 Q-Q2,
Q-B3; and the game was drawn.
Their 5th game varied with 5 B-K3,
Q-N3; 6 N-N5, N-KB3; 7 BxB, QxB;
8 N-Q6+, K-K2; 9 NxB+, RxN; 10
B-Q3, N-B3; 11 O-O, P-KR4; 12
N-Q2, P-R5; 13 P-KR3, P-KN4; and
Black looks well enough, though he
lost through his later play. In their
7th game Morphy played 6 N-QB3
(instead of the N-N5 of the 5th game).

124 *Paulsen — Morphy*

Black now went wrong with 6 ...,
QxP?; 7 N(4)-N5, BxB; 8 R-QN1,
QxR; 9 NxQ. More accurate than this
was Basman's 6 ..., N-QB3 against
Hartston at Hastings 1973-74, which
continued 7 N(4)-N5, BxB; 8 PxB,
QxP+; 9 B-K2, K-B1; 10 R-KB1,
N-B3; 11 Q-Q6+, K-N1; 12 RxN,
PxR; 13 R-Q1, P-KR4; 14 R-Q3,
Q-B8+; 15 K-B2, P-R5; 16 N-B7,
N-K4; 17 NxR, Q-B5+; 18 K-N1,
NxR; 19 QxN, P-N3; 20 Q-B4, B-N2;
21 N-B7, Q-K6+ with equality.
Finally, one more modern example of
this development but in a deferred
form: Hamann - Hartston, Menorca
1974, went: 1 P-K4, P-QB4; 2
N-KB3, P-K3; 3 P-Q4, PxP; 4 NxP,
N-QB3; 5 N-QB3, P-QR3; 6 P-KN3,
Q-B2; 7 B-N2, B-B4; 8 NxN, NPxN; 9
Q-N4, P-N3!?; 10 O-O, P-QR4; 11
N-R4, B-Q5 and Black arrived at a
fianchetto of his KB by a roundabout
route, though White stands better
and eventually won.

6 N-N3	B-N3
7 O-O	KN-K2
8 N-B3	P-QR3
9 B-B4	P-K4
10 B-K3!	BxB
11 PxB	O-O
12 Q-R5	Q-K1

Not N-N3; 13 RxP!, RxR; 14 R-KB1
and White stands better.

13 P-QR4	N-N3
14 QR-Q1	Q-K2
15 N-Q5	Q-Q1
16 P-R5	P-Q3

von der Lasa pointed out that Black
could not play 16 ..., NxP because of
17 NxN, QxN; 18 RxP!, RxR; 19
N-K7+, K-B1; 20 NxN+, PxN; 21
Q-R8+. Just as good was 18 N-K7+,
NxN (forced); 19 RxBP.

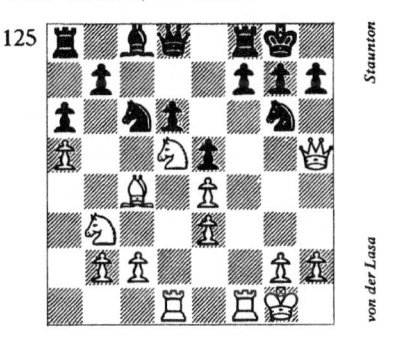

125 *Staunton — von der Lasa*

17 P-R3??

Missing the win by 17 N-N6. If then
17 ..., R-N1 White's combination
goes like clockwork with 18 RxBP!,
RxR; 19 R-KB1. A more complex
reply is 17 ..., NxP but the combination is still on, e.g. 18 RxBP!!, when
the continuations to consider are: (i)
18 ..., RxR; 19 BxR+, KxB; 20 NxR,
NxN; 21 QxRP, threatening R-KB1+
(ii) 18 ..., NxB; 19 RxR+ and NxN.
(iii) 18 ..., QxN; 19 R(1)-KB1!!, RxR
(or NxB; 20 RxR+, NxR; 21 Q-B7+);
20 BxR+ and BxN. Possibly White
overlooked the 19th move in this last
variation. Staunton now defends the

vulnerable KBP and White's chances evaporate like the morning mist.

17	B-K3
18 R-R1	R-B1
19 Q-K2	K-R1
20 P-B3	N(B)-K2
21 QR-Q1	P-B4

The once weak pawn now strongly undermines White's centre.

22 N-N6	BxB
23 NxB	R-QB3
24 PxP	NxP
25 P-N4	N-N6
26 RxR+	QxR
27 Q-N2	RxN
28 QxN	Q-K2
29 Q-B3	R-B1
30 N-Q2	R-B1
31 Q-N3	P-R3
32 N-B4?	P-Q4
33 N-N6	

Not 33 RxP, Q-KB2 showing that White would have done better on his previous move to play N-K4.

33	P-Q5!

See Diagram 126

A splendid conception, which leads to the complete occupation of the centre by the Black pieces.

34 KPxP	PxP
35 R-KB1	

If 35 PxP, N-B5; or if 35 RxP, Q-K7.

35	R-Q1

126

Staunton

von der Lasa

36 PxP	RxP
37 Q-QB3	Q-Q3

Black is now well centralised and threatens R-Q6. White cannot reply 38 R-B3, because of 38 ..., N-R5; 39 R-K3, R-Q8+; 40 R-K1, N-B6+.

38 Q-R3	Q-Q1
39 Q-K3	R-Q6
40 Q-K4	Q-Q3
41 R-B3	

There were possibilities of slightly longer resistance by 41 N-B4, Q-N6+ 42 Q-N2, Q-R5; 43 R-B3 (or K-R2, Q-Q1 threatening Q-B2+), N-B5; 44 Q-KB2, NxP+.

41	Q-B4+
42 K-B1	Q-B8+
	Resigns

It is mate after 43 K-B2, R-Q7+; 44 K-N3, Q-N8.

57

STAUNTON & OWEN - LOWENTHAL & BARNES
Consultation game, London, February 1856
Evans Gambit

1 P-K4	P-K4
2 N-KB3	N-QB3
3 B-B4	B-B4
4 P-QN4	BxP
5 P-B3	B-R4
6 P-Q4	PxP
7 O-O	P-Q3

Black's best move is probably KN-K2 to meet 8 PxP with P-Q4 and 8 N-N5 with P-Q4!; 9 PxP, N-K4. This line was known from a few of Anderssen's games of this period but never became popular, probably because of a general 19th century fear of the open K-file and because it involves returning the pawn. The Compromised Defence 7 ..., PxP is not as bad as it sounds or as it was thought to be when it was so named, but a century of analysis still tends to find in favour of White after 8 Q-N3, Q-B3; 9 P-K5, Q-N3; 10 NxP.

8 Q-N3!

This could well have been played on the previous move, to forestall the defence mentioned in the previous note; it is then one of the current critical lines of the Evans Gambit. The objection to Q-N3 has always been that it is decentralising and permits the resource N-QR4 to Black in many cases; analysis on the other hand supports the move quite strongly. The text move was originally proposed by the Irishman, George Waller, in the *Chess Player's Chronicle* in 1848 and was further analysed in the *Deutsche Schachzeitung* and the *Chess Player's Companion* in the following year.

8	Q-B3

Black can also try Q-Q2?! or Q-K2! but White always gets good attacking chances.

9 PxP?

It is now regarded as correct to play 9 P-K5!, PxP; 10 R-K1!, the last move being introduced by Morphy in a casual game at Birmingham in 1858, and was therefore not known at the time when the present game was played. The variation has since been analysed practically to mate for White.

9	B-N3
10 B-QN5	

P-K5 is no longer any good. In a casual game in New York, Thompson - Morphy, in 1857, after 10 P-K5, PxP; 11 PxP, Q-N3; 12 B-R3, B-K3; 13 QN-Q2, KN-K2, Black consolidated and then went over to a brilliant counterattack. Staunton and Owen show good judgment in avoiding this line.

10	B-Q2
11 P-K5	PxP
12 R-K1	KN-K2
13 PxP	Q-N3
14 B-Q3	

In contrast to Thompson, the White players retire their bishop to embarrass the Black Queen.

14	Q-R4?

Here Black could have moved into the lead with the coup B-KB4!; 15 N-R4, N-Q5!; 16 Q-R4+ (better than BxB, NxQ; 17 NxQ, RPxN), Q-B3; 17 QxQ+, PxQ; 18 NxB, N(2)xN; 19 N-B3, but a pawn is a pawn in such positions. Now the game becomes very complicated.

15 R-K4	N-N3
16 QN-Q2	B-K3
17 Q-R4	B-Q4
18 R-KN4	P-KR3?

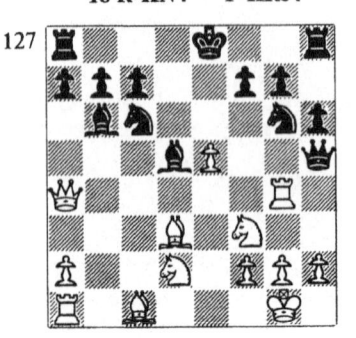

Lowenthal & Barnes
Staunton & Owen

By adding a weakness on KN3 to the already precarious situation of their Queen, the Black partners unwittingly provide the motif for a beautiful combinative onslaught.

19 RxN!!   BxN

Not PxR; 20 P-N4, Q-R6; 21 B-B1.

20 NxB	PxR
21 P-N4	Q-R6
22 BxP+	

Q-K4, threatening the combination in the last note, now fails against 22 ..., O-O-O; 23 B-B1, R-Q8.

| 22 ...... | K-Q1 |
| 23 Q-KB4 | |

The incarceration of Black's Queen makes his defeat certain.

23	N-K2
24 B-B7	K-B1
25 B-R3	N-B3
26 B-B8!	

A most attractive blow. With Black's Queen already *in angustis* White goes hunting for Black's cornered KR. RxB in reply fails against 27 B-K6+.

26	N-Q1
27 BxP	NxB
28 BxR	NxB
29 Q-B5+	K-Q1
30 Q-B6+	K-K1

H. Staunton

J.J. Lowenthal

58

LOWENTHAL & FALKBEER - STAUNTON & RANKEN
Consultation game, London, August 1856

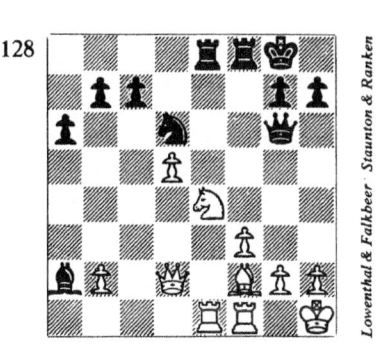

128

A position arising from a Scotch Gambit.

23 ......   B-B5!

White's KR has little choice.

24 R-KN1

The White King now looks suspiciously caged in and Black forces a neat exploitation of this important factor.

24 ......   RxN!
25 RxR   QxR!

A highly efficacious temporary sacrifice of the Queen.

26 PxQ   NxP

Threatening smothered mate if the Queen runs.

27 B-K3

Or 27 R-Q1, NxB+; 28 K-N1, NxR; 29 QxN, R-B8+; 30 QxR, BxQ; 31 KxB, K-B2 with an easily won ending for Black.

27 ......   NxQ
28 BxN   R-B7
29 B-B3   BxP

The presence of opposite coloured bishops only accentuates Black's superiority, for he obtains great pressure on the KNP.

30 P-R3   P-KR4
31 P-R4   K-B2
32 R-Q1   P-B3
33 R-Q2   BxP+
34 K-N1   RxR
35 BxR   B-K5

White resigned after a few more unimportant moves.

59

ANDERSSEN & ALLIES - STAUNTON & ALLIES
Consultation game, Manchester, 6th and 7th August 1857
French Defence

Anderssen reported on this game in the *Deutsche Schachzeitung* of 16th August as follows: 'On Thursday, 6th August, the Manchester Tournament was interrupted; Staunton had arrived and we were to play our consultation game. Staunton led on one side with his fellow Englishmen, Boden and Kipping, the latter the secretary of the local club. The opposition consisted of myself, Horwitz and Kling.

'Staunton's game was very cramped until a piece sacrifice (put forward by Kipping) gave him some air. The offer was justified by the gain of three pawns, and a most difficult position arose in which victory was unclear for either party. At this point an accident occurred which soon turned the game in favour of the English. It had been decided to play 'touch-and-move' and each side had an umpire present to enforce this rule. At the decisive moment Kling, overcome by excitement, picked up a piece and moved it, and we felt constrained to adhere to this, although it cost us the exchange. The game was adjourned at 11 p.m. and continued next day when it took an ever more unfavourable turn for us. At 6 p.m. it was again adjourned and later resigned by the foreign party. All in all, it lasted 18 hours, of which time the losing side consumed but a sixth!'

1 P-K4	P-K3
2 P-Q4	P-KN3

The Modern Defence! See the introduction to the book of that name by Keene and Botterill.

3 B-K3	B-N2
4 N-Q2	

Anderssen and Staunton had crossed swords in this variation once before — in the 5th game of their semifinal match in the 1851 London tournament. On that occasion Anderssen had preferred 4 B-Q3, and Staunton continued with the uncompromising P-QB4, but after 5 P-QB3, PxP; 6 PxP, Q-N3!? (a 19th century Poisoned Pawn!); 7 N-K2, QxNP; 8 N(1)-B3, Q-N3; 9 R-QB1, N-QR3; 10 N-N5, White obtained immense compensation for the pawn and went on to win.

4 ...... N-K2

5 B-Q3	P-N3

The Black allies resolutely avoid a premature P-Q4 and concentrate on maintaining the maximum flexibility for central pawn breaks.

6 N-K2	B-N2
7 O-O	P-Q3
8 P-QB3	N-Q2
9 Q-N3	

The Queen is misplaced on this square. It would have been more promising to retain the option of playing Q-K1 and ultimately Q-KR4.

9	O-O
10 P-KB4	P-Q4

Now this move is good since, after the inevitable response P-K5, Black has the twin thrusts P-QB4 and P-KB3 available. Another reasonable possibility was 10 ..., P-QB4.

11 P-K5	QR-N1
12 QR-B1	P-QB4

129 *Anderssen & Allies / Staunton & Allies*

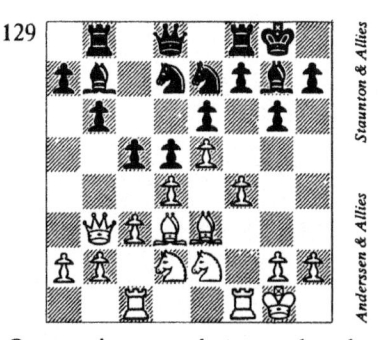

Once again we can but marvel at the striking modernity of Staunton's lay-out of the Black game. (Anderssen's notes show that the leaders of the respective sides were undoubtedly the two international masters.) The double fianchetto and the refusal to commit the Black central pawns would have been regarded as advanced concepts even for the Hypermodern masters of the 1920s. Indeed, such ideas were not fully accepted until the 1970s! For example, Garcia - Larsen, Siegen, 1970: 1 P-K4, P-KN3; 2 P-Q4, B-N2; 3 P-QB3, P-N3; 4 B-K3, B-N2; 5 N-Q2, N-KB3; 6 B-Q3, O-O; 7 P-KB4, P-Q3; or, even closer to the mark: A.H.Williams - Keene, Woolacombe 1973: 1 P-K4, P-KN3; 2 P-Q4, P-Q3; 3 N-QB3, B-N2; 4 P-B4, N-QB3; 5 B-K3, N-B3; 6 B-K2, O-O; 7 N-B3, P-K3; 8 P-KR3 (more fruitful was Q-Q2 followed by O-O-O, P-K5 and eventually P-KR4), N-K2; 9 O-O, P-N3; 10 N-Q2, B-N2; 11 B-B3, P-Q4; 12 P-K5, N-Q2; 13 N-K2, P-QB4; 14 P-B3,

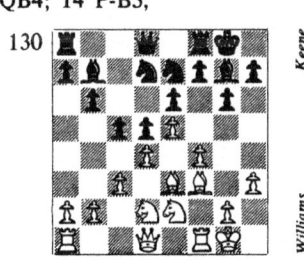

130 *Williams / Keene*

14 ..., Q-B2; 15 P-KN4, QR-B1; 16 Q-K1, B-QR3; 17 R-B2, and now P-B3! would have given Black an initiative (a break-out which Staunton did not miss on the 20th move in the present game).

13 Q-R3

The displacement of the White Queen confirms the criticism of White's 9th move.

13	P-B5
14 B-QB2	P-QR3
15 P-KN4	P-QN4

Of the rival pawn-rollers Black's packs the heavier punch, since any movement of the White K-side necessarily involves a weakening of his own King's defences.

16 N-KN3	KR-K1
17 P-N4	PxP e.p.
18 PxP	R-QB1
19 B-Q3	Q-N3
20 Q-N2	P-B3!

Black's position looks cramped and Anderssen claimed this factor as proving a White advantage at this point but, as Nimzowitsch was to teach sixty years later, it is not absolute control of space which is significant, but the possibility for a break-through. In this position all the break-through possibilities lie with Black.

21 QR-K1   Q-B3

A typical Staunton move, preparing a diagonal attack. (Compare move 31 in Game 23, move 26 in Game 42, move 16 in the 4th London Tournament game against Horwitz, quoted in the notes on the Staunton System, and finally move 16 in Game 49).

22 N-N1	PxP
23 BPxP	BxP!?

An ingenious sacrifice (suggested by Kipping and sanctioned by his general) intended to throw a harsh searchlight onto the weaknesses in the White King's field; though it may be too risky, P-QR4 and a slow Q-side push being preferable, it is nevertheless a good practical try. This was the sacrifice for which Anderssen said Black got three pawns but, as will be seen, they only collected two and left the third.

24 PxB   NxP
25 Б-QB2

B-K2? allows P-Q5 with advantage.

25 ......   R-B1

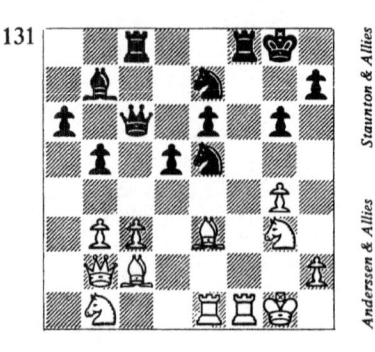

131

Staunton & Allies
Anderssen & Allies

Faced with the threats of P-N5, N-B6+ and NxNP, White's most sensible course appears to be to offer the exchange to eliminate Black's menacing knight.

26 B-N5?

The move said to have been made by Kling in a fit of over-excitement, but Anderssen's criticism of it is somewhat harsh. The move looks powerful indeed and the refutation is extremely refined and difficult to visualise. If the White allies adhere to the precept of sacrificing the exchange, outlined in the previous note, this plausible move also appears decisive in that it simultaneously attacks both Black knights. But one subtle point has been overlooked. Much better would have been 26 B-Q4, when N-B6+; 27 RxN, RxR leaves White in control of the important diagonal Q4-KR8, while 26 ..., NxP to obtain three pawns for his piece, open his KB4 for a knight and create the future possibility of P-K4, is adequately met by 27 B-Q1!

26 ......   N-B6+
27 RxN   RxR
28 B-Q1

Recognising the error of the 26th move. If instead 28 BxN, Black can force a win with a deep and beautiful Queen sacrifice which the White players had obviously omitted from their calculations: 28 ..., Q-N3+; 29 K-R1, Q-B7; 30 R-K2 (or R-KB1), RxN!!; 31 RxQ, P-Q5+; 32 B-K4, BxB+; 33 R-N2, RxR; 34 QxR, BxQ+; 35 KxB, PxP and the passed QBP forces White to surrender a minor piece, leaving Black the exchange ahead in the ending. If instead 30 Q-B1, RxN!; 31 PxR, P-Q5+; 32 B-K4, BxB+; 33 RxB, Q-B6+; 34 K-R2, QxR and Black stands much better. After the retrograde text Black can escape with his booty (rook and two pawns for two minor pieces) and stands better, since the White pieces are disorganised and his King exposed.

28 ......   Q-B4+
29 K-N2   R-KB2
30 K-R3   Q-Q3
31 Q-K2   R-QB3
32 Q-K3   B-B1

With White's minor pieces lacking useful squares, Black's twofold task is to mobilise his central pawns by P-K4 without permitting undue weaknesses to arise and to exert pressure against White's sensitive QBP.

33 K-N2   R-B2
34 P-N4

Now in the event of P-K4 by Black, they have B-N3 available, attacking Black's QP.

34 ......   N-B3
35 Q-Q2   R(QB)-Q2
36 B-N3   N-K4

The career of this powerful knight, threatening to come to QB5, KB6 or to annex White's KNP, must be cut short, but the resultant exchanges help Black.

37 B-KB4	RxB!
38 QxR	N-Q6
39 Q-K3	NxR+
40 QxN	R-QB2

After the letting of blood Black's advantage is manifest. White has shed the bishop pair, his weaknesses now extend to the dark squares, and the knight pair is notoriously inefficient in combat with a rook.

41 Q-K3	K-N2
42 N-Q2	P-K4

At last!

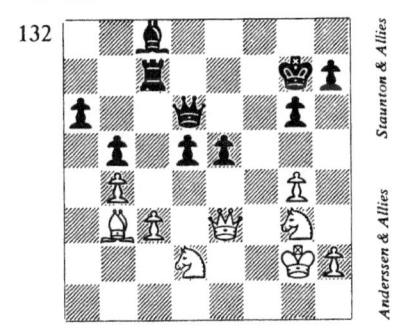

132

The advance of Black's central pawns spells doom for White. Their march can only be impeded with the intervention of White's QN, but if it loses contact with QN1 the QBP becomes indefensible.

43 Q-N5

White embarks on a final, desperate attack, abandoning the QBP. However, given the solidity of Black's position and the lack of co-ordination amongst the White pieces, its failure is a forgone conclusion.

43	Q-K2
44 N-R5+	K-R1
45 N-B6	B-N2
46 K-N1	RxP
47 P-R4	K-N2
48 N-R5+	K-B2
49 Q-R6	K-K1
50 N-N7+	K-Q2

Staunton was never afraid to send his King for a stroll. The Black King's flight deprives White's attack of its primary target, and the push of the KRP is exposed as a further weakness.

51 QxRP	R-N6+
52 K-B2	RxP
53 K-K2	R-N7+

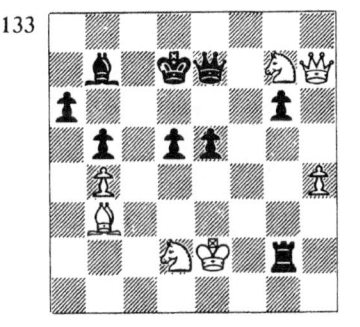

133

At this point, after 18 hours play, **White resigned**. Black already possesses the huge material superiority of rook and three pawns for two knights, and after 54 K-Q1, he has the choice of augmenting this surplus by R-N5 or of switching to the attack with Q-B2. After this marathon effort Staunton proposed to play a match of a few games with Anderssen, but the Professor of Mathematics from Breslau was obliged to return to Germany and the projected games never took place.

60

STAUNTON - WORRALL
Match game, London, 1859
Odds of Queen's Knight (remove White's QN)
Queen's Fianchetto Opening

In the following game Staunton employs a 'hypermodern' strategy, which was not to be fully elaborated for a further seventy years, and shows a profound understanding of an opening variation that, although pioneered by Nimzowitsch, did not become popular until its enthusiastic adoption by Bent Larsen. This game also forms a valuable contrast to the more conventional games played at the odds of a piece (e.g. Games 28 and 40) where the victim's demise is usually brought about as a result of some obvious tactical error. In this game Staunton thoroughly outplays his opponent, although ceding him a piece handicap, and the only crass error committed by Worrall, and it is an error of the positional variety, is the exchange of his KB on move 19.

1 P-QN3

A move much favoured by Owen, both as White and as Black, and it was from him no doubt that Staunton acquired an interest in it. Owen often found the satisfactory deployment of the QN something of a problem, as in the opening of a match game for the Provincial Challenge Cup against Gossip, played at his Hooton Rectory in 1874: 1 P-K3, P-Q4; 2 P-QN3, N-KB3; 3 B-N2, P-K3; 4 N-KB3, B-Q3; 5 P-B4, P-B4; 6 N-B3, O-O; 7 N-QN5, B-K2; 8 B-Q3, P-KR3; 9 B-B2, P-R3; 10 N-R3. The opening thus had its own particular attractions when White was playing without a QN.

1	P-K4
2 B-N2	N-QB3
3 P-K3	B-B4

Black develops his pieces centrally and 'sensibly' according to the precepts of the time, but Staunton expertly demonstrates that these 'well placed' pieces in fact represent a target for the advance of White's potentially mobile central and Q-side pawns.

4 N-K2	P-Q3
5 N-N3	B-K3
6 P-QR3	KN-K2
7 B-K2	O-O
8 O-O	P-B4?

At this stage Black should have taken time off for the precaution P-QR4!, which would have dampened down the 'lust to expand' of White's Q-side pawns. The injudicious double advance of Black's KBP also weakens his defences along the dark long diagonal.

9 P-Q4	B-N3
10 P-QB4	PxP
11 PxP	B-Q2

With a pawn on QR4 instead of KB4 Black could now have secured his centre by P-Q4. As it is, White threatens P-Q5, and 11 ..., P-Q4? fails against 12 P-B5, B-R4; 13 P-QN4. In view of this Black must expend a tempo to salvage his QB.

12 P-N4   P-QR4

Somewhat too late, but by now the KB also was in jeopardy from White's pawn mass.

13 P-N5	N-N1
14 R-B1	P-B3
15 P-B5	PxBP
16 QPxP	

Opening the significant diagonal for his QB. Already White has considerable positional compensation for his piece.

16	B-B2
17 Q-Q4	R-B3
18 B-B4+	

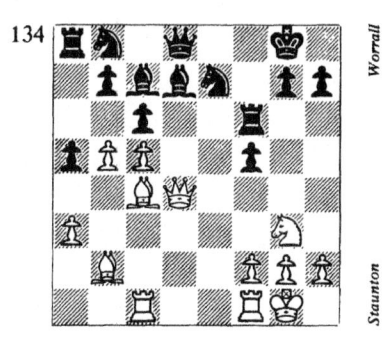

134 *[board diagram — Worrall (top) / Staunton (bottom)]*

Black's position is precarious. If now incautiously 18 ..., K-R1; 19 QxR!, PxQ; 20 BxP mate.

18 ......　　N-Q4
19 R-B3

Playing for the attack. White threatens 20 P-N6, forcing BxN; 21 RxB with tremendous pressure against Black's KNP. It was also possible to recoup material with 19 BxN+, PxB; 20 QxP+, menacing Black's QNP and his KR, but the course adopted by Staunton is undoubtedly more consistent.

19 ......　　BxN?

An awful move which voluntarily drags White's rook into a most attacking post. 19 ..., R-N3! was the best defensive try.

20 RxB

White's pieces converge against Black's vulnerable KN2 square.

20 ......　　K-R1
21 Q-R4

The Black KR obviously cannot move.

21 ......　　B-K3
22 R-K1　　B-B2

Not N-Q2; 23 RxB, RxR; 24 BxP+, K-N1; 25 B-B6+, K-B1; 26 Q-R6+, K-B2; 27 QxP+, KxB; 28 Q-N7 mate.

23 BxN　　PxB
24 BxR　　PxB

Or QxB; 25 QxQ, PxQ; 26 R-K7, and Black is helpless.

25 Q-R6　　Resigns

There is no conceivable defence to White's mating threats. One of the most impressive odds games on record and a remarkable anticipation of the 'diagonal attacks' which are usually linked with Nimzowitsch and Larsen.

INDEX OF OPENINGS

	page
Anderssen's (Reverse Sicilian) Opening	131
Benoni Defence	55
Bird's Opening	55, 78, 108, 122, 124
Bishop's Opening	36, 44, 46
Centre Counter	22
Dutch Defence	3
English Opening	5, 19, 62, 86, 92, 109, 113, 116, 126, 127
Evans Gambit	42, 103, 151
French Defence (modern Defence)	154
Giuoco Piano	51, 119, 142
King's Gambit (Muzio Gambit)	87
King's Indian Defence	59
King's Indian Opening	125
Odds Games:	
Odds of QR. Bishop's Opening	14, 105
Odds of QN. Bishop's Opening	83
Evans Gambit	20, 75
Queen's Fianchetto Opening	158
Sicilian Defence	26
Odds of Pawn and Two Moves	27, 40, 81, 84, 97, 99, 104, 138
Odds of Pawn and Move	50
Philidor Defence	22
Ponziani Opening	101
Queen's Gambit	72
Queen's Gambit Declined	62, 65, 67, 69, 72
Queen's Indian Defence	75
Queen's Pawn Counter-Gambit	7
Reti System	112, 125
Ruy Lopez	143, 147
Scotch Gambit	38, 117, 137
Sicilian Defence	19, 47, 53, 58, 64, 90, 93, 107, 109, 120, 129, 130, 140, 147, 148, 149
Two Knights Defence	33
Vienna (Falkbeer Counter) Gambit	133

GENERAL INDEX

	page
Alekhine, A.	69
Anderssen, A.	1, 14, 15, 17, 18, 19, 20, 21, 29, 42, 109, 117, 119, 120, 124, 126, 130, 131, 140, 148, 151, 154, 157
Andersson, U.	93, 109, 112, 124
Bachmann, L.	6
Barcza, G.	124
Barnes, T.W.	22, 151
Basman, M.	55, 148, 149
Beeby, T.	15
Bell's Life	6, 8, 10
Bilguer, P.R. von	1
Bird, H.E.	3, 4, 11, 17, 18, 19, 23, 117, 122
Bledow, L.	1, 13
Boden, S.S.	19, 23, 154
Bohn	16
Botterill, G.	148, 154
Breyer, J.	4
Brien, R.B.	6, 20, 23, 29, 138
Brighton Chess Club	13
Bristol Chess Club	1, 78, 81
British Chess Association	13
British Chess Magazine	6, 11, 12
Brodie	17, 18, 29, 86
Bronstein, D.	144
Brown, J.	6, 29, 97
Buckle, H.T.	6, 8, 12, 16, 17, 19, 29, 124
Byrne, R.	59, 125, 144
Capablanca, J.R.	47, 90, 109
Carlisle, 5th Earl of	1
Century of British Chess	6, 15
Chess Life-Pictures	6, 8, 11
Chess Monthly	24
Chess Player's Chronicle	6, 8, 11, 16, 20, 24, 138, 151
Chess Player's Companion	4, 8, 16, 28, 151
Chess Player's Handbook	2, 15, 16, 24, 36, 101
Chess Player's Textbook	16
Chess Praxis	23, 24
Chess Studies	13
Chess: Theory and Practice	25
Chess Tournament	20
Chess World	3
Chess World	24
City of London Chess Magazine	11
Cochrane, J.	7, 8, 29, 42, 43, 44, 46, 47, 50, 64, 117
Coles, R.N.	72, 90, 107
Cook, N.	16
Cook, W.	67
Deacon, F.	19, 24

Deschapelles, A.	7
Deutsche Schachzeitung	151, 154
Dictionary of National Biography	1, 16
Divan, The	5, 8, 14, 16
Donaldson, Rev. J.	6, 138
Ebralidze	3
Edge, F.M.	21, 22
Electric Telegraph Co.	12
Evans, Capt. W.D.	12, 42, 85, 99, 101
Evolution of the Chess Openings	67
Falkbeer, E.	23, 153
Field, The	23, 81
Fine, R.	58, 59, 60, 61
Fischer, Bobby	3, 10, 21, 33, 58, 130, 140, 147
Fraser, W.	7
Gilbert, Sir J.	20
Golombek, H.	15, 21, 126
Gordon, Rev.	138
Gossip, G.H.D.	158
Greville, Brooke	8, 29
Handbuch	1, 15, 144
Hannah, J.W.	13, 29
Hanstein, W.	13, 17
Harding, T.D.	36, 43, 133
Harrwitz, D.	10, 13, 14, 17, 19, 20, 21, 29, 67 97, 99, 101
Hartston, W.R.	36, 55, 87, 149
Horae Divanianae	81
Horowitz, I.	33
Horwitz, B.	1, 3, 4, 5, 10, 11, 13, 14, 17, 18, 19, 21, 29, 38, 90, 93, 95, 106, 107, 109, 113, 147, 154
Illustrated London News	11, 20, 24
Jaenisch, C.F. von	17, 19, 20, 29, 133, 137
Janowski, D.	90, 144
Jaques, Messrs.	16
Karpov, A.	148
Kean, Edmund	2, 11
Keene, R.D.	72, 88, 107, 116, 124, 144, 148 154, 155
Kennedy, E.S.	17, 18
Kennedy, Capt. H.A.	12, 13, 17, 18, 19, 29, 84
Kenny, C.	14, 29
Keres, P.	38, 87, 133, 137, 144
Kieseritsky, L.	8, 17, 18, 19
Kipping, J.S.	23, 154
Kling, J.	13, 154
Kolisch, I.	4, 124, 130
Konig, I.	127
Korchnoi, V.	59, 147
Labourdonnais, L.C. de	6, 7, 8, 15, 47, 53, 68, 72, 83, 84, 88
Larsen, B.	36, 53, 120, 124, 155, 158, 159

Lasa, T. von der	1, 3, 8, 17, 20, 29, 143, 148, 149
Lasker, Em.	15, 42, 46, 95
Lee, Sir Sidney	1
Lewis, W.	7
Liverpool Chess Club	13
Ljubojevic, L.	109, 117
London Chess Club	6, 13, 16, 17
Lowe, E.	14, 15, 17, 18, 19, 29, 104, 127
Lowenthal, J.J.	8, 10, 17, 18, 19, 21, 22, 23, 29, 124, 142, 151, 153
Macdonnell, Rev. G.A.	6, 8, 11
McDonnell, A.	6, 7, 15, 47, 48, 53, 54, 72, 83, 84, 88, 105
Marshall, F.J.	33, 44
Mayet, K.	13, 17, 18, 67
Medley, G.W.	16, 29
Mongredien, A.	12, 13, 29, 80, 83
Morphy, P.	1, 2, 3, 7, 10, 13, 15, 16, 21, 22, 23, 24, 33, 42, 47, 83, 84, 126, 128, 131, 138, 148, 149, 151
Mucklow, J.	17, 18, 19
Murray, H.J.R.	11, 13, 15
Nethersole, Mrs. F.	16, 24, 25
Newham, S.	17, 18
Nimzowitsch, A.	3, 15, 47, 50, 63, 69, 78, 79, 81, 92, 93, 102, 104, 109, 132, 139, 158, 159
Northern & Midland Chess Assoc.	21
Olafsson, F.	117
Owen, Rev. J.	22, 23, 138, 151, 158
Paulsen, L.	148, 149
Penrose, J.	116
Perigal, G.	12
Petroff, A.D. von	17, 20
Petrosian, T.	3, 59, 69, 72, 75, 86, 102, 109
Philidor, F.A.D.	3, 15, 36, 53, 58, 81, 82
Pillsbury, H.N.	42
Popert, H.W.	6, 29, 36, 38
Portisch, L.	69
Potter, W.N.	11, 12, 38
Quinteros, M.	93, 112
Ranken, C.E.	12, 19, 153
Regence. La	8, 24
Reti, R.	3, 4, 15, 124, 126
Ribli, Z.	124
Rives, de	20, 38
Rockferry Chess Club	20
Romih, M.	92
Rubinstein, A.K.	69
Saint-Amant, P.C.F. de	1, 2, 3, 7, 8, 9, 10, 17, 20, 23, 29, 30, 31, 51, 53, 55, 58, 62, 64, 65, 67, 69, 72, 78, 92, 113, 126

St. George's C.C.	13, 17
Salmon, Rev. G.	23
Saxe, Marshal	13
Sergeant, P.W.	6, 8, 15
Skipworth, A.B.	26
Smyslov, V.	143, 144
Spassky, B.	10, 59, 75, 130
Spreckley, G.S.	12, 13, 29
Stanley, C.H.	7, 29, 41
Staunton System, The	4, 5, 107, 108, 110, 113
Steinitz, W.	1, 3, 5, 10, 13, 38, 46, 47, 59, 93, 101, 109, 126, 147
Szen, J.	17, 18, 19, 130, 131
Taimanov, M.	109, 140
Tal, M.	55
Tarrasch, S.	47, 67
Tartakover, S.	59, 88, 113, 114, 115, 134, 135, 137, 138
Taverner, T.	7, 29
Tchigorin, M.	42, 47, 101
Tomlinson, G.	10
Tuckett, T.	10, 12, 29
Walker, George	6, 7, 12, 13
Walker, Greenwood	6
Waller, G.	151
Westminster Chess Club	6
Whiteley, A.	55
Williams, A.H.	155
Williams, E.	1, 4, 5, 10, 13, 14, 17, 18, 19, 29, 78, 81, 108, 109, 113, 120, 122, 124, 129, 131
Wilson, Capt. H.	9, 10, 30
Winawer, S.	144
Wormald, R.B.	25
Worrall, T.S.	24, 29, 158
Worrel	9, 30
Wyvill, M.	17, 18, 19, 127, 131
Yorkshire Chess Assoc.	1, 11
Zytogorski	6, 27, 29, 40

'Figures of the Age'

Herr Lowenthal   M. de Riviere   Mr. Wyvill, M.P.   Herr Falkbeer   Mr. Staunton   Lord Lyttelton   Captain Kennedy

From photographs by Signor Aspa (Leamington Chess Club) and Mr. Russell   First published on 14th July 1855

L.Kieseritzky
1806 - 1853

P.R. von Bilguer
1815 - 1840

S.S.Boden
1826 - 1882

D.Harrwitz
1823 - 1884

H.T.Buckle
1821 - 1862

H.E.Bird
1830 - 1908

J.A. de Riviere
1830 - 1905

Rev. W. Wayte
1829 - 1898

L.Paulsen
1833 - 1891

R.B.Wormald
1834 - 1876

T. von Heydebrand
und von der Lasa
1818 - 1899

P.T.Duffy
1834 - 1888

L.C. de Labourdonnais
1795 - 1840

C.F. von Jaenisch
1813 - 1872

W. Lewis
1787 - 1870

G. Walker
1803 - 1879

Two portraits of
A. Anderssen

P.Morphy
1837 - 1884

W.N.Potter
1840 - 1895

L.Hoffer
1842 - 1913

J.H.Zukertort
1842 - 1888

W.Steinitz
1836 - 1900

Baron Kolisch
1837 - 1889

C. de Vere
1845 - 1875

Rev. G.A. MacDonnell
1830 - 1899

LIST OF ILLUSTRATIONS

Staunton's marriage register entry	4 - 5
Staunton	9
Staunton (Illustrated London News, 1874)	25
Staunton	45
Saint-Amant	57
The Staunton - Saint-Amant match in Paris	77
Mongredien	81
The Staunton - Horwitz match	91
Horwitz	96
Harrwitz	100
Anderssen	118
Lowenthal	142
Staunton - Lowenthal	152
Group (14th July 1855) — Lowenthal, de Riviere, Wyvill, Falkbeer, Staunton, Lord Lyttelton, Capt. Kennedy	167
L.Kieseritzky	168
P.R. von Bilguer	168
S.S.Boden	169
D.Harrwitz	169
H.T.Buckle	170
H.E.Bird	170
J.A. de Riviere	171
Rev. W.Wayte	171
L.Paulsen	172
R.B.Wormald	172
T. von Heydebrand und von der Lasa	173
P.T.Duffy	173
L.C. de Labourdonnais	174
C.F. von Jaenisch	174
W.Lewis	175
G.Walker	175
A.Anderssen	176
P.Morphy	177
W.N.Potter	177
L.Hoffer	178
J.H.Zukertort	178
W.Steinitz	179
Baron Kolisch	179
C. de Vere	180
Rev. G.A.MacDonnell	180

Illustrations in this book have been obtained from various sources, in particular 'The Illustrated London News', 'Chess Life-Pictures', 'Anderssen' by von Gottschall and 'Aus Vergangenen Zeiten' by Bachmann. Our thanks to Messrs. J.Guisle, G.Balbo and P.J.Balbo for their kind help in obtaining further material.

Printed in Great Britain
by Amazon